THE ROMANCE OF WILLIAM MORRIS

J. Pittendreigh MacGillivray: *William Morris*. From a sculptural relief
made in 1886.

THE ROMANCE OF

William Morris

BY CAROLE SILVER

OHIO UNIVERSITY PRESS
ATHENS, OHIO

Library of Congress Cataloging in Publication Data

Silver, Carole.
  The romance of William Morris.

  Bibliography: p.
  Includes index.
  1. Morris, William, 1834–1896—Criticism and
interpretation.   I. Title.
PR5084.S5   1982   821'.8   82-2278
ISBN 0-8214-0651-5   AACR2
ISBN 0-8214-0706-6 pbk.

CONTENTS

ILLUSTRATIONS

ACKNOWLEDGMENTS

In the course of research, I have incurred numerous obligations which it is a pleasure to acknowledge. The New York Public and British Libraries and those of Columbia University and the University of Toronto were most gracious and helpful. I am indebted to the Tate Gallery for permission to reproduce four paintings from its fine collection of Dante Gabriel Rossetti and to the Birmingham Museums and Art Gallery for allowing me to include a photograph of a Morris and Company tapestry in their possession. The Society of Antiquaries of London generously permitted me to quote from two unpublished manuscripts of William Morris. My thanks are also due to John Stasny, editor of *Victorian Poetry*, for permission to reprint, in revised form, a section of Chapter Three which originally appeared in that journal. A portion of Chapter Two also first appeared as an article—on "The Defence of Guenevere"—in *Studies in English Literature: 1500–1900*. That journal kindly allowed me to reprint a condensed and altered version of the essay. Last, I am indebted to Yeshiva University for a President's Award and a Summer Research Grant both of which provided funds for travel and technical assistance.

I owe as much, and perhaps more, to individuals. Twenty years ago Jerome Buckley suggested that I prepare a paper on Morris for his doctoral seminar; three years ago he proposed a title for this book, thus providing its genesis and terminus. Carl Woodring has played an equally important role; his encouragement and astute criticism have been richly present through all stages of the work. I am grateful to the Morris scholars who have exhibited the fellowship that Morris himself espoused. Chief among them is Joseph Dunlap; John Hollow, Norman Kelvin, and Frederick Kirchhoff have also been of considerable assistance.

For the time and valuable insights they have contributed, I wish to thank my colleagues and friends. To Nina Auerbach, Laurel Hatvary, Robert Keane, and Peggy Porder, I am deeply indebted. To Judith Neaman, I am profoundly grateful. My thanks are also due to Muriel Bennett and Isabel Balson who provided assistance in preparing the manuscript and to the amiable staff of the Ohio University Press. Finally, I am grateful to two books and those who wrote them. I wish to express my indebtedness to E. P. Thompson's *William Morris: Romantic to Revolutionary* and to William E. Fredeman's *Pre-Raphaelitism: A Bibliocritical Study*. Both are works without which my own would have been difficult, if not impossible, to write.

INTRODUCTION

As for romance, what does romance mean? I have heard people mis-
called for being romantic, but what romance means is the capacity for a
true conception of history, a power of making the past part of the
present.

> William Morris
> Address at the Twelfth Annual Meeting
> of the S.P.A.B.—3 July 1889

THE TITLE of this book, *The Romance of William Morris*, implies a cluster of attitudes about Morris's conception of his
life and of the literary, visual, and societal works that issued from
it. For because of the culture of his era, one still marked by its
romantic legacy, and because of his individual psyche, Morris
perceived the self and the world with the eyes of a latter-day
romantic. Through the genre of romance, he strove to create them
both anew.

The medieval romances Morris admired drew upon and linked
together the varied disciplines of their world—areas as diverse as
venery, architecture, and the art of love. So too did Morris. Thus,
to concentrate primarily upon one aspect of his work, his literary
achievement, is to open oneself to the charge of fragmenting or
compartmentalizing the concerns of a figure whose impulse was
integration and whose vision was holistic. However, closer investigation of Morris reveals that the same basic impulses and
aspirations dictated what he tried to achieve in whatever field
he chose, that what he wrought in design, for example, was
integrally related to what he created in social theory. Interwoven
in the poems and romances Morris wrote throughout his life are
the strands of all his other thought. In these poems and romances,
he most clearly reveals the ideas and feelings that shape his work
in decoration and design, in the preservation of architecture and
culture, in ecology, in socialism.

The relations between Morris's literary achievements and his
designs are a case in point; the same spirit informs both. Each, in

its way, emphasizes repetition framing subtle variation. The reiterated themes and refrains of the 1858 *Defence of Guenevere* volume and the strong structural repeats of many of the patterns manifest the same impulse. In both the literary and visual arts, Morris alternated energy and stasis, strove for "flat" rather than shaded, soft effects, and employed circularity as a structural principle. In each medium, Morris valued and heightened detail, investing it with a significance beyond the literal. The meticulous attention to the choice of color for a tiny dot within a pattern or to the composition of a group of flowers that never bloomed together in the world of nature finds its reflection in romances that the casual reader may well deem carelessly imaginative. Selecting and intensifying detail so that it became symbolic, Morris strove to see reality from changed perspectives.

Moreover, in literature and art alike, Morris drew on history and the world of nature but then sought to transform them. His knowledge of medieval history and belief informed his poetry and prose romances; his command of the technology and history of textile design illuminated his patterns—and led him to describe himself as both an "artist" and an "archaeologist." In both areas he transmuted his historicism into something beyond servile imitation; in his romances he made myth from history; in his designs he made new patterns from historic elements. In the same way, when he described or drew upon the world of nature, he structured, stylized, or evoked its forms. His fidelity was less to external nature than to the truths revealed by the inner eye.

In both the literary and visual arts, Morris moved from his somewhat literal Pre-Raphaelite style of the late 1850s to the more formalized and richly patterned one of his later years. The same developments in form and idea—here, a shift from verisimilitude to the depiction of the symbols and archetypes that transcend reality—affected both media, though at different chronological times. Peter Floud indicates that in design Morris began with an early closeness to naturalistic rendering, moved through several varieties of formalism, and ended his career with a return to a new, transformed naturalism.[1] In his literary work, Morris passed from the vivid realism of the poems of *The Defence* to the formal intricate design of such poems as *Love is Enough* (1873). His epic of 1877, *The Story of Sigurd the Volsung* and the highly stylized romances of the late 1880s and early '90s manifest new kinds of formalism, and the return to naturalism is mirrored in the folkloric, realistic bent of the last romance, *The Sundering Flood*.

The accusation that after *The Defence of Guenevere* Morris never again created realistic literary figures distorts Morris's development and ignores his intentions. In both his poems and patterns he had ceased to emphasize the "real" and chose instead to capture the archetypal and iconic. His romantic and Pre-Raphaelite concern with art as the embodiment of dream—an interpretation rather than an imitation of life—became the impetus behind much of his work.

The same respect for the embodiments of the imagination, the same love for history and nature dictated Morris's role as a preserver of architecture. His efforts in 1877 to found the Society for the Protection of Ancient Buildings, or "Antiscrape" as it was called, arose from his awareness that the wave of restoration sweeping England was mechanical, unhistorical, and unnatural—an obfuscation of the cultures of the past. Morris was angry at those who renovated romanesque, gothic ("romantic"), and later structures because they placed considerations of money before those of art. He was incensed at the ignorance of the architects, clergymen, and public who accepted stripping and destroying as restorative. He was enraged at the violation of architectural organicism by those who removed what they considered later accretions and replaced them with office-designed, mechanically accurate replicas of buildings of any given century. The destruction of a twelfth-century tower at Canterbury, because it differed in style from the fifteenth-century building which had evolved beside it, struck him as foolish. The replacement of the structure with a nineteenth-century model of a theoretically appropriate fifteenth-century tower struck him as sacrilegious.

The convictions about preservation Morris held—that man is accountable to the works of earlier ages, that the arts and artifacts of the past are merely vested in the present, not owned by any single generation but by all mankind—are indications of his underlying sense of man's communal responsibilities. The active measures Morris undertook—his endless letters to the press, his refusal to supply new glass in aid of restoration, his rendering of advice and money to those who tried simply to repair ancient buildings—are demonstrations of his belief in an historical inheritance that should not be destroyed. Similar convictions led him to warn of the despoliation of man's legacy from nature. An early ecologist, he campaigned against the stench of industry, the pollution of the waterways, the destruction of the woodlands.

E. P. Thompson has shown how Morris's romanticism lay at the base of the communism he embraced in 1883.[2] The same intellectual roots—romanticism, utopianism, and anti-mechanism—that fed his other activities, nourished his Marxism; the values that he brought to poetry, design, and preservation are identical to those he sought in socialism. From the time that he began to write, Morris lauded "fellowship"; he described the ideal comradship and the nobility of those—like Svend and Gertha in the early romance tales—who sacrificed their individual needs to save their worthy nations. Just as early, Morris praised egalitarianism, expressing his dislike of despotism and of any realm, however mythical, in which a great gulf yawned between the rich and poor. From the beginning, he believed in the integrity and educability of the ordinary human being and abhorred the institutions that exploited him. He seems always to have valued the simplicity of life, be it the idealized rusticity of pastoralism or the normal work and life of country people. Always present was his sense that work *was* life, performed not out of necessity but for identity, ennoblement, and joy.

Marxism appealed to two of Morris's essential psychic needs which were expressed but could not be fulfilled in other areas of life. Perhaps unconsciously, Morris found in it a substitute for lost religious faith, perhaps more consciously, an organizing principle which would explain the ebb and flow of history. Just as Morris needed to shape fiction and make patterns, so he was impelled to forge an order in which he could believe. As a young man, he had been intended for the ministry; he had been attracted, although briefly, to the Oxford movement; he had never lost his capacity for intense commitment. To him the essence of religion was a habit of responsibility to some thing or ideal outside the self. First he strove to be responsible to art, then to romantic love, and finally (as he defined it in *The Manifesto of the Socialist League*) to a "religion of Socialism."

In much the same way, Morris needed to believe that history was a valid way of knowing. Disliking the "civilization" of his era, he had always sought in other times and places the feelings and ideas that would redeem his age. For most of his adult life he had held an intuitively dialectical and cyclical view of history. His perception of a pattern of historical recurrence marks *The Earthly Paradise*; his awareness of repeated waves of progress and decline shapes *Sigurd*. Marxist history supported Morris's own preferences for early cultures, allowed for the ethical and human factors he would not deny, and predicted the coming of the golden age that he desired. Moreover, in indicating that historical progress involves backward as well as forward movement, in suggesting that the best of older principles would be conserved to reappear, transformed and purified in a future world, it satisfied both Morris's preservationist and revolutionary impulses. Thus,

Morris found in communism a way of seeing history as logical, intelligible, and purposive.

When Morris became a socialist, the traits and values that had wrought his other works shaped his private Marxist vision. As he had devoted himself to making poetry and patterns, so he set himself to making revolution. From 1884 to 1890, he spent much of his time in studying the documents of "scientific socialism," in writing for and editing one of its major journals, in lecturing on its premises and aims, in agitating for its acceptance. As he had opposed "escape" in his verse romances of the 1860s, so he opposed palliative trends in socialism, condemning measures, such as parliamentary cooperation, he thought were escapist. As he had loved the past and future rather than the present, so in socialism he concentrated on the pre-industrial world and on the restoration of its spirit in the loosely federated groups that would constitute the ideal society to come.

It is not surprising that the man who found in communism a guide to life should have been so long committed to the genre of romance. For romance, as Northrop Frye says, is a revolutionary literary form, a complement to rather than evasion of socialist thought.[3] Romance harmonized individual and communal interests; it suggested—or could be made to suggest, as it did in the hands of Morris—the social responsibility of the individual, his role in building man's only earthly paradise, a free society on earth. It avoided the isolated or escapist point of view Morris had found vitiating other genres of romantic literary art, making them feverish and dreamy or narrow and crabbed because their creators were deficient in social integration. It was born from the art of the people, employing their folklore and customs, and it was accessible to their imaginations. Moreover, as a literary form without discontinuity, romance tied the traditions of the past to those of the present and future.

Yet another appeal which romance held for Morris was that it stood between the mythic and the modes of realism. It humanized pure myth and set implicitly mythical patterns into a world of human experience, while it idealized the human content. Liberal, intense, and popular, romance was also natural, arising from and interacting with the order of nature. Frye describes the structure of its narrative as cyclical (manifested in the cycle of nature) and dialectical (moving from the natural to touch or intersect with the apocalyptic realm above it).[4] Romance's structural design filled the aesthetic needs of a man attuned, as Morris was, to the earth's calendar and cycle.

Coincident with its distillation of the natural order was the world romance depicted. Although that world might vary, it was far removed, by definition, from the sterile, mechanistic realms that Morris so abhorred. With its imagery of innocence, its benevolent, parental deities, and its childlike people, romance met Morris's criteria for art, since he believed the childlike part of man produced works of imagination. It was nostalgic, since it yearned for an imagined golden age; yet it was forward looking, since its protagonists would grow to build a new society. The many facets of romance thus satisfied Morris's political, social, and artistic cravings.

Yet still more central to the life and thought of Morris were the classic themes of romance—love, fate, and death. The ways in which he dealt with these motifs reveal both his artistic and his psychic growth.

The need to feel responsible to something outside himself led Morris, in the 1850s, to idealize romantic love. Like Shelley, Browning, and Rossetti, he saw eros as a religious experience, a union of two souls, a way to heal the wounds of life; he believed in love's transcendent power. In addition, he sought from passion a discovery of identity, a knowledge of the female soul within his soul, a reunion of all aspects of the self—the revelations of love's immanent power.

Romantic passion was to transform those who experienced it, often through redemptive suffering. More godlike than the vanished Christian god or the indifferent pagan deities, it was to give a meaning to reality. Yet, even as a young man, Morris sensed that the erotic passion that transformed could also ruin and destroy. As his marriage floundered, he became increasingly aware that endless yearning coupled with eternal satisfaction did not and could not flourish on the ordinary earth.

By the 1870s, Morris had begun to feel that the power and presence of love were not enough. Love was still best. It was stronger than the social forces that might seek to bind it, but it was insufficient—and unattainable—as life's guide and goal. These reasons prompted him to postulate new, earthlier varieties of tenderness. Changeless passion became a future hope—rather like the golden age of statelessness—while its functions were subsumed by other concepts: those of friendly love, of healthy animal desire, of fellowship. Friendly love, or the respect, trust, and affection between male and female peers, and fellowship, or the permanent and kindly bonding with a group, became the barriers against the wasteland of the world. As he substituted these more general, achievable ideals for the desire for perfect passion, Morris demonstrated the growth of his mind and art.

Perhaps inevitably, when Morris felt that eros was the only

antidote for the vicissitudes of time and change, he was much troubled by the power of fate. Fate too would play a major role in his aesthetic life, and, as with love, he would begin with a concern for individual destiny and move to an absorption in larger, more collective patterns. Although not speculative nor drawn to the abstract, Morris shared, initially, the feeling of many of his contemporaries that there were no certainties that man could reach. He resisted the notion of man as a human automaton, but he viewed him as a being diminished by and vulnerable to the forces of time and change.

Uneasy with relativism but unable to believe in a designing providence, Morris sought to find a pattern in the material world around him. His first explorations, those of the 1850s, yielded answers of despair. *The Earthly Paradise* (1868–70) announces that time and change are rulers of this world; few can survive their pangs and even love does not outlast their visitations. Art can offer the illusion of a triumph over fate, but, like love's, its power is limited. The northern wizard of the "Apology" can create— "Folk say"—the momentary image of three fruitful seasons in a brutal winter; the poet strives "to build a *shadowy* (my italics) isle of bliss / Midmost the beating of the steely sea." Despite the artist, time and change erode the things man values most.

Nevertheless, Morris saw the necessity of the agencies that most tormented him. He recognized that changelessness could be the mark of death or of the psychic death in life that was far worse. He observed that time, although primarily destructive, could bring new birth and life. By the late 1870s and *Sigurd*, Morris had turned toward stoic resignation. He saw change as the law of life; he viewed man's duty as acceptance and endurance.

The evolution of Morris's thought from a romance conception of the power of fate to an epic and heroic one was completed by his conversion to socialism. Adopting a Marxist faith in progress, albeit of a cyclical rather than linear kind, Morris came to see time and change as purposive universal laws. Almost Tennysonian in his hope for "the one . . . divine event to which the whole crea- tion moves," he visualized the occurrence as the outcome of successful revolution: a paradise rebuilt on earth. Thus, for Morris, fate became a Marxist reading of history. The destinies of nations and of those within them depended on the maintenance of socialist values. If societies contributed to a Marxist future, their seeds would germinate until its time had come. By means of Morris's creative transmutation, communism became epic romance: its events were prefigured in history; its figures were heroes; its outcome was reunion and rebirth.

Finally, in his later years, Morris came to terms with death. In youth, he had been fascinated by death's violence and beauty and found heroism in those who faced their end unflinchingly or chose it to preserve their higher values. Relinquishing his faith in a conventional heaven, he had flirted with, but not assented to, a belief in a pagan lovers' paradise. By the end of the 1860s, he was torn between the love and the fear of death. Understanding but not condoning man's desire to escape death, he saw it as a state far preferable to psychic and emotional paralysis, as an end to the woes of love and fate. In the early 1870s, as the tension in his marriage grew, Morris became even more attracted to and yet afraid of his demise. Only with the gradual restoration of his faith in life, in the late 1870s, could he effectively resolve his powerful ambivalence.

But Morris needed a far richer answer to the question of mortality. In the 1880s, he again repudiated both the concepts of the immortality of individual souls and of eternal life in an otherworldly paradise; he had found alternatives. His acceptance of death and his vision of immortal life are best expressed by Thiodolf, his persona in *The House of the Wolfings*, the historical romance of 1888. Death is merely a "changing" of life; to die heroically for the benefit of the group insures one's survival in the memory of one's people and in that of all the children of the earth. Man's immortality is, thus, through others, through the growth of the entire human race, and through the earth itself, for one becomes part of the eternal cycle of the fertile world of nature. The individual may pass, but the earth and man remain.

Eighty-six years after his death, Morris's contributions to art, literature, and society remain. Though we have not achieved his holistic vision nor embodied it in the full, integrated world that he desired, we still can read and see his works and so preserve a part of his romance.

ONE

THE HOLLOW LAND

I N THE CONCLUDING lines of "Sir Peter Harpdon's End,"
Lady Alice de la Barde hears outside her window a minstrel's
song "of love and fate and death."[1] From the earliest years of his
literary career until his death in 1896, William Morris was to vary
the strains but repeat the burden of the song he had created for his
imaginary minstrel. Though he would change his source materials, develop his unique literary style, and experiment with
numerous genres and techniques, he would retain his preoccupation with the thematic trinity he had announced in his early
works. His quest for answers to the problems posed by the powerful forces of love, fate, and death would lead him to numerous
explorations of the relationships among them, as well as to in-
vestigations of the realms in which they could be best studied.

Morris would remain fascinated with the Middle Ages, in
which love, fate, and death were writ so large. Although he would
expand his work to include the medieval visions of the classical
world and a medievalized future, he would never cease to be involved with that past which seemed, to him, most meaningful.
Yet, always aware of the pastness of the past, he would not attempt to escape to it or to avoid the realities of his own era. Instead, he would seek to find and identify emotions and situations
common to past and present and applicable to the future, those
enshrined in the myth, folklore, and legend that he believed
demonstrated the continuity of the human spirit. Less a histori-
cist than a myth maker, he would attempt to embody his dreams,
creating literature that would satisfy himself and speak to his
own era. Always a complex and enigmatic figure, he would struggle to resolve the tensions created by his dialectical mind.

The historical and personal origins of Morris's literary
themes, medieval yearnings, and habit of mind are not difficult to
trace. Although he believed that he was "born out of . . . [his]
due time" (3:1), he was clearly an offspring of the romantic revolution and its Victorian re-evaluation. Born in 1834, the eldest son
of middle-class parents, he partook of the Victorian passion for
the medieval and romantic from an early age. He had read all

1

Scott's *Waverley* novels by the time he was seven and had even acquired his own miniature suit of armor. By the time he was fourteen, he had developed a love for the Gothic in art and architecture. Even at Marlborough, which he attended from 1847 to 1851, he was more interested in reading archaeology and architecture and in exploring the prehistoric sites around him than in pursuing his assigned studies.

Influenced by Marlborough's High Church leanings, by the antiquarianism of the Oxford Movement, and by such books as Pugin's *Contrasts,* he entered Exeter College, Oxford, in 1853 with the intention of taking orders. Both his Anglo-Catholicism and his devotion to religious art developed through his friendship with Edward Burne-Jones. With Ned Jones at his side, he began to learn something of Celtic and Norse mythology; with Ned Jones, too, he discovered the primary documents of Victorian Gothicism, Ruskin's *Stones of Venice* and Carlyle's *Past and Present.* Two summer trips to the continent, in 1854 and 1855, impressed upon him the glories of Gothic cathedrals and medieval art. Yet by 1855, he began to abandon organized religion for the religions of beauty and nature.

In 1855, he discovered the pictorial and literary power of the group known as the Pre-Raphaelite Brotherhood. He saw paintings by Hunt, Millais, Madox Brown, and Rossetti, read Ruskin's praises of their truth to nature, and even obtained a copy of the Brotherhood's magazine, the *Germ.* The Pre-Raphaelites, especially Dante Gabriel Rossetti whom Morris met in 1856, were major influences on the young man. Pre-Raphaelite painting helped him crystallize his sense of rebellion against Victorian ugliness; Pre-Raphaelite themes and techniques were assimilated into his own consciousness. Morris admired and imitated what James D. Merrit characterizes as the keynotes of the poetry in the *Germ:* the constant and brilliant use of descriptive details, sensuous and highly colored imagery, imitation of the tone and structure of ballads, and the use of symbolic overtones—numerological, Christian, or esoteric.[2] As important, in the Pre-Raphaelite fascination with tragic love, with imminent or actual death,[3] and with the crucial moment which determines one's earthly fate, he found echoes of his own preoccupations. He found himself in sympathy with both of the antithetical aspects of the Brotherhood, its realism and its romanticism; both could appeal to a mind itself divided.

The first important fruits of Morris's literary and visual exposure to past and present may be found in the prose tales written for the *Oxford and Cambridge Magazine* of 1856. Designed by

Morris and his friends, chiefly Oxonian, as a "Crusade and Holy Warfare against the age"[4] and as a successor to the *Germ*, the magazine presented to a small public, three articles, five poems, and eight tales by the young Morris.[5] Poems and tales alike reveal Morris's interest in love, fate, and death and the beginning of his complex attitudes toward them. They reveal his reading as well. Influenced not only by the chivalric romance and Northern myth and folklore he loved, he utilizes the full tradition of romantic Gothic literature. He borrows mood, tone, and detail from the German romances of Meinhold, Tieck, Hoffmann, and La Motte Fouque, and he is well acquainted with the works of Edgar Allan Poe. His borrowings, for the most part, are fragmentary, and the surprise of Morris's early tales is how skillfully he invents his own narratives. The tale of "Golden Wings" might have been a brief romance told by Malory; "Svend and His Brethren" might have been a section of a Norse chronicle, and "Gertha's Lovers" (especially the chapter titled "What Edith the Handmaiden Saw from the War-Saddle") might well have been a translation of a saga. They are original works which appear so "typical" that the reader expects to find their analogues among the books Morris was reading.

Morris does use traditional *topoi* and details from them. Benjamin Thorpe's *Northern Mythology*, one of Morris's favorite books, is the acknowledged source of "Lindenborg Pool," as well as of the names Siur, Cissela, and Valdemar in "Svend and His Brethren," another Northern tale. But Morris merely uses the names themselves, inventing entirely new characters to bear them. Even when he derives "Lindenborg Pool" from Thorpe's brief account of "The Sunken Mansion" the differences are more striking than the similarities. Just as Morris's treatments of traditional romantic and Victorian themes are strikingly personal, so too are his transmutations of his literary sources.

Thorpe presents a brief redaction of the Danish legend of an unfathomable lake:

"The Sunken Mansion"

In the neighbourhood of Lindenborg, near Aarhuus, there is a lake which no one has hitherto been able to fathom. Of this lake the following story is current in the neighbourhood. Many years ago there stood in the place where the lake now is, a proud, ancient castle or mansion, of which the only trace remaining is a road that led to the gate, but which is now lost under the waters of the lake. On one holyday-eve, when the family were from home, the servants of the place indulged in great revel and merriment, which at length proceeded so far, that in their state of drunkenness they wrapped a swine up in bed-linen, placed a cap on its head, and laid it in the master's bed. They then sent a message to the priest, summoning him to come without a moment's delay to administer to their master, who lay at the point of death. The priest was instantly there, and, observing no deception, read to the swine and did everything required by his vocation; but when he was about to administer the sacrament, all present burst into a fit of laughter, and the swine snapped the bread out of his hand. In terror he hurried from the place, but forgot to take his book with him. Just as he was hastening through the outer gate, the castle clock struck twelve, when a cracking and crashing began in every side and corner of the building. When he turned round the mansion had sunk and the lake rushed forth from the abyss. As he stood gazing, through fear and wonder unable to proceed, there came a little stool floating on the water to the border of the lake, on which lay the book that he had left in the mansion.[6]

This straightforward account becomes a Gothic story, strongly influenced by Poe, in Morris's hands. Creating a first person narrator, also used for drama and immediacy in "Golden Wings," "The Hollow Land," and "Frank's Sealed Letter," Morris centers his tale less on the grotesque events than on the narrative consciousness. As R. C. Ellison remarks, Morris is always interested "in the behavior of his characters within the contrived situation, their solution to the dilemma of life and death."[7] Morris's Victorian narrator becomes Thorpe's thirteenth-century priest, while simultaneously retaining a nineteenth-century identity. Morris is as much concerned with the narrator's awareness of his double identity as with the events the narrator witnesses.

Descriptive elements, merely sketched by Thorpe, become significant images in Morris's tale. The wild May night on which the narrator attempts to fathom the pool echoes his unresolved guilt at killing a man on the same night ten years earlier. External nature reflects inner emotion in Morris's description of the landscape surrounding the pool. Reminiscent of the lair of Grendel's mother in *Beowulf*, it is marked by grotesque weeds and shrubs that seem derived from Browning's "Childe Roland":

. . . a rank crop of dreary reeds and segs, some round, some flat, but none ever flowering as other things flowered, never dying and being renewed, but always the same stiff array of unbroken reeds and segs, some round, some flat.

(1:245–46)

Described in Morris's insistent, rhythmical prose, the land

around the pool becomes a mythical wasteland, the pool itself an entry to hell.

Morris adds the incident of the priest's journey with a debauched jester and amplifies the account of the revels into a lengthy description of a nightmare rout, obviously modeled on Poe's "Masque of the Red Death." Creating an almost hallucinatory mood, he describes the masked, transvestite figures, their mad laughter and dancing, and the strange apartment through which they move. His ending is equally intensified. The narrator-priest is wounded by the boar to whom he has unwittingly given the last rites, thus gaining his stigmata and atoning for the murder he has committed, and must fight his way out of the castle. And the castle's fall is seen as a judgment of God in a way different from Thorpe's Christian tale. The priest's Bible is not returned to him, for Morris's emphasis is not on God's mercy but on primitive supernatural vengeance. The dark tarn that is Lindenborg Pool is the result of a fall, like that of the House of Usher: "Then while the east grew bright there arose a hissing, gurgling noise, that swelled into the roar and wash of many waters, and by then the sun had risen a deep black lake lay before my feet" (1:253).[8] Morris ends his tale with an embarrassingly clear echo of Poe's.

The techniques Morris uses in this tale are reutilized with similar effects in the other stories written for the magazine, the plots of which are entirely his own. In all the tales, vivid, carefully delineated details are placed within imaginary and timeless realms and often framed by dreams and visions. "A Dream" is a medieval dream-vision, and sleeping and waking dreams are vital components in "The Story of the Unknown Church," "Gertha's Lovers," "The Hollow Land," and "Frank's Sealed Letter." The effect of dream exists even within the tales which do not ostensibly contain it. All capture the associative flow of dream, all shift scenes and metamorphose characters without logical transition or explanation.

Just as the use of dreams provides a unique blend of aesthetic distance and immediacy, so, too, does the way in which Morris utilizes his narrators. While often using first-person narration for immediacy, he will create aesthetic distance by having the speakers describe their past from the point of view of old age or death. Walter, the mason of "The Unknown Church," tells his story after he is dead, as does Lionel in "Golden Wings." Florian speaks of "The Hollow Land" after he has left the ordinary world to enter it. Even when the narrators are living participants in their own adventures, they are psychically distant from themselves and separate from others.

Yet Morris's details have the inexplicable intensity of dream images. Like the mason of "The Unknown Church," who in his dream can see a bunch of gold and red wall flowers though they are on a distant castle built above a far off cliff, so the reader can see distant objects as clearly as he can see foreground details. Foreground details are often amazingly vivid. Morris's journalistic description of "The Churches of North France: Shadows of Amiens" (1:349–66) is less real and intense than his imaginative transformation of Amiens into the unknown church. The Last Judgment the mason is carving on his church is clearly based on what Morris saw at Amiens, but a powerful transformation of the reality. So, too, Morris's accurate descriptions of nature are either arranged or heightened to become unnatural. The landscape of which the unknown church is the center is as much a picture in an illuminated manuscript as an earthly phenomenon:

> The Abbey where we built the Church was not girt by stone walls, but by a circle of poplar trees . . . ; moreover, through the boughs and trunks of the poplars we caught glimpses of the great golden corn sea, waving, waving, waving for leagues and leagues; and among the corn grew burning scarlet poppies, and blue corn-flowers; and the corn-flowers were so blue, that they gleamed, and seemed to burn with a steady light, as they grew beside the poppies among the gold of the wheat. Through the corn sea ran a blue river, & always green meadows and lines of tall poplars followed its windings.
>
> (1:150)

Even the colors are preternaturally intense. They are the brilliant hues of stained-glass windows or of Pre-Raphaelite paintings. Morris's use of colors as private symbols begins to manifest itself in the early tales, and red is established, quite traditionally, as the color of passion and violence. Green is the color of hope and happiness found in the green garments of Morris's heroines, the green air of the Hollow Land, and the green raiment and armor donned by Florian and Red Harald in "The Hollow Land" when they have forgiven each other for misinterpreting the judgment of God. Morris's palette is also well laden with white, which maintains its associations with purity; purple, for empire and penance; blue, for the heavenly or divine; and gold, associated with life's brilliance and value.

"The Hollow Land," often considered inexplicable, derives both its power and its meaning from Morris's color symbolism. Red Harald, enraged at the murder of Swanhilda, his mother, by Florian and his family, paints God's judgments—garish scarlet and yellow pictures, on the walls of Florian's ruined castle. When

Florian questions him about his painting, he screams that the colors he has chosen, yellow and red, are "gold & blood" (1:284), that they represent God's condemning them both to hell on earth. Their penance and forgiveness are symbolized by the painting of "purple pictures and green ones," symbols of their mourning and atonement and of the hope that God will "change both . . . [them] and . . . [their] works" (1:287). The epiphany that frees them from their purgatorial state, permitting Florian to return to the earthly paradise of the Hollow Land, is symbolized by the funeral procession of a king. The dress of the dead king, his knights and lords, in which the scarlet, purple, and gold of passion and empire prevail, are juxtaposed against their opposites, the white and golden garb of churchmen and the green and white of maidens' garments. The revelation is in the harmony that comes of the dialectically opposed colors themselves.[9]

Seasons, too, take on the symbolism that will adhere to them in Morris's later volumes; Morris's fascination with the cycle of the earth and its message of birth, growth, and death is already evident. The lovers, Margaret and Amyot, in "The Story of the Unknown Church" are united in death in the golden haze of early autumn, the harvest and decline of the year. Florian is expelled from the Hollow Land on "a horrible grey November day" (1:281), an external correlative to his physical aging and emotional despair. Swanhilda is murdered in the dead of winter, ironically, on Christmas Eve. (Later, we learn that she has been transported to the Hollow Land.) The final reunion of Ella and Lawrence, in "A Dream," occurs as the bells toll in the new year; they sink to white ashes and the promise of a final rebirth.

Here, too, as in later works, Morris correlates external events and details with inner emotions and states of mind. At times he is heavy-handed, as when thunder and lightning punctuate Svend's warnings to his evil subjects. At times he is far more subtle, as when the mason of the church sits by his dead friend, focusing intensely on the vines outside the window. He is waiting for the red leaves of the vine to fall, in an unconscious premonition of the impending death of his friend's beloved.

Thus, early in his career Morris has gathered a body of techniques which will create the unique effect of the later poetry and prose. He has also found one of his central themes, for the tales center on love, triumphant or rejected, defying society or yielding to the duties it imposes, and usually unconsummated in the characters' lifetimes. Like Browning, as Morris interpreted him in reviewing *Men and Women* for the *Oxford and Cambridge Magazine*, Morris believes that life's goal is "love for love's sake, the only true love" and adds a fervent prayer that "some of us attain to it before we die!" (1:340–41). Stimulated by protestant earnestness, romantic enthusiasm, and chivalric worship, he aspires to "intense" and "unmixed" passion (1:340). Love is more than enough; it "should go before everything, before all friendship, all duty, all honour even" (1:189). Yet Morris does not suggest that the outcome of erotic passion will be happiness. The lovers in the tales know that each person needs someone "to love him infinitely, to think his thoughts, be one with him" (1:184), but they seldom achieve what, to Morris, is perfect union: "Body and soul together again" (1:167).

Morris's male lovers are seldom triumphant in their life adventures. Instead they are figures like Browning's Childe Roland,[10] whom Morris visualized as "a brave man doing his duty, making his way on to his point through all dreadful things . . . [though] he will be slain certainly, who knows by what unheard-of death" (1:339), or like Palomydes. The latter figure, questing for a reward that evades him, also becomes Morris's archetype of the knight who spends his life in devoted service to a lady who rejects him. Mackail, describing Morris's use of the Palomydes motif, notes that "the subject was one for which he felt a singular and morbid attraction, that of the unsuccessful man and despised lover."[11] Leuchnar in "Gertha's Lovers" and Hugh in "Frank's Sealed Letter" are the first of the many heroes modeled on Palomydes. Each resembles him in his "bitter useless striving after love" (1:21); each believes that his life has been shaped or warped by the pain of his unrequited passion.[12] The women in the tales, whether they are the virgins and princesses of folklore and legend or the fatal women of Gothic tradition, suffer equally. Whether they love or reject the knights who win them, they, too, are denied full satisfaction in life.

Almost all the lovers in the tales—Cissela and Siur in "Svend and His Brethren," Ella and Lawrence in "A Dream," Lionel and Alys in "Golden Wings," and Gertha and Olaf in "Gertha's Lovers"—are separated or destroyed by forces beyond their control. Only Florian and Margaret are lastingly united and they are joined not in the ordinary world but in the earthly paradise of the Hollow Land. Cissela and Siur must sacrifice erotic passion to social duty. She becomes a peace-queen, taking King Valdemar as her husband to preserve her endangered race and to redeem them from a curse. Lawrence and Ella are separated by her taunts and by the pride which makes her send her knight on a fatal quest. Yet even her imperfections seem less like inner flaws than the commands of a power outside herself, the mandates of a destiny which ordains such separations.

Fate is also responsible for the love triangle, a configuration with which Morris was fascinated before he had even met Jane Burden or she and Rossetti had fallen in love. Although in "Svend and His Brethren" Cissela must choose the king, regardless of his worth, in two other tales the tragic situation is that two good men are in love with the same woman. Lionel, the hero of "Golden Wings," recognizes that he is taking Alys away from a knight he considers both stronger and better than himself—the man who has rescued her from rape and fire. Both Olaf and Leuchnar fall in love with Gertha at first sight, but Leuchnar, considering Olaf more noble, sacrifices his love for his friend's. Despite the behavior of the heroes, the triangles result in their deaths.

Indeed, Morris's lovers are denied consummation by death, as, in this first literary work, he establishes what will become a lasting tension in his later volumes: the connection between sexual passion and violent or unnatural death. Margaret and Amyot are separated by the demise of both; he dies of a mysterious illness contracted in the Crusades, she, of grief at his death. Olaf is slain in battle, and Gertha, waiting until her duties as queen are finished, joins him in death. In the most direct connection made between erotic love and death, Lionel is murdered for eloping with Alys.

The world in which the characters reside is far from hospitable to love. Instead, it is a realm torn by family feuds or stained by battle. The pervasive image is of blood, mingling with the landscape and coloring the waters of the sea. Even in depicting heroic battle, Morris emphasizes shattered skulls, slit throats, and gore. Often, his preoccupation with mutilation and decay becomes excessive. He describes how one warrior grinds his boot into the face of a dead king and then drinks his victim's blood; how a torturer, equipped with knife, pincers, and cleaver, removes a young man's eyes and cuts off his hands; and, most grotesquely, how Florian, in "The Hollow Land," rises from the ground, his helmet and body encrusted with the slimy earth and coiling worms of physical decay. Morris's view of the brutality of life is made clear by the description in "Golden Wings" of the lover slaughtered before the eyes of his lady: "Then one thrust me through the breast with a spear, and another with his sword, which was three inches broad, gave me a stroke across the thighs that hit to the bone; and as I fell forward one cleft me to the teeth with his axe. And then I heard my darling shriek" (1:308). In the earthly world, Morris indicates, sensuous love and violent death go hand in hand; the passion to which all men should aspire brings comfort only in the grave or in a world beyond it.

Love's monument is the tomb. It grants immortality to lovers, signifying both the triumph of art (its ability to make legend out of human suffering) and love's consummation in death.[13] The figures whose union life does not permit are married in death, carved side by side on a tomb. Margaret and Amyot become the husband and wife they never were on earth in the tomb carved by the mason, whose completion of this tribute to tragic love is marked by his own demise. A mighty, though unfinished, church is built as a shrine for the bodies of Olaf and Gertha. The ashes of the reincarnated Ella and Lawrence are buried in a marble tomb wrought by those who, having heard their tale, "carved their figures lying with clasped hands" (1:175) in a tribute to their reunion in death. The implicit symbolism of the tomb is made explicit in "Svend and His Brethren" when Svend, who has been willing to sacrifice his love for Cissela in life, refuses to sacrifice it in death. When Cissela dies, Siur will not carve King Valdemar's figure next to hers on the royal tomb. He will not grant the King the eternal marriage in death that Siur believes is his own right.

Morris clearly utilizes Rossetti's concept of a fleshly reunion of lovers in heaven, the idea which underlies "The Blessed Damozel" (a poem Morris printed in the *Oxford and Cambridge Magazine*). He indicates his fascination with heaven as "a rose garden full of stunners," a fantasy of which his friend Swinburne writes.[14] A heaven for lovers provides consolation and reunion to those severed or rejected on earth. Hugh, cruelly scorned by Mabel, in "Frank's Sealed Letter," retains his sanity by believing Frank's message that "remembered love will be a very bright crown to you up in Heaven" (1:315). The advice Frank's letter offers Hugh—to let the memory of love remain, however cruelly one has been rejected—is based on the belief of a reward and reunion in paradise. Leuchnar, in "Gertha's Lovers," can accept Gertha's earthly preference for Olaf and die content in her kindness, for he is persuaded that he will have a heavenly reunion with her.

In all, Morris sees this earth as a place to endure trials and frustrations, not to enjoy rewards. His early tales might be called *Bildungsromane* of love, since their young protagonists develop by suffering the woes of passion. "A Dream" traces the growth of Ella as she transforms herself from cruelty and vanity to goodness, learning duty in her reincarnations as a nurse and as a queen. Simultaneously, it describes the development of Lawrence as he compensates in his reincarnations for being unable to do the knightly duties of his first life. In most of the tales, growth is traced as the male figures choose between passion and duty and win or fail in the world.

Morris's protagonists become heroes because of love or because of its frustrations. After his *enfance*, Lionel performs deeds for his lady, striving to be worthy of her love, growing as he does so. Siur in "Svend and His Brethren" becomes wise and courageous when, sublimating his passion for Cissela, he educates her sons by King Valdemar. Florian begins to learn from the lips of his beloved, Margaret, that he has mistaken the judgment of God and been wrong to kill or seek revenge. Leuchnar in "Gertha's Lovers" learns the worth of sacrifice by loving. His passion for Gertha thaws his hard heart and turns him away from a cynical belief in "the faithlessness of Adam's sons" (1:188). When he woos Gertha for Olaf rather than for himself, he moves further in the direction of self-sacrifice and heroism. As he spends his life in service, first to Olaf and later to Gertha, he becomes Morris's outstanding example of the rejected lover ennobled by the tribulations of his unrequited passion.

The lady Leuchnar loves and the women in the other early tales are more than simply educative forces. They are images of the soul itself, either of the dark aspects of the self—seen as a fatal woman—or of the benevolent feminine anima—envisioned as a beautiful virgin or princess. Morris's images of the beloved as the soul in the form of a woman are clearly influenced by Rossetti's. He knew and admired Rossetti's tale "Hand and Soul," with its clear statement that "earthly love . . . [was] a mutual recognition of twin souls, which used a woman as the soul's symbol."[15] More generally, Morris recognized that many of the poems and romances he loved described the passion for a beautiful woman as the exploration of the writers' own souls—that women, whether cruel or ambiguous or good and true, embodied animas. He was to use repeatedly, in the course of his literary career, the idea that rightful love was a mystic union not only of the bodies and souls of man and woman but of the separate aspects of the human personality. "Body and soul together again" (1:167) symbolizes the reintegration of the male and female aspects of the self.

The theme is first sketched in "A Dream," where the lovers must undergo reincarnation to achieve it, but the image of the pure or benign anima is most fully drawn in the character of Margaret, Florian's mysterious beloved. She awaits him—mystically knowing who and what he is—in the dream world of the Hollow Land.[16] Their bond is shown by the fact that in wounding her, he wounds himself. When he strikes her hand with a sword and she bleeds, he discovers that he, too, is bleeding. She tries to heal and teach him; because of his flaw, his unforgiving nature, he cannot learn the lesson of love. Not yet ready to reintegrate himself, he is cast back into the world to do penance. He cannot even remember Margaret or his love for her until his guilt has been purged. Their final union, upon his return to the Hollow Land, is clearly symbolic. As they approach the palace ordained for them, they see over a gateway, "two figures of a man & woman winged and garlanded, whose raiment flashed with stars" (1:290). The figures are both those of Cupid and Psyche—ancient symbols for the lover and the soul—and their own images. The reintegration of self, the perfect love of man and his pure anima, is described in Morris's exquisite, paradisaical ending: "And then we walked together toward the golden gates, and opened them; and no man gainsaid us. And before us lay a great space of flowers" (1:290).

The opposite of the pure anima is the dark anima, first seen in Morris's works as Mabel, the fatal woman in "Frank's Sealed Letter." She is a cruel lady, incapable of loving anyone but herself, but she is irresistibly beautiful with "heavy sweeping black hair" and "dreamily passionate eyes" (1:310). While she is clearly seen as unworthy of Hugh's passion, he senses that she cannot be other than she is. She is fated to be fatal. The tragic incidents of which he dreams are warnings of what will happen if he does not deal with his passion for her in an appropriate way. He is to accept his involvement with the dangerous and ambiguous aspects of himself as a necessary stage in his development. Though he can neither understand nor accomplish his ultimate goal, the shedding of the dark anima and the finding of the benign one, he has begun the quest for personal wholeness.

Thus, in the tales written for the *Oxford and Cambridge Magazine*, Morris begins to develop his accounts of the human struggle for the integration of the psyche. He brings the struggle to fuller life in the poems he writes for *The Defence of Guenevere and Other Poems*, his next volume. By working within the rich literary traditions which center upon love, fate, and death, he is able to provide a substantial framework for his emotions. By using materials from Malory, Froissart, and folklore, and by revitalizing legendary characters and incidents, he is able to clarify and objectify his own life journey.

TWO

IN DEFENSE OF
GUENEVERE

I

UNLIKE THE early prose tales and much of Morris's other verse, the works of his 1858 volume, *The Defence of Guenevere and Other Poems*, are replete with qualities which appeal to twentieth-century readers. Brief, intense, concentrated distillations of experience, these poems often contain the conversational tone, the idiosyncratic idiom, and the dramatic effects that excite modern readers. They are—or can be made to appear—complex, ambiguous, paradoxical, and ironic. Of all Morris's poems, those of *The Defence* come closest to satisfying contemporary criteria for poetic excellence.

The Defence volume, however, is significant for other reasons. It introduces the techniques in poetry and the ways of developing source materials that Morris will reutilize in later works. It reiterates many of the themes which had been sketched in the tales and were to become the constants in the pattern of his poetry. Much of the volume's impact comes from Morris's use of the same techniques he had already utilized in the tales: the brilliant Pre-Raphaelite imagery, the vivid description of landscape, the symbolism associated with color, and the use of symbolic details within simplified but weighted backgrounds. These, when supplemented by his tense, stuttering rhythms and the compression natural to poetry, create powerful works in verse.

Although the poems of *The Defence* are not without metrical inaccuracies, Morris's prosodic flaws pale in the light of his use of imagery and symbolism. For example, the refrain of the lyrical "Two Red Roses Across the Moon" is a functioning multiple image; the same words evoke a lady's song, a knight's battle cry, and the device emblazoned on his shield.[1] The same device is used in "The Gilliflower of Gold," where the ramifications of the central image become even more complex. The phrase which

13

forms the poem's refrain, *"la belle jaune giroflée"* (1:90–91), refers, firstly, to an image of an actual flower "stain'd with red" because there are crimson streaks on its yellow petals; secondly, to an image of the floral token which the knight who narrates the poem wears in his tourney helm and which is stained with the blood of his opponents; thirdly, to the physical characteristics of the golden-haired, red-lipped lady he loves and in whose honor he fights. As he remembers her "quiet head/ Bow'd o'er the gilli-flower bed" (1:91), he associates her beauty with that of the blossoms.[2] Other images are subtly symbolic. In "The Wind," the dramatic monologue of a crazed Norse knight, the image of an orange "with a deep gash cut in the rind" (1:107) which lies in the green hangings of the speaker's chair, combines pictorial and em-blematic qualities. Its visual source is probably John Everett Mil-lais's painting, *Isabella*,[3] in which the lovers share a blood orange in token of the tragedy to come, but Morris adapts the image to his own ends. The bleeding orange becomes the insane speaker's correlative of the woman he has loved and perhaps stabbed; the green drapery reminds him of the grass covered hill on which the crime occurred.

As Walter Pater noticed in his essay on "Aesthetic Poetry," nature is seldom objective in Morris's poetry. The landscape is always sympathetic, a comment upon or reflection of the emo-tional states of the characters depicted. As the lover in "Summer Dawn" waits for "one word" (1:144) from his beloved to illumi-nate his life, so the responsive earth on which he sings his *aube* awaits the dawn and the sunlight.[4] The howl of the wind in "The Wind" is an echo of the mental tempest of the poem's mad speaker. The sickness and blindness he attributes to the wind are his own; the wind's vain search for the lily seed is his own inter-nalized quest for the woman he has loved and lost. The sun blazes upon the heat of Guenevere's passion in "The Defence of Guene-vere" and upon Launcelot's in "King Arthur's Tomb." In the latter poem, Guenevere's realization of her sin is prefigured by the gray blight of the hills at which she gazes.

Developing his color symbolism, Morris at times anticipates French symbolist poetry. Poems such as "The Blue Closet," "Two Red Roses Across the Moon," and "The Gilliflower of Gold" attain their effects and enhance their themes through Mor-ris's use of color. In many of the poems color is associated with the past or with powerful emotion and juxtaposed against the colorlessness of present reality or of the ordinary levels of exist-ence. Sometimes a brightly colored object is pinpointed against a gray background. The object is thrust into the foreground, de-manding attention, in the faint light of a gray dawn or twilight.[5]

In the gray rain-drenched world of "The Haystack in the Floods," the only color is of the villain Godmar's pennon with its "three/ Red running lions" (1:125). The intense colors of "The Blue Closet"—a poem that attempts to capture the impact of Rossetti's watercolor in words—are set off by the gray night, dusty snow, and ivory pallor of the dead lover who enters the closet to claim its inhabitants. Objects function as they do in Pre-Raphaelite paintings: they are not merely decorative, but symbolic in intention, although their meanings are not always explicated. The reader senses that they are significant, but, as in dream, their precise meanings remain elusive.

As in the tales, Morris borrows qualities from the literary works he admires. He is greatly inspired by themes and images from the poems and paintings of Rossetti, to whom he dedicated *The Defence*. From Browning, Morris learns the form of the dramatic monologue, imitating, in poems such as "Concerning Geffray Teste Noire," the conversational beginnings, associative transitions, and cacaphonous music of the author of *Men and Women*. He utilizes forms and materials probably derived from the medievalized ballads of Elizabeth Barrett and Sir Walter Scott.[6] Yet, through a process of synthesis and intensification, he makes what he borrows his own. For the tone of the volume differs from his contemporaries. In Morris's own era, critics attempted to define its quality, agreeing that it was almost unique in English poetry. Swinburne spoke of its "passion," Dixon Scott of its tension of "nerves" and Pater of its quality of "delirium."[7] None, however, fully analyzed the thematic and tonal devices which made it so.

The particular intensity of *The Defence* volume is partially created by Morris's use of irony and by his conjunctions of opposing images, those of love and beauty played against images of horror and death.[8] Morris's use of verbal and dramatic irony is skillful, but his chief strength lies in the way he ironically reverses expected situations and events. The unanticipated parting that Jehane and Robert share "Beside the haystack in the floods" (1:128) is one famous example of this technique. Situational irony pervades "Riding Together," in which a crusader's anticipated ride to victory becomes a last ride to a pagan prison, and "The Sailing of the Sword," in which the narrator's plea that her knight return to his "white maid" (1:103) is answered in a manner different from her expectations, as her lover returns *with* a pale maiden other than herself. In two cases, the titles Morris chooses for his poems ironically alter their meaning. "The Eve of Crecy" is the title of a poem about a knight's dream of love, reward, and victory on the night *before* the famous battle; if the reader ignores the title or fails to notice that the knight is French, Morris's irony is lost. "The Judgment of God," a title which leads the reader to believe that the poem's narrator will face an ordeal-by-combat with prayer and a conviction of his cause's rightness, is an ironic statement of the knight's determination to win by craft and treachery, if necessary.

Morris's pleasure in dramatically reversing the reader's expectations—a technique perhaps learned from Gothic literature—extends even to his descriptive passages. He will develop and embroider an image and then shatter it. For example, the first stanzas of "Golden Wings" carefully amplify images of peace and beauty: a lovers' gard, waving banners on a tower, sweet red apples, swans feasting on cake, and a carved and softly cushioned pleasure boat. In the final stanzas, the images are dramatically reversed:

> The apples now grow green and sour
>   Upon the mouldering castle-wall
>   Before they ripen there they fall:
> There are no banners on the tower.
>
> The draggled swans most eagerly eat
>   The green weeds trailing in the moat;
>   Inside the rotting leaky boat
> You see a slain man's stiffen'd feet.
>
>   (1:123)

Like the prose tales, the poems of *The Defence* volume are filled with events and images that juxtapose loveliness and brutality. In "Concerning Geffray Teste Noire," the idyllic setting of Verville forest with its hazel copses, primroses, and shimmering dragonflies frames an account of the discovery of violent death. In "The Haystack," the penultimate tableau is of beautiful Jehane—arms outstretched and lips parted for a kiss—watching her lover slaughtered like an animal before her eyes. In "The Wind," "The Gilliflower of Gold," and "Rapunzel," Morris connects the beauty of flowers with the terrible beauty of blood. His vision is epitomized in Rapunzel-Gwendolen's description of the combat she has witnessed from her tower. She sees:

> One knight lean dead, bleeding from head and breast,
>   Yet seem'd it like a line of poppies red
>   In the golden twilight, as he took his rest.
>
>   (1:69)

The interconnections between beauty and violence, erotic love and death are, of course, made thematically as well as imagistically. The traditional divisions of the volume: the Malory poems (those derived from *Le Morte D'Arthur*), the Froissart poems (those derived from the *Chronicle*), and the "fantasies" or "dreamlight" poems[9] (those which I call fairy tale poems, since they stem from folklore and legend) are unified by their common preoccupation with these themes. Moreover, to further unify *The Defence*, Morris pairs and triples poems. Concerned with two contrasting structural patterns, one in which love triumphs over fate and death, another in which it is altered or destroyed by them, he will often have one poem answer another. "The Gilliflower of Gold" and "The Eve of Crecy," though similar in rhyme scheme, stanzaic form, and refrain, offer opposite views of love, fate, and death. After winning a bloody tourney, the knight of the Gilliflower muses on the lady he adores and now may win; before fighting the battle of Crecy, a contest he will lose, Sir Lambert of France dreams of the lady he loves and can never attain. Two ballads similar in technique, "Welland River" and "The Sailing of the Sword," deal with the plights of lovesick ladies; the first is the tale of a woman who successfully wins back her absent knight from a rival, the second of a deserted maiden who fails to do so. Two of the fairy tale poems, "The Blue Closet" and "The Tune of Seven Towers," share similar elements of tone and atmosphere. Both are poems about the destructive passion which leads to death. Beneath the music of the first lies the myth of the demon lover; the song of the second is that of the demon lover's female counterpart, the fatal woman. Although "A Good Knight in Prison" and "Spell-Bound" differ in style, both are centered on captive knights whose fantasies and frustrations are bound up with their dreams of their absent ladies. In the first poem, the knight is freed and attains his bride; in the second, he remains trapped in his prison, enthralled by his futile love.

Thus, by pairing poems, Morris connects and builds motifs both within divisions and among them. While each division focuses on a different poetic world and each establishes its unique tone, the central themes of the entire volume remain constant.

II

The vast creative and destructive power of earthly love is the subject of the Malory poems. Morris's preoccupation with rejected lovers and fatal women mingled with his excited discovery of Southey's edition of *Le Morte D'Arthur* to create two of the most powerful poems of the division, "The Defence of Guenevere" and "King Arthur's Tomb." Counterpoised against these, he wrote two additional poems, again based on Malory, which examine the tensions between earthly and heavenly love, "Sir Galahad: A Christmas Mystery," and "The Chapel in Lyoness." Additionally, he began but did not complete a number of Arthurian works, "The Maying of Queen Guenevere," "Saint Agnes [sic] Convent," and "Sir Palomydes' Quest."[10]

The influence of *Le Morte D'Arthur* pervades them all. Morris is fond of developing hints and implications from his source into major incidents or motifs in his own poems. He attempts to create original works that elaborate upon yet are true to what he envisions as the essence of the source with which he is dealing. Thus, the Malory poems are poems of brilliant, flashing color, the colors of chivalry and heraldry; their settings—bowers, tourney fields, and chapels—are drawn from Malory's realm of magic and romance. Even the structure of the poems, complex, elaborate, contrapuntal, attempts to capture the richness of Malory's interwoven tales; their utterance imitates what Morris thought was the quality of *Le Morte D'Arthur*'s stylized prose. Investigating the effects of love on character, Morris examines the motivations of Malory's figures, analyzing emotions at which Malory only hints. Concerning himself, before Tennyson, with the mixture of love and sin that marked the final days of Arthur's court, Morris dramatizes the tragedy and examines the reasons for it.[11] "The Maying of Queen Guenevere," a fragment seemingly intended as the first poem in a cycle, presents a brief picture of the frustration of Meliagraunce in loving Guenevere who "laughs aloud" (1:xix) at his passion for her. Thus, it introduces the Meliagraunce incident in "The Defence." "Sir Palomydes' Quest" seems intended as a treatment of the plight of Iseult and Palomydes, both paralleling and contrasting with the relationship between Guenevere and Launcelot. In Palomydes, Morris had found an image of the worthy but unloved lover of a fatal woman;[12] in Guenevere he now found both the Pre-Raphaelite image of beauty and the romantic concept of the fatal woman, loved and desired by all—but doomed to destroy herself and those who adore her. Meredith Raymond suggests that the four Arthurian poems form two pairs of diptychs[13] and that Guenevere is the central figure in the first group. Her portraits in "The Defence" and "King Arthur's Tomb" illuminate each other. By understanding the queen's complex nature as revealed in the first poem, the reader can more fully comprehend her actions in the second.

"The Defence" and "King Arthur's Tomb" are integrally related to each other, though each can stand on its own. They are also closely related to Malory, for Morris both alludes to his source and weaves an elaborate counterpoint around it.[14] As Laurence Perrine indicates: "Morris has . . . taken one of Malory's characters in a moment of stress and brought her intensely alive."[15] He has based his poem on Malory's account of Guenevere's second trial for treason and adultery, a crisis arising from her harboring of Launcelot in her chamber. In the course of her defense, Guenevere mentions her first trial, the result of Meliagraunce's accusation that she has lain with one of the ten wounded knights captured during her kidnapping. In both cases, with Malory's story in mind, the reader realizes that although the queen is unquestionably guilty of adultery, the specific charges against her are false. Gauwaine's accusation—that Launcelot and Guenevere had been making love in her chamber when they were trapped there by Agravaine and his companions—is probably incorrect.[16] Malory first has Launcelot announce his intention of going to speak with the queen and then refuses to discuss the next occurrence:

And then, as the French book saith, the queen and Launcelot were together. And whether they were abed or at other manner of disports, me list not hereof make no mention, for love that time was not as is nowadays.[17]

Malory is not being coy, for on an earlier occasion he tells us plainly that "Sir Launcelot went unto bed with the queen . . . [and] took his pleasance and his liking until it was in the dawning of the day."[18] He simply does not *know* what happened on this specific occasion, and he suggests, moreover, that sexual intimacy need not have occurred:

But the old love was not so; men and women could love together seven years, and no lycours lusts were between them, and then was love, truth, and faithfulness: and lo, in likewise was used love in King Arthur's days.[19]

Morris probably read Malory as suggesting the queen's innocence in this instance and built from it one of the fine ironies of the poem. Morris follows Malory in indicating that the second accusation against Guenevere is equally untrue. She is "innocent," for it is Launcelot, rather than one of the wounded knights kidnapped with her, who has entered through the barred window of her chamber and enjoyed her favors. Thus, Launcelot can truthfully, if ironically, swear with certainty "that this night there lay none of these ten wounded knights with my lady,"[20] and she can do the same. Meliagraunce is "shent" (1:8) for selecting the wrong man.

Moreover, Guenevere hews down Gauwaine's proof of her guilt in this incident—the presence of blood stains on her bed—more conclusively than just by suggesting that a queen does not need to offer proof of innocence.[21] The blood is Launcelot's, but Guenevere provides a suggestion of its origin calculated to arouse sympathy for her. She will not say she has been forced, she tells us: not in this way will she defend "The honour of the lady Guenevere" (1:7) even on judgment day. But this is just what she implies; she suggests what she wishes her audience to believe—that Meliagraunce, "Stripper of ladies" (1:7) has attempted an assault on her virtue—but that she is too much a queen to discuss it.

Yet, far more important than her specific objections to Gauwaine's charges are Guenevere's revelations of her true inward nature.[22] The moral ambiguities within the poem are quite deliberate; they stem from Guenevere's character, not Morris's uncertainty about it. The queen does not know whether she is morally guilty; she is uncertain of the rightness of her position, certain only of the strength of the love that has placed her in it. She can defend her love, indeed, she will not deny its worth or power, but she cannot always defend the adultery that it has caused; thus she attempts at times to deny the latter and always to minimize its importance. She hints at her actions, half confessing through double-meaning statements, slipping, through the imagery she uses, into temporarily admitting adultery, then withdrawing into a stance of innocence and ostensibly retracting the statements she has made. Denying, finding excuses, equivocating, she always stops short of full confession. The keynote of the poem—and of Guenevere's character—is the poem's first word, "But" (1:1). With it, we are thrown into the whole moral structure of Guenevere's nature.

The quality of Guenevere's argument is revealed at the very beginning of the poem. The meaning of her first statement to the judges who have decided to burn her at the stake is certainly double:

> God wot I ought to say, I have done ill,
> And pray you all forgiveness heartily!
> Because you must be right, such great lords—
>
> (1:1)

On one level she is sarcastically flattering her audience, saying that the lords in their wisdom and rank are not to be contradicted; but she may also mean that she *has* sinned and *should* ask forgiveness. That she does mean the latter, as well as the former, is shown by her next argument. When she asks the lords to identify with her in the matter of the "choosing cloths" (1:2), she is asking them to understand her moral dilemma and the reason for her wrong choice. The lords are to suppose they were about to die, "quite alone and very weak" (1:1), and were then to choose between heaven and hell, without knowing which was which—just as she has had to do. In describing the instruments of choice, she subtly slants the argument. One of the two cloths is described as "blue,/ Wavy and long, and one cut short and red" (1:2). "No man could tell the better of the two" (1:2), says Guenevere, but this is untrue. All—especially those acquainted with Morris's color symbolism —would do as she had done and choose "heaven's colour, the blue" (1:2); all would be shocked to discover that blue, with its connotations of spirituality, means hell.[23] Guenevere is ostensibly pleading that the wrong choice in her life was made unwittingly, but she is also suggesting that the choice was logical and the one all would have made. Her argumentative skill almost makes the reader forget that she *is* confessing; in saying that she had chosen hell, she means not only unhappy love, but adultery, a path of action that will lead to hell. She seeks to excuse her sin by suggesting its universality, and she blames it upon the moral confusion in the universe: things are not what they seem. But she still must admit that, whatever the cause, she has done wrong.

The refrain which follows the incident appears at first to be Guenevere's repudiation of what she had just admitted:

> Nevertheless you, O Sir Gauwaine, lie,
> Whatever may have happened through these years,
> God knows I speak truth, saying that you lie.
>
> (1:2)

But it may be interpreted in another way as well. The queen, answering the letter rather than the spirit of Gauwaine's charge, may well mean that she has been innocent in the particular incident of which she is accused, though guilty on other occasions.[24] When the refrain next occurs, after her confession of her love for Launcelot, its second line is slightly altered. "Whatever may have happened" (1:2) becomes "Whatever happened on through all those years" (1:5). The statement is no longer conditional; Guenevere is openly confessing her love, perhaps even her adultery, though again protesting her innocence on the particular occasion cited. Uttering the refrain one last time, she moves back to the conditional tense ("Whatever may have happen'd") but stresses the length of time she and Launcelot have loved and suffered—"these long years" (1:10). Her stressing of the long years brings to mind Malory's defense of her affair—its delayed and inevitable consummation. But it brings to mind, as well, the many years of the lovers' dalliance. Ambiguity is reintroduced every time Guenevere utters the refrain.

The queen reveals herself even more directly when her speech works against its intentions, when she slips into saying too much. She says more than she intends when she pleads for kindness from Gauwaine, asking him to "Remember in what grave your mother sleeps" (1:6)—ostensibly not to condemn her to his mother's ignominious death. Her conscious point is that punishing adultery brings nothing but shame and fear to the avengers of it; she implies that Gauwaine is already haunted for his deed. But, in so doing, she slips into identifying herself with Gauwaine's unfortunate but guilty mother, Margawse. Again, in discussing her interview with Launcelot in her chamber, in describing them as "children once again, free from all wrongs / Just for one night" (1:9), she suggests other nights less free from wrong.

But Guenevere's most important revelations are made through the images in which she describes herself and her love. Suggesting that her beauty is a "gracious proof" (1:9) of her innocence, she equates her external loveliness with her inner spiritual perfection in the time-honored medieval tradition. But the images in which she describes herself are the sensual ones of "Body's Beauty" rather than "Soul's Beauty." We are shown the "passionate twisting of her body" (1:2), and she demands that her male judges notice the rising of her breast, "Like waves of purple sea" (1:8), the movement and brightness of her hair, the grace of her long throat and rounded arms, and the shadows lying in her hand "like wine within a cup" (1:8). The long red-gold hair and pillarlike neck suggest Elizabeth Siddal, Rossetti's model and mistress, but, more significantly, they suggest the opulent sensuousness of Guenevere's own nature.[25]

The terms in which she describes the growth of her love for Launcelot are both descriptions of madness and images of a fall. On her first meeting with him, she has been "half mad with beauty" (1:4). Overwhelmed with joy at the fertility of the spring, she has exchanged kisses with him. The birth of nature has been paralleled by the birth of passion. Love has overpowered her, making her lips "curl up at false and true," her soul seem "cold and shallow without any cloud." She informs her judges that, in internal chaos, she has moved beyond the accepted rules for human conduct. Her marriage vow has become only "a little word, / Scarce ever meant at all" (1:3), for she has forgotten the significance of marriage. She admits that with moral sense, public opinion, and religious and legal sanctions unimportant to her, her only stay has been love; there is nothing to keep her from adultery.

Loving Launcelot is described as the process of "slipping"

> . . . slowly down some path worn smooth and even,
> Down to a cool sea on a summer day;
> Yet still in slipping there was some small leaven
>
> Of stretched hands catching small stones by the way,
> Until one surely reached the sea at last,
> And felt strange new joy as the worn head lay
>
> Back, with the hair like sea-weed; yea all past
> Sweat of the forehead, dryness of the lips,
> Washed utterly out by the dear waves o'ercast.
>
> (1:4)

Sliding down a path "worn smooth and even" perhaps because so many have taken it, she has been initially ambivalent about her fall. She has stretched out her hands to catch "small stones" with which to temper it, but she has yearned to immerse herself in the sea. The sea, when reached, has substituted "strange new joy" for fear, frustration, and anticipation. It is a joy in love—a distinctly sexual passion suggesting the release of spent desire.

Ironically, her self-vindication backfires; in pleading "temporary insanity," in dwelling upon the mitigating circumstances, she convinces the reader that she has done what she will not quite openly admit. One of the strengths of the poem is that her central argument—moral confusion—is what convinces the reader that she is an adulteress. The reader is to appreciate her consummate rhetoric, her methods of handling her judges—she seduces, cajoles, and threatens them—and the variety of pleas by which she seeks to win sympathy and time, but he is not to ignore her duplicity. For example, what she says she will say and what she does say are quite different. She states that she will not review the past, but her purpose is to do just that, slanting events to win her audience's sympathy and their belief in the omnipotence of love. She says that she has told her judges everything:

> all, all, verily,
> But just that which would save me; these things flit.
>
> (1:10)

She has not done so, for she breaks off her argument just at the point at which she would have to incriminate herself, telling of Launcelot's plans for their flight and life together. She cannot do so without revealing that she knows that Launcelot will come to rescue her. She can say with some accuracy, "All I have said is truth, by Christ's dear tears" (1:10), for she has omitted important evidence and made statements whose double meanings have allowed her confession to go unheard. Skillfully, she gives her auditors, and many readers, the impression that she could prove her total innocence if she chose, that she has left the strongest part of her case unstated.

Guenevere's defense is not, of course, to be fully believed. In this sense, the poem's title is ironic. Guenevere intends a speech of self-vindication, but her words and actions persuade the reader of her adultery. The final turn of the poem, however, reinforces its ultimate ambiguity. The reader is forced to recognize that the adultery is less meaningful than the love itself. One believes in her love for Launcelot, in the overwhelming power of the passion that has undone her. The most persuasive part of her argument is her defense of the necessity of erotic passion:

> Must I give up for ever then, I thought,
>
> That which I deemed would ever round me move
> Glorifying all things; for a little word,
> Scarce ever meant at all, must I now prove
>
> Stone-cold for ever?
>
> (1:3)

Love, the force that moves the world and the impetus behind all being, is the difference between life and death in life. "Bought/ By Arthur's great name and his little love" (1:3), Guenevere has been forced to seek love outside her marriage of convenience and with a man other than her kingly, chilly husband. Thus, she must be partially pardoned and fully sympathized with. She has indeed suffered, and she realizes that passion has undone her, driving her —except for a few sea-moments—to pain and near madness. She does not yet recognize in her cruelty to her opponents, her glee at the death of Meliagraunce, and her threats to destroy her enemies and the kingdom, the signs of her moral and emotional deterioration. All that she as yet knows is that passion is her *raison d'être* and that, to preserve it, she will stop at nothing. The rest of the lesson will come in "King Arthur's Tomb."

On the other hand, what the reader is to recognize in "The

Defence of Guenevere" is the power of an ambiguous figure who is beyond morality, who represents the poet's mixed anima, creative and destructive, deadly and life-giving both. Morris's genius is in his refusal to render a smug verdict upon her. His testimony, as well as hers, is to the formidable power of erotic passion which can dissolve all other values in it.

Morris's profound psychological grasp of illicit romantic passion is displayed once again in "King Arthur's Tomb." The poem is both a sequel to the "Defence" and a further analysis of the love that leads to death, this time as it affects both Launcelot and Guenevere. The poem's source is Malory's account of the last meeting of the lovers, though, as David Staines indicates, Morris has telescoped several incidents in the final pages of Malory.[26] But his inspiration is visual as well as literary, for the poem's imagery comments on Rossetti's watercolor, *Arthur's Tomb*, which Morris had purchased. The painting shows a tormented Launcelot leaning over a tomb with the figure of Arthur carved on it; Launcelot's lips are seeking those of the queen who kneels, resisting, in the foreground. The lovers are confined and trapped by the apple trees surrounding them and separated by the cold marble of the tomb. In the grass of the foreground is a coiled snake—a major image in Morris's poem—which untwists itself near Guenevere's form.[27]

Both Rossetti's painting and Morris's poem, thus, seem to illustrate Malory's terse lines: "Wherefore, madam, I pray you kiss me and never no more." "'Nay,' said the queen, 'that shall I never do.'"[28] But Rossetti's single scene becomes a triptych in Morris's poem. Two separate panels frame the central tableau. The first is devoted to Launcelot's trip to Glastonbury and to his shining memories of the "old garden life" (1:11) which he shared with Guenevere, the second to the queen's mingled memories of her past love and the pain it has brought, thoughts which have haunted her on the night before she and Launcelot meet at Glastonbury. Thus, the poem contrasts the past of each of the characters, utilizing brilliant, heraldic color to suggest its vitality and beauty, with their present states, seen as the cold grays and blacks of bleak reality. For example, Launcelot's visual memory of the queen, shining in the morning light, clothed in green and holding scarlet lilies like Saint Margaret, forms an ironic contrast to her image when he meets her at Glastonbury in the poem's present:

> all her robes were black,
> With a long white veil only; she went slow,

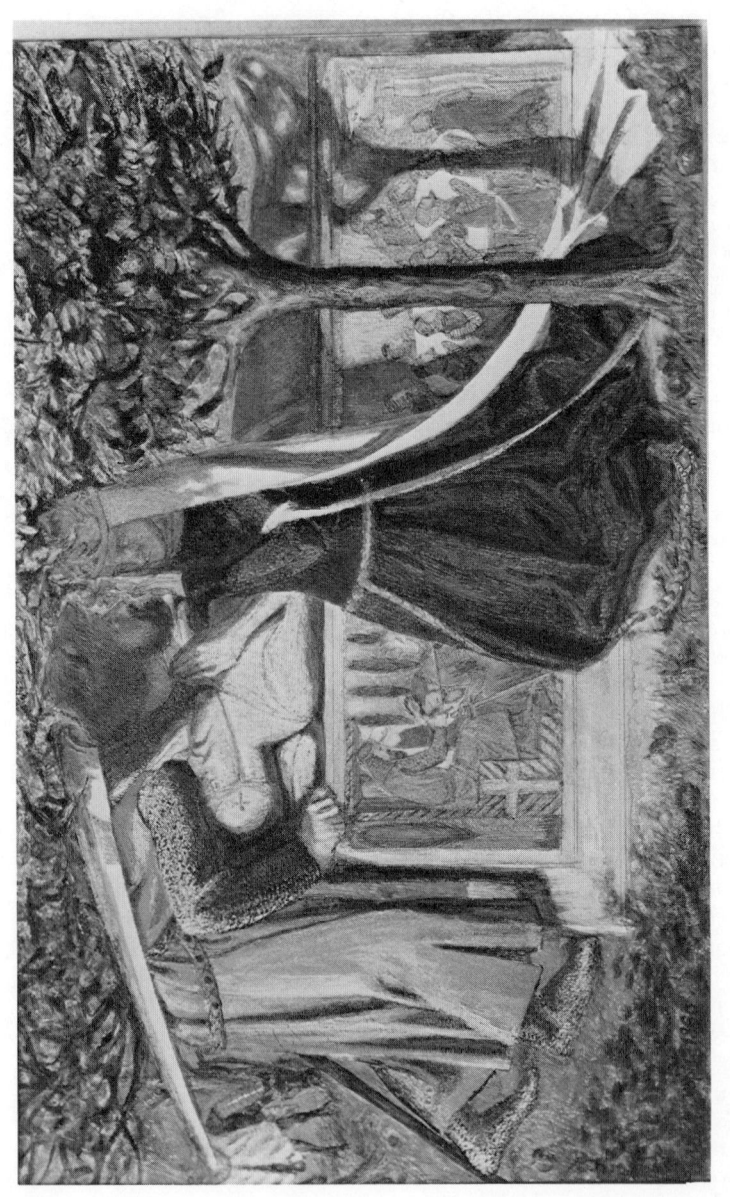

Dante Gabriel Rossetti: *Arthur's Tomb*. Watercolor of 1855. (Courtesy of The Tate Gallery, London.)

As one walks to be slain, her eyes did lack
Half her old glory, yea, alas! the glow

Had left her face and hands;

(1:15)

The contrast between past and present is further sharpened by
the poem's lack of logical transitions.[29] The utterance is an attempt to capture the time-sense and impact of dream, specifically
of nightmare. Scenes and memories shift in dream logic; time is
either blurred or frozen into everlasting moments. For the severing of the lovers is seen as a nightmare to both, and it will be over
only when they die.

In "King Arthur's Tomb," Morris fully develops the *Liebestöd*
theme that he had sketched in the early prose tales. The love that
leads to death and partakes of it is emphasized by the many
images of entwinement that run through the poem.[30] The lovers'
beings are entwined and their entanglement is destroying them,
but their separation means their deaths. When separated from
Guenevere, Launcelot is dead-alive. Yet, when they meet and she
rejects him, he asks her to slay him instead. As he arises from his
swoon, bloodied on the hands and head, he has been symbolically
crucified. When Guenevere renounces her lover, all she desires is
death: her wish is granted, for the poem ends with the tolling of
her bell of passage. For the lovers enmeshed in their tragic passion, the only resting place is the tomb.

Guenevere comes to self-knowledge before her end. When, in
the central scene, she comes forth to meet Launcelot at the tomb
he does not know is Arthur's, she knows that "a blight/ Had
settled on her" (1:14–15). The blight is spiritual as well as physical, for she comes persuaded of her sin and sickness, determined
to renounce Launcelot forever—destroyed by the love that had
once made her bloom.

Unlike Malory's character who confesses her sin with calm
dignity, Morris's Guenevere must go through an intricate process
of self-vindication leading finally to self-recognition. She begins
by offering a defense of her actions, this time with God and
Launcelot as her audience. Though she insists, "I am not mad,
but I am sick; they cling, / God's curses, unto such as I am" (1:17),
she realizes only gradually that she has become what she had predicted she would become in the "Defence," if she were guilty of
adultery:

A great queen such as I
Having sinn'd this way, straight her conscience sears;

And afterwards she liveth hatefully,
Slaying and poisoning, certes never weeps,—

(1:5)

At Glastonbury, she has been unable to weep, and her beauty, the "gracious proof" of her innocence, has faded. The agony of guilt has consumed her and made her cruel. She has become what her attendants call her, a "tigress fair" with "claws" (1:20).

Moreover, while Launcelot's thoughts have been of love and freedom, hers have been meditations on damnation. Fearing a hell which would be a continuation of the worst moments of her earthly life, an eternity of being called a harlot by a churl, she has come to ask God's pardon. The God she prays to is no disembodied spirit to her; she loves His beauty, yearns to kiss His feet, and coaxes Him as if He were her lover. She reminds Him, as she has reminded her judges in "The Defence," of how beautiful she is. And she sees Him as an object of erotic passion: "I cannot choose/ But love you, Christ, yea, though I cannot keep/ From loving Launcelot" (1:16). Indeed, she sees the two as rival lovers and she wishes to be allowed to keep both. Unable to resolve her conflict, she strikes out at Launcelot and, through him, at herself. Entwined as they are, in scourging him she beats herself, and in humiliating him she shames herself.

Her justification is that God has given her the grace, in renouncing Launcelot, to save his soul. Guenevere may, indeed, have to purge Launcelot's spirit and her own by fire, but the smell is not of redemption but of burning flesh, as Morris dwells on the agony of the renunciation. Guenevere's opening words to Launcelot, when they meet at Arthur's tomb, establish the tone of her attack. "Well done!" she says sarcastically to her lover, who kneels in exhaustion near the monument; it is right to pray "For Arthur, my dear lord, the greatest king/ That ever lived" (1:16). Attempting to wound Launcelot by her sudden preference for her husband, she refuses her lover a single, final kiss of parting. Instead, with God's name on her lips, she ironically offers him a more sexual greeting:

Across my husband's head, fair Launcelot!
Fair serpent mark'd with V upon the head!
This thing we did while yet he was alive,
Why not, O twisting knight, now he is dead?

(1:17)

Her confession of past adultery and sneering suggestion that they make love on the tomb are not unexpected, but her description of Launcelot as a twisting serpent is initially surprising. Her taunt is connected both with Rossetti's painting and with Launcelot's coat of arms, which in a cancelled portion of "The Defence" is described as "the great snake of green/ That twisted on the quartered white and red" (1:xx). Guenevere finds her lover's heraldic emblem symbolic of his behavior. She sees him as the serpent in the garden, the tempter of herself as Eve, and the cause of her fall.[31]

She initially refuses to accept the responsibility for loving Launcelot, though she cannot disavow the passion itself. She argues that the affair has been Arthur's fault and Launcelot's, not hers. Arthur has been cold to her, merely kissing her "in his kingly way" (1:18) and thrusting her at his friend as he tells her to cherish the knight who is his "banner, sword and shield" (1:18). Launcelot, she indicates, has been all too eager to accept her. Attacking him, she insists that she has been the one to suffer and that he has forced her into a life of lies, ruined her in her role as queen, and dishonored her person and reputation. Projecting her own guilty view of herself onto him, she accuses him of emotional disloyalty, of thinking her changeable in love and mood, "uncertain as the spring" (1:19).

As the poem continues, and Guenevere's self-awareness increases, she admits the validity of her last charge, ascribing it, correctly, to her own sense of self and to the perceptions of her attendants. Her plea for their forgiveness: "Forgive me! for my sin being such . . . / Made me quite wicked" (1:20) marks the beginning of her understanding of her condition. While Launcelot has envisioned her as the pure Saint Margaret, she sees herself as the woman of Samaria and as Mary Magdalen. When she imagines

> . . . Mary Magdalen repenting there,
> Her dimmed eyes scorch'd and red at sight of hell
> So hardly 'scaped, no gold light on her hair
>
> (1:20)

the image is of herself. She cannot see the glory of repentance, only its pain, for the agony is all that she has experienced. The last step in self-realization occurs when, remembering a joust in the "old garden days," she hears the names called out by the opposing knights—"Iseult" and "Guenevere" (1:22). "The ladies' names bite verily like steel" (1:22), she screams, for they remind her of Iseult's and her own adultery.

But as she moves from identifying herself with God to recognizing herself as a fallen Eve, a Magdalen, and a common harlot, she is driven almost insane by the realization. Thus, she bursts into a brutal, obsessively repetitive attack on her lover. Compulsively repeating Arthur's description of Launcelot as his "banner, sword and shield," she calls her lover a banner and shield besmirched by the *bend sinister* of bastardy and a "crooked sword" (1:22) that has scarred its bearer's arm. Reiterating her charges, she damns him as a Malay blade secretly "poison'd with sweet fruit" (1:22), as a reaper's sickle stained with the deadly hemlock it has cut, and, in both cases, Arthur's murderer. Branding Launcelot as a false protector of Arthur and herself—*traitor* to both—she will not even permit him to imagine peace through death. He "dare not pray to die," she screams, "Lest . . .[he] meet Arthur in the other world" (1:22).

When she sees Launcelot swoon and believes him dead, her own ordeal is over. Wishing for her own demise, she echoes Malory's queen in lamenting the absence of the kiss of parting she has refused to give her lover: "Never, never again! not even when I die" (1:23).[32]

Obsessed by guilt, revenging herself upon her lover and herself for her discovery that earthly love can destroy, repudiating that love, but still chained to it, Guenevere gains the only possible release from her pain. The bell that Launcelot hears as he returns to consciousness is the knell announcing her death.

Although erotic love is seen as blasting the bodies and souls of those enslaved by it in "King Arthur's Tomb," Morris does not find a comfortable solution in espousing celestial love as its alternative. Meredith Raymond is correct in stating that the second pair of Malory poems, "Sir Galahad: A Christmas Mystery" and "The Chapel in Lyoness," examine "spiritual love and heavenly grace," thus balancing the first pair.[33] But "Sir Galahad" and "The Chapel" emphasize the trials and frustrations of eros, and the rewards of heavenly love seem strangely weak.

Galahad, the virgin knight, replaces Guenevere as the central figure in the poems and both his character and his adventures are less closely linked to Malory than were Guenevere's. Morris's real interest is firmly rooted in this world, and his Galahad is a man of it, suffering the pains and doubts of earthly existence. Morris either creates his own Malory-like incidents or greatly amplifies brief statements from his source. For example, while Malory mentions that Galahad is benighted in a deserted hermitage, the episode in the hermitage which constitutes the "Christmas Mystery" is Morris's invention. Morris's concerns are psychological rather than supernatural; he traces the thoughts of the virgin knight during "the longest night in all the year" (1:24)—which is also the dark night of his soul. While the rebirth associated with Christmas does come to Galahad, the emphasis falls on his pain as much as on his promised redemption. Galahad thinks much upon his chastity, wondering "what thing comes of it" (1:24). He compares his plight to those of Palomydes and Launcelot and initially decides that it would be better to be Palomydes, who has the hope, even if vain, of ultimately winning Iseult's love, or Launcelot who, despite his sin, has "Guenevere's arms, round, / Warm and lithe, about his neck" (1:25). His most vivid memory is of an unknown knight taking leave of his lady before departing on the quest of the Sangreal. Their "last kisses" sink into Galahad's mind, provoking his intense loneliness and frustration. His most powerful grief arises at the thought that "no maid will talk/ Of sitting on my tomb" (1:25). Though comforted by Christ, who reassures him that God's love is best and that sexual love, vain and illicit in the lives of Palomydes and Launcelot, cannot offer the rewards of heaven, Galahad cannot fully and freely renounce earthly love. He will indeed refrain from the vain lusts of the flesh, but his quest for the Grail becomes, as Ralph Berry indicates, more a sexual sublimation of his desires than an alternative to them.[34] Most significantly, "Sir Galahad" ends on a note of defeat. Morris makes clear, long before Tennyson's bitter treatment of "The Holy Grail," that the pursuit of a purely spiritual goal can bring destruction. The reader learns that Sir Lionel and Sir Gauwaine have been shamed, Sir Lauvaine wounded, and that "poor merry Dinadan" lies "hack'd and dead" (1:30); "In vain they struggle for the vision fair" (1:30). Galahad's successful quest and triumph are never witnessed.

"The Chapel in Lyoness," while indicating Galahad's movement toward perfection, does not show that he has lost his frustrations or relinquished his sympathy for erotic love. Its central theme is the motif Morris had reiterated in the early tales: the hope for a fleshly reunion of lovers in a paradise devoted to them. Sir Galahad finds Ozana Le Cure Hardy lying wounded within a deserted chapel. Like the maimed king in the Percival romances, Ozana is suffering a wound of the soul, a result of a failure or inability to aid his mysterious lady,[35] and Galahad diagnoses the malady. Lamenting that "there comes no sleep nor any love" (1:33), Ozana yearns for death and a heavenly reunion with his lady. It is Galahad who frees him, bringing him a rose sprinkled with dew and the precious water of rebirth, symbols of purification and salvation. Only after Galahad has blessed him and given him the kiss of passage, can Ozana, pressing a lock of hair from the head of his beloved, find the peace of death. It is the virgin Galahad who sees the vision of Ozana's reunion with his lady. He sees Ozana's "wasted fingers twine"

> Within the tresses of her hair
> That shineth gloriously,
> Thinly outspread in the clear air
> Against the jasper sea.
>
> (1:34)

Galahad's question, uttered when the knight has died—"Ozana, shall I pray for thee?" (1:34)—requires a negative answer. Ozana, in a heavenly rapture that has little to do with God, needs no prayer, for he has been united with the woman who is his soul. It is Galahad, the lonely visionary, who needs the reader's prayers and evokes the reader's sympathies.

Thus, in the Malory poems, does Morris establish his concern with the deadly effects of desire and the desirable elements of death. Finding few rewards in either heaven or earth, he creates a group of tormented, frustrated, and memorable characters. Through the figure of Galahad, he adds to the portraits of rejected lovers the image of the hero doomed to isolation, but sympathizing with the pains of others. In the portrait of Guenevere, he not only creates a superb fatal woman, but depicts the ambiguous nature of the anima herself. In all the poems of the group, he reveals his considerable, if precocious, understanding of the conflicts within the human psyche.

III

Morris's Froissart poems continue and intensify the exploration of the interrelationships between erotic love and death. The three most important poems of the division, "The Haystack in the Floods," "Sir Peter Harpdon's End," and "Concerning Geffray Teste Noire,"[36] are narratives of the destruction of passion by the brutality of war. Though they at first appear to contrast the purity of the medieval love ethic with the violence of the era in which it existed, they subtly indicate the destructive force of the ideal itself.

Stamped by their source, Lord Berner's translation of Froissart's *Chronicle*, the poems catch the atmosphere of Froissart's world. To move from the works inspired by Malory to those derived from Froissart is to travel from a mythic realm of romance to a world of the grimmest reality. For life, as Morris sees it through the *Chronicle*, is made up of treachery and violence, of ambush and surprise, of blood and death. Brilliant color vanishes from these works; they are studies in tones of gray, simpler in diction, starker in outline, more matter of fact in tone than those influenced by Malory.

The reader has only to compare "King Arthur's Tomb" and "The Haystack in the Floods" to see these differences. Both poems deal with similar events: a last meeting, a final kiss, the conquering of love by death; yet their tone and atmosphere are entirely different. Compared to "King Arthur's Tomb," "The Haystack in the Floods" is a poem of understatement; the contrast between the events and emotions depicted and the poet's re-strained utterances about them leads one to imagine the horrors that occur in a way one might not, were they more fully drawn. The calmly reportorial quality, the terse relation of the facts, and the stark realism of the account lead to the shock ultimately experienced.

The incident and characters of "The Haystack in the Floods" are Morris's creations, but they are deeply grounded in the world of the *Chronicle*. Even Gascony, near whose borders Robert and Jehane are trapped, is significant to a reader of Froissart. As an English possession, it represents safety to the lovers. Ironically, they have almost arrived at its boundaries when they are captured. Although Froissart does not mention a knight called Robert de Marny, Morris indicates that Robert has fought for the English at Poitiers in 1356, a battle Froissart describes. Though no Jehane is imprisoned in the Chatelet or subjected to the water trial for witchcraft,[37] Froissart relates the horrors of the prison and the uses of the trial, making the ramifications of Jehane's choice clear. Godmar, on the other hand, is associated with villainy to a reader of the *Chronicle*. Morris's character is none other than Godmar du Fay, a powerful French baron who fought against Edward III at the battle of Blanchtaque, when the floods were up and the opposing armies met knee-deep in water. When Godmar was finally defeated, he "fledde and saved hymselfe,"[38] leaving his men to be slaughtered and his name to be censured by Froissart. Thus, the hatred of the English and their allies, the baseness, cowardice, and cruelty manifested by Morris's character are more fully understandable if the reader knows, as Morris did, Godmar's Froissartian history.

Froissart provides a frame of reference wherein Morris's poems become fully plausible. Morris invents incidents for the "Canon

of Chimay" (1:75) to include in his collection. He tells the incidents as Froissart might have done, as well. Events are seen
externally; the reader is left to imagine the emotions that motivate
actions. Jehane, unlike Guenevere, does not reveal the inner
workings of her mind. The reader witnesses her physical and
emotional fatigue as reflected in her riding, moving, and sleeping, as well as in her brusque, exhausted speech, but is not
permitted to enter her consciousness. Her courage is seen through
her actions, and the process of decision working within her is left
unchronicled. She has already made her decision. She has chosen
death for herself and her lover over life as Godmar's mistress.

　　The point of the poem is less her choice than her ability to stick
to it despite the pressure put upon her. Her passive strength, the
keynote of her character, is sharply opposed to Guenevere's active
histrionic power. When Godmar gives Jehane the choice of
Robert's life in return for her sexual submission, her answer is a
quiet no. She

> 　　　　　　. . . turn'd her head away,
> As there were nothing else to say,
> And everything were settled.
>
> 　　　　　　　　　　　　　　(1:126)

To Godmar's threat of rape, her answer is direct—if
malicious:

> 　　　　　A wicked smile
> Wrinkled her face, her lips grew thin,
> A long way out she thrust her chin:
> 'You know that I should strangle you
> While you were sleeping; or bite through
> Your throat, by God's help—'
>
> 　　　　　　　　　　　　　　(1:126)

Her only cry of anguish is directed to God, and Jehane fully
understands the consequences of the act she must perform. All her
choices involve sin. Jehane's capitulation will lead to the murder
of Godmar and her own suicide, her resistance will result in
Robert's immediate death and in her own demise. Since she
"cannot choose but sin and sin,/ Whatever happens" (1:126–27),
she chooses the act which she believes will best preserve her honor
and her love: to be Robert's slayer and the victim of the judges of
the Chatelet. Thus when Godmar gives her an hour in which to
choose her fate, she sleeps to regain her courage for the ordeal fac-

ing her. She is unyielding even in the face of Godmar's mounting anger and the direct threat of death. She "sighed quietly,/ And strangely childlike came, and said: 'I will not'" (1:127).[39]

The ideal love of Robert and Jehane precipitates the destruction of both lovers. Passion dictates their attempt to kiss and hastens Robert's death, for Godmar cannot bear to see what he construes as another act of defiance. Since Jehane's lips can only touch her lover's sleeve, Robert is denied the marvelous kiss of passage, so important to Morris's heroes. As in the tale of "Golden Wings," the lover is slaughtered like an animal before his lady's eyes:

> she saw him [Godmar] bend
> Back Robert's head; she saw him send
> The thin steel down; the blow told well,
> Right backward the knight Robert fell,
> And moan'd as dogs do, being half dead.
>
> (1:128)

Violence replaces sexuality[40] and Godmar finds sadistic satisfaction in watching the mutilation of Robert's body as he "turn'd grinning to his men,/ Who ran, some five or six, and beat/ His head to pieces at their feet" (1:128). Witnessing this scene destroys Jehane. When she is told that she will be returned to the Chatelet and put to death, she does not care. Her state of shock, with its foreshadowings of her impending madness and death, is a form of death in life:

> She shook her head and gazed awhile
> At her cold hands with a rueful smile,
> As though this thing had made her mad.
>
> (1:128)

The poem closes with the narrator's incrementally charged refrain:

> This was the parting that they had
> Beside the haystack in the floods.
>
> (1:128)

And, by its end, both the setting and the parting have taken on new significance. The rain, a traditional symbol for the renewal of life, becomes a contrast to the dry-eyed and deadened lovers; the cold of the weather has become the chill of death; the haystack, a place associated with love, is now an ironic lovers' tomb. The parting is final, a symbol of all the severances caused by human passion and human cruelty. Most important, the erotic love that has promised to be a source of life and courage is revealed as a source of death.

Again, in "Sir Peter Harpdon's End," Froissart's account of the enmity between France and England frames a tale of the tragedy of two lovers. Although the hero and heroine are the products of Morris's imagination, they are connected to persons mentioned in the *Chronicle*. Peter Harpdon, "a Gascon with an English name" (1:53), may be the nephew of Sir John Harpedon, an important English knight, himself associated with failure.[41] Lady Alice is identified as a de la Barde, a member of the powerful Gascon family whose allegiance shifted back and forth between England and France. Sir Bertram de Guesclin, Constable of France, and Sir Oliver de Clisson are historical personages whom Morris paints with considerable accuracy. Guesclin, noble, imperious, but capable of cruelty, and his equally noble but more compassionate companion fight side by side through numerous battles recorded in the *Chronicle*. Even the year in which Morris sets the events of his poem is significant. Not merely for decoration does he have Peter chronicle recent history and catalogue the English leaders who are lost:

> At Lusac bridge
> I daresay you may even yet see the hole
> That Chandos beat in dying; far in Spain
> Pembroke is prisoner; Phelton prisoner here;
> Manny lies buried in the Charterhouse;
> Oliver Clisson turn'd these years agone;
> The Captal died in prison; and, over all,
> Edward the prince lies underneath the ground,
> Edward the king is dead; at Westminster
> The carvers smooth the curls of his long beard.
>
> (1:37)

Morris is establishing both the condition of the English forces and the time of the poem's events. In a cancelled section of the poem the exact date of the siege of Peter's fortress, "Tenth of November" (1:xxvii), is mentioned, although the year is not indicated. But the events of which Peter speaks have occurred by 1377, and the additional statement in the poem that the monks who owe allegiance to Peter are still only "wishing well for [Pope] Clement" (1:49), the French candidate who became Pope in 1378, limits the action of the poem to November 1377. As Froissart states, it was in the autumn of 1377 that the tide of war turned against England. Sir Bertram de Guesclin and Sir Oliver de Clisson began their campaign to attack the "dyvers lytell forteresses"[42] held by English sympathizers. The lonely Poictou castle that Peter must defend is one of their objectives. Significantly, the weakened, mouldering castle becomes a symbol of the decay of English power in France. Peter's personal tragedy is to be seen within the context of a larger one, England's loss of France.

Peter's nobility lies in his resistance to change, his refusal to turn French though all around him are deserting the English cause. Associating himself (as the English did) with the Trojans, who fought well for love in the face of defeat, he states his admiration for "the straining game/ Of striving well to hold up things that fall" (1:43). His cousin Lambert serves as an ironic foil to him, for Lambert, whose heraldic emblem of "Three golden rings/ On a red ground" (1:40) reveals his love of "ease and money" (1:43), has switched sides for the rewards that he expects. However, his underlying motivation is sexual jealousy. He hates Peter for being handsome and for having attained the love of Lady Alice. He lies about Peter's having pro-French sympathies primarily to damage Peter's relationship with Alice and to separate the lovers. When Peter chooses to mutilate rather than kill Lambert, he causes his own death.[43]

When the situation is reversed and Peter becomes Lambert's prisoner, Lambert's cruelty is heightened. As Dianne Sadoff has observed, Lambert's torture of Peter is primarily sexual.[44] Like Godmar relishing the idea of the tormenting of Jehane's body, Lambert dwells on the appearance of Peter's corpse after hanging. He climaxes his sadistic diatribe with a perverse suggestion: "I am Alice, am right like her now,/ Will you not kiss me on the lips, my love?" (1:51). Thus, the theme of the kiss of parting is now introduced as ironic travesty. To Peter, who has lived for love, the absence of Alice's kiss or of that of a "beautiful lady" (1:53) to serve as her substitute in wishing him Godspeed on the road to death is the cruelest torment of all. The world's thwarting of love and the pain of life's frustrations are symbolized by Peter's dying, like Launcelot or Robert, without the final kiss of passage.

In the final scene of the poem, Lady Alice's fantasy of receiving "one kiss" (1:54) from Peter to help her sleep is interrupted by a Squire bringing her the news of his death. The *Liebestöd* motif is sounded; like Launcelot and Guenevere, Peter and Alice are so entwined that their separation is death. Like Jehane, Alice desires release and reunion with Peter through her own demise. The kiss Peter had been unable to give her is to be supplied by a fleshly Jesus, who will comfort her—as a lover would—and let her reunite with Peter in a physical lovers' heaven. But Alice, who wishes only to die, is forced to survive. The final ironic turn of the poem is that in her shock and near madness she hears men singing, not of Peter but of "Launcelot, and love and fate and death" (1:60). They sing, not of the new hero just passed but of one long dead, shutting out, as all men do, the events that have occurred around them. They sing of a great love past, not knowing of the equally great passion mourned before their eyes. The romance world of Malory becomes a comment upon the brutally realistic world of Froissart.

Yet, not content with simply juxtaposing the medieval visions of romance and realism represented by Malory and Froissart, Morris creates, in "Concerning Geffray Teste Noire," a sustained tension between elements derived from each. In "Geffray Teste Noire," a dramatic monologue reminiscent of Browning and replete with details from the *Chronicle*, Morris inserts a tale of chivalric love inspired by Malory. Interweaving an account of the discovery of the skeletons of two lovers with Froissart's story of the campaign against Geffray, the head of a group of bandits ensconced in the impregnable castle of Ventadour,[45] Morris emphasizes the connections between the capacity for romantic passion and the brutality he finds characteristic of the Middle Ages.

As John of Castel Neuf[46] tells Alleyne, his audience, an incident to be relayed to Froissart, "the Canon of Chimay," he reveals his private obsession with desire and death. In a world he sees as filled with slaughter, good does not overcome evil: the wicked Geffray dies in bed with his fortress still intact; the Jacquerie burns the innocent women who seek refuge in a church, and two young lovers who have long ago travelled through the woods (in which John now waits to trap Geffray) have been ambushed and slain.

As John attempts to find some meaning in an unjust or ambiguous world, he offers a love service to the bones of an unknown lady. His is a strange necrotic fantasy, as his imagination brings her bones to life. The poem does indeed illustrate "the Victorian theme of [the] resuscitation of the past through the artist's imagination," but its strange quality does not come, as Margaret Gent suggests, from the fact that John's "lady will not come fully to life."[47] John envisions her not as dead but as deadly. Clothing her in the trappings of fatality, he imagines her "most

pale face, that brings such joy and sorrow/ Into men's hearts,"
"her long eyes where the lids seem like to drop," and her lips that
kiss "like a curved sword/ That bites with all its edge" (1:79–80).
To him she becomes a fatal Iseult, as he sees her drinking the red
wine of passion as if "some wild fate might twine/ Within that
cup, and slay . . . [her] for a sin" (1:80). John falls in love with
an image that holds within it the "indissoluble union of the
beautiful and the sad," described by Mario Praz.[48] While she
blends the aesthetic and the sensous, rapidly changing moods and
transient passions, hers is the burden of a desirability that can
only torment her worshippers.

Significantly, she has had another lover and John becomes, in
his own mind, her Palomydes, worshipping her to the point of
self-abasement. John has chosen to adore a figure he paints as
tormented and tormenting, deadly and devouring, and he has
been warped by his erotic passion. Tangled in the dream of her
hair, he dedicates his remaining years to enshrining her fatal
image.

Thus he proceeds to memorialize his dead lady and her accepted lover by sending their story to be recorded by Froissart.
They are, ironically, denied a place in the *Chronicle*. Additionally, John creates a chapel and a tomb for them at his own cost.
The lovers are married in the tomb; in an evocation of the early
prose tales, they are carved upon it "with stone-white hands/
Clasped fast together hair made bright with gold" (1:81), united
in death as they could not be in life. But Morris now changes the
meaning of the tomb symbol he had used in "The Unknown
Church," "A Dream," and "Svend and His Brethren." The sign
of the consummation of love in and through death becomes an
emblem of its defeat by time and death. The "assertion of mortality"[49] that ends the poem: "This Jaques Picard, known through
many lands,/ Wrought cunningly; he's dead now—I am old"
(1:81), stresses the impermanence of beauty, memory, and love
itself.

Other less important Froissart poems reiterate the triumph of
fate and death and stress the denial of the possibility of lasting
erotic fulfillment or release. Sir Lambert's dream on "The Eve of
Crecy" is a false one; he will not gain his Marguerite. Lord Roger
in "The Judgment of God" may justify his treachery through his
love for Ellayne, but there are hints that even if he succeeds in his
combat, he will be destroyed. Still other minor poems, which may
be considered Froissartian since they imitate the style of the
Chronicle or are based on historical events, press home Morris's
point.

For example, in "Shameful Death,"[50] the account of the hanging of Lord Hugh, the narrator's brother, and of the narrator's life spent in avenging the murder, is not the only tragedy. Alice, Lord Hugh's young bride, had died of grief, and her demise is another shameful death to be avenged. In "Old Love," the fall of Constantinople becomes an external correlative of the failure of love. Like John of Castel Neuf, the aged knight, Sir John, has devoted his life to the chivalric adoration of his liege's lady. The fall of Constantinople is a mirror image of his realization "that things outwear . . . [he] thought were made for ever" (1:87); it marks the end of his faith in the permanence of all things—even of the love that ruled his life.

If erotic passion can triumph at all, Morris says, it cannot do so in the grimly brutal world of Froissart or in the realm of Arthurian romance. Thus, for further examination of the problems of fate and death and for a fuller exploration of the life journey, he creates a third division of poems which inhabit the realms of folklore and fairy tale.

IV

The third division of *The Defence of Guenevere* consists of such poems as "Rapunzel," "The Sailing of the Sword," "Golden Wings," "Spell-Bound," "The Wind," "Father John's War-Song," "Two Red Roses Across the Moon," "The Gilliflower of Gold," "The Blue Closet," "The Tune of Seven Towers," and "Welland River." All take place within the indeterminate medievalized world of fairyland; many lack clear explanations of causes and events. Some are in ballad form, but even those that are not suggest ballad qualities: they pose questions they do not answer or pass over certain incidents to concentrate on others. The light of dream shines over them all. Closest in spirit to Morris's early prose tales, they have the precise detail and conceptual ambiguity of stories like "The Hollow Land."

While the fairy tale poems derive minor motifs and details from such sources as the Grimms' *Märchen* and Benjamin Thorpe's *Yule-Tide Tales*, Morris merely alludes to these works. Except for "Rapunzel," the narratives and important episodes are his own; in all cases his interpretations of events have little to do with their originals.

Only within the fairy tale world of pure imagination is success in love seen as possible. Five poems within the division illustrate the triumph of passion over threats of imprisonment, war, or death. The promise of wedded bliss rings through a pair of brief ballads, "Two Red Roses Across the Moon" and "The Gilli-flower of Gold." The two ballads are the joyous lyrics of trium-phant lovers who will gain their ladies after they have won their battles. "The Little Tower" promises the same reward, though their brief narrative of love's battle with and escape from a society opposed to it, ends before the ordeal of the siege begins. However, despite the narrator's confidence, the reader does not know with *certainty* if the couple will be happily united, or if, instead, their fates will be similar to those of Robert and Jehane or of Lionel and Alys in the tale, "Golden Wings." An uncertain outcome mitigates the joy of "Father John's War-Song," a poem partic-ularly interesting for the connections it makes between the har-vest of corn and sexual union.[51] Father John will clearly gain the son he desires through the union of Maiden Mary and her knight, Roland, but the battle for home and harvest is yet to be waged.

Again, two poems derived from the Grimms' *Märchen* slightly undercut their themes of success in love. Morris's "Welland River," based in part on the Grimms' tale, "Roland,"[52] uses the riddle and recognition motifs common to folklore. But the em-phasis falls equally on the plight of the faithful woman, pregnant and deserted by her lover, and on their happy reunion. The same is true of Morris's fascinating version of the Grimms' "Rapun-zel."[53] In Morris's rendition of the tale, external action is avoided and the psychological development of the hero is stressed.[54] Morris makes his poem a bridequest, following the pattern he had first utilized in "The Hollow Land." The poem is an unusual account of the search for the beloved who is the rightful anima. In a work that looks forward to Morris's later bridequests,[55] Sebald, the hero, responds to a vision of his beloved, must seek her through the wastelands and forests of the world, and must free her from imprisonment and slavery before he may wed her. As Robert Stallman notes, the poem clearly centers on a rite of initiation,[56] but the despair of the young man "riding out to look for love" (1:65) and the condition of his beloved, indicate Morris's preoc-cupation with the possibilities of frustration and failure. Sebald, scorned and mocked by a people who accuse him of evading reality, must undergo a year of blindness and passivity before he truly begins the process of maturation. Rapunzel must suffer a total deprivation of love, the sight of brother slaying brother, and the violations of the witches before she can be freed. The impli-cation with which the poem ends is that Rapunzel's experience cannot be totally erased. "Even now," says she, happily wedded to Sebald, "a harsh voice seems/ To hang about my hair" (1:74).

The last words of the poem are those of the witch; they are a re-
minder of what Rapunzel has escaped, but they inject a note of
menace into an otherwise joyous conclusion.

Even in the fairy tale world, however, tragedy outweighs joy.
Morris envisions mysterious wizards, unknown invaders, anonymous imprisoners who hold their victims in bondage or death.
The sympathetic figures in the poems are spellbound captives,
separated from those they love or doomed to violent death. The
forces that destroy them are externalized as fate. Separated from
his beloved on the night before his wedding, enchanted by a mysterious wizard and transported to a supernatural land, the knight
in "Spell-Bound," wears out his days musing on his beloved. His
first hope, that she will quest for and free him, yields to his
despair as well as to his recognition of impending death. The
same theme of mysterious imprisonment and impending death is
echoed in "In Prison," the poem, originally part of "Frank's
Sealed Letter," which Morris reutilizes to end the *Defence*
volume.

Two paired poems, both related to Rossetti watercolors which
Morris purchased in 1857,[57] again suggest the mysterious power
of fate. "The Tune of Seven Towers" is the song Morris writes for
the painting's lady—a red-robed beauty who sits holding a
musical instrument, while a young man in a green doublet stands
watching her. Morris names the figures Yoland and Oliver and
captures some of the tense, mysterious nature of the painting in
his poem. Like Ella, in "A Dream," Morris's Yoland is about to
send her lover on a fatal quest to a haunted castle. She cannot tell
him either why she is unhappy or why he must fetch her coif and
kirtle from the towers that day. Her actions remain unmotivated
and her behavior is a curious blend of love and cajolery. But, offering him a kiss as his guerdon, she sends him to his death.
Simply fated to be fatal, she is as much a victim as her lover.

"The Blue Closet," another comment on a painting, tells the
tale of a dead lover who comes to claim his lady. Rossetti's painting is of four ladies, similar in appearance, playing and singing.
Its claustrophobic quality finds its equivalent in the poem. The
song the ladies appear to be singing in Rossetti's painting and are
singing in the poem, a *Te Deum* appropriate to Christmas Eve, is
not the important musical theme of "The Blue Closet." Instead,
the theme is the *Liebestöd* as Queen Louise, the imprisoned lady,
expresses her desire for union with Arthur, her dead lover. The
poem partially inverts the situation of Rossetti's "Blessed
Damozel," and Louise's wish for union through death is granted.
While the bells toll their premonitions of her passing, and the red

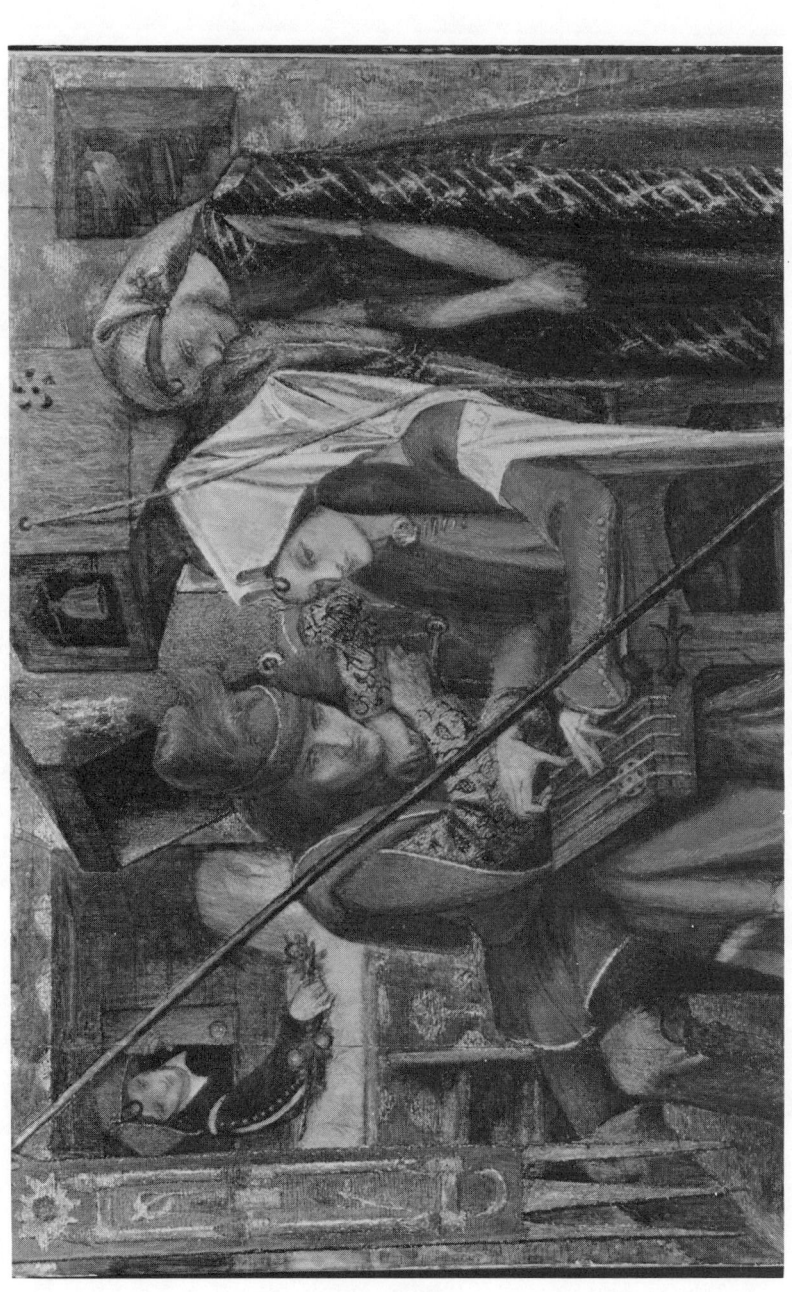

Dante Gabriel Rossetti: *The Tune of Seven Towers.* Watercolor of 1857. (Courtesy of The Tate Gallery, London.)

The Blue Closet.

Dante Gabriel Rossetti: *The Blue Closet*. Watercolor of 1857. (Courtesy of The Tate Gallery, London.)

lily from the underworld springs up through the floor of the chamber, the dead lover comes for his bride. In a somewhat ghastly reunion (the lover too has been held captive by a mysterious sorceress), Arthur leads Louise and her companions off to the land of death. Though his source may well be the demon-lover figure, and the corpse-like quality of his face is fully described, he is neither evil nor malicious. Again, it is the mysterious force of fate which is responsible for the events of the poem. The deaths of Jehane in "Golden Wings" and Margaret in "The Wind" are likewise treated as acts of fate. The reader never knows with certainty what irrational or impersonal force causes the women's destruction.

In all, the most powerful poems of the fairy tale division show the downward turn of the wheel of fortune and the tragic love and death connected with it. What is true of the division is equally valid as a description of the entire *Defence* volume. Despite the varied sources, forms, and styles within it, the volume is almost obsessive in its repetition of themes.

Morris, in so insistently repeating these themes, reveals much about himself. The poet who sees love as capable of being either a creative or destructive force is a psychological realist, but the one who intensely identifies with the agonies of Palomydes and Launcelot expects to suffer and derives emotional satisfaction from his pain. The poet who paints women as formidable as Guenevere and Jehane, as helpless and enslaved as Rapunzel and Queen Louise, fears and worships strangely. Indeed, the nervousness and ambivalence of Morris's sexual desire is reflected in the agonized sensousness of the poetry. The split between Morris's fear of love and his ardent yearning for it explains, in part, the *Defence* volume's intensity.

More significantly, Morris does not understand the anima for what she is, a force within the self. His fatal women and fairy princesses—clearly malign and benign animas—are not fully recognized by him as externalizations of his divided self. Communions and reunions between the male and female aspects of the self do not last or are not complete in most of the poems, simply because Morris is unable to integrate his personality. What Barbara Gelpi says of Rossetti's poetry is true of the Morris volume written so heavily under his master's influence: because Morris cannot bring his divided self into unity, his poems are full of internal drama and well-created tensions.[58] The *Defence* volume is, as Dixon Scott suggests, a precocious one, full of the *angst* of youth. Its violence is the fantasy violence of the young and its passion is the heightened fever of a vigorous man. Superimposed upon these youthful emotions are the insights of maturity, and the balance is exciting but precarious.[59]

As Morris's chronological and emotional growth continued, his poetry naturally changed. Morris's problems were complicated rather than resolved in the nine year interval between *The Defence* and *The Life and Death of Jason,* his next published work. But by the end of this interval he had assumed the appearance of stability and control; he had modulated and repressed the more obvious manifestations of his split self. Poetically, his mask was more firmly in place, his expression of emotion more controlled and subdued. He moved, as well, from essentially dramatic modes to narrative episodes, from the intense to the more diffuse, from, as Pater called the journey, "dreamlight to daylight."[60]

THREE

THE LOSS OF EDEN

I

TO MOVE FROM the world of *The Defence of Guenevere* to that
of *The Earthly Paradise* is to journey from the brilliant
phantasmagoric realm of troubled adolescence to the more solid
though shadowed land of maturity. In the nine years which separate these two works, Morris changed the coloration and tonal
quality of his poetry, subduing its brilliance and moving to a
more sober and elegiac mood. Gradually, he shifted the genre in
which he worked, selecting the medieval narrative romance as his
vehicle, not only in emulation of Chaucer, but with an awareness
that it reflected the dreams of men in a declining medieval world.
To Morris, the fourteenth century was a waning age not unre-
lated to the declining Victorian world he perceived in the late
1860s.

When Morris re-emerged before the public with *The Life and
Death of Jason* in 1867, presenting them with a romance intended
as part of *The Earthly Paradise*, he must have seemed a poet
rather different from the creator of *The Defence*. Gone were the
occasional metrical stutterings of the earlier volume, as were the
cacophonies in diction which, while contributing to the vigor of
the poems, had displeased some of his contemporaries.[1] Gone
were the brief lyric symphonies in color, the scenes merely
touched with narrative, the ballads, and the little dramas. Convinced that Keats and Tennyson had done all that was possible
with the lyric, believing that he could never match their mastery,
he concentrated less on the lyric mode and gradually turned to the
narrative. Still affected by Malory, profoundly moved by
Chaucer, he sought to revitalize the form they had utilized, that of
the medieval verse romance.

Morris's change in mood precedes his change in mode. The
first signs of a new elegiac tone, one often darkening from melancholy to despair, are visible in "Scenes from the Fall of Troy," a
series of dramatic monologues Morris planned but did not complete or publish.[2] The "Scenes," designed and partially written in

47

1858, are similar in diction and dramatic method to such poems of *The Defence* as "Sir Peter Harpdon's End." Indeed, a speech of Peter's forecasts the appeal of Troy to Morris as well as his approach to the subject:

> There! they were wrong, as wrong as men could be;
> For, as I think, they found it such delight
> To see fair Helen going through their town:
> Yea, any little common thing she did
> (As stooping to pick a flower) seem'd so strange,
> So new in its great beauty, that they said:
> 'Here we will keep her living in this town,
> Till all burns up together.' And so, fought,
> In a mad whirl of knowing they were wrong;
> Yea, they fought well, and ever . . . did they struggle sore,
> Quite sure to slip at last; wherefore, take note
> How almost all men, reading that sad siege,
> Hold for the Trojans.
>
> (1:42–43)

Like his idol, Chaucer, and his fictional character, Peter, Morris found in the fall of Troy a symbol of the decline of the medieval world and of heroic England. His sympathies are with the Trojans, traditionally the ancestors of the British. But Morris dwells less on the failed heroism of the Trojans than on the despair that gradually overwhelms them, destroying their lives, hopes, and fears. The beauty and brutality of life which Morris had depicted in *The Defence* are shrouded, in "Scenes," in a gloom that makes the Trojans question even the premises for living.

In Morris's Troy, even violence and death are insufficient outlets for despair. As the war drags wearily on, action itself becomes pointless. The Trojans become spellbound victims, gradually deprived of energy and will; the Greeks, passive yet changeless and implacable, are the agents of the nemesis overtaking the city. Intrigue has debased the antagonists and, with the death of Hector, "all has come to stabbing in the dark" (24:30). Even Helen, the wonder of the world, is weary and guilt-ridden. The arming song she sings, a version of which appears in *The Earthly Paradise*,[3] is one of the gloomiest of *carpe diem* lyrics. With its repeated injunction to love now—"for who knoweth/ What thing cometh after death"—it bitterly indicates that "life and love in age grow cold" (24:40), and that the earthly world is a place of futile battles and debilitating lovers' quarrels. For Helen, who like Guenevere is a model of the destructive power of love and a symbol of the dark anima, love is not enough. Passion is blighted by her sense of her fatality, her premonitions of future misery, and her concern with the bitterness of death. Even when she mistakenly believes that peace has come to Troy, she is haunted by fears of the fading of beauty and the mutability of love.

Paris, who in the first scene in Helen's chamber ("Helen Arming Paris") can still believe that life and passion will triumph, becomes increasingly death-haunted and death-desiring. When in scene five ("Helen and Paris") he again stands in Helen's closet, he laments that he is "all as dead" (24:38). In an ironic comment on the first scene, Morris demonstrates through Paris that "death indeed is strong/ When this same shadow of him can slay love" (24:38). Paris's passion for Helen cannot make him wish to live; with the fall of Troy inevitable, he yearns for release from life. More surprising, however, is that in the second version of scene five, Paris desires death as a welcome release *from* erotic passion. Crying out for the kiss of passage: "One kiss at last, one bitter bitter kiss,/ O life and death together" (24:39), he goes forth to meet his fate.

Thus, in "Scenes from the Fall of Troy," erotic love is shown as destroying all who aspire to it: Troilus, Achilles, Polyzena, Cassandra, and Andromache as well as Paris and Helen. The purpose of Helen's flight with Paris had been to escape a loveless relationship with Menelaus. Echoing Guenevere, Helen justifies her actions by stating that it was Paris "Who taught me how to love, when long ago/ I had forgotten that the world was fair/ And I was fair" (24:4). She, like the other victims of love, has yielded to a force that is "life and death together," offering a taste of honey, but bringing poison in its wake.

Helen's torment is the cruelest, for she is forced to live. Finding a triumphant Menelaus in the chamber she had shared with Paris, she is forced to aid in the slaying of her present husband, Deiphobus, and is then raped in the bloody bed by the Greek husband she hates. Devoid of hope and fear, Helen enters a state of death in life. A mere shell of her former self, she is sent to the ships that will return her to a Greece that will be her psychic and physical prison.

Thus, in "Scenes," Morris moves beyond an elegiac lament for loss into a nihilistic statement of the meaninglessness of all things. Morris has written of a society destroyed and hinted that those who have ruined it will have only a Pyrrhic victory. He has shown love—the sustaining force in the self and in the world—obliterated and the anima as an enslaved captive with no hope of being freed. Why he chose not to complete "Scenes" becomes evident. Morris abandoned a work too revealing of his personal (and perhaps social) despair and chose to mute, though not to abandon, the themes which had dominated the poem. Moreover, finding in medieval romance a form in which he could achieve psychic distance from himself, he began to change his genre.

The change is reflected in the first published, though not first written, of the verse romances, *The Life and Death of Jason* (1867), which had grown too long to be an *Earthly Paradise* tale, and was therefore separately published.[4] The story of Jason is foreshadowed in "Scenes" when Helen imagines the Greek rowers singing the tale "Of Argo and the Golden Fleece, and Her / That made and marred them all in a short while, . . . / Medea the Colchian" (24:3). While Morris's romance loosely follows its source, the *Argonautica* of Apollonius Rhodius, Morris enjoys, as he had in "Scenes," combining Greek and medieval elements. *Jason* becomes a Victorian conceptualization of a medieval romance on a Greek theme.

While Morris's contemporaries reveled in the style and form of *Jason*, his use of the genre of medieval romance has been condemned in our own time. Seeking to follow what he believed were the conventions of medieval romance, Morris deliberately emphasized action and plot. Dedicated to lucidity and narrative speed, he pared his diction and simplified his metrics for the sake of clarity. He deliberately reduced his characters, stripping them of all but essential traits, creating types rather than individuals. He wanted his audience to concentrate not on striking single lines or individual passages, but on large overall units and memorable cumulative effects. Thus the complex psychological portraits, brilliant colors, and richly freighted brief images so prominent in *The Defence* volume are muted or diffused.

The genre Morris chose, however, did allow him to stress patterns and motives which he believed were timeless and universal. His use of the romance manner freed him from artistic restraints, permitting him to present strong passions which, in the context of ordinary Victorian life, would have seemed inappropriate and allowing him to explore realms of consciousness which might otherwise have been closed to him. Most significantly, the mythic and folkloric matter of romance contained what he considered the constant elements within the human spirit: man's endless quests for immortal life or love, his conquest by or rescue from the fate that threatens him, his love encounters with benign or malign beings of another order, the journey from womb to tomb that constitutes man's life.

Substituting a gentle elegiac tone for the intense gloom of "Scenes," Morris is again preoccupied in *Jason* with love, fate, and death. His main interest is in the fated and fatal passion of Jason and Medea, and his sympathies are clearly with the woman. Indeed, a title more reflective of the poem's theme might have been the Love and Death of Medea. The romance springs to life only when she appears; hers are the joys and torments with which the poet empathizes.

Jason is essentially passive, an agent and victim of the implacable fate that rules the poem. His basic drives are for rest and peace, and the desire for glory which impels him to the quest for the Golden Fleece is external, leaving his essential character unchanged. Though far from ignoble, he is seldom truly heroic. As a lover he is restless and shallow, and, although he is willing to reciprocate Medea's passion for him, his love is never as intense as hers. To him, eros is a lovely but "unasked gift" (2:111) from the gods. When he rejects Medea for Glauce, he is repudiating the heroic way of life. While Jason's attraction to Glauce is portrayed in a form parallel to that of his earlier meeting with Medea, the purpose of the stylistic parallel is ironic: to compare the rightful passion for Medea and the noble deeds it causes with Jason's less mature desire for Glauce and his concomitant wish to escape from the life of challenge, action, and responsibility identified with Medea.

Jason's desire to evade maturity and responsibility is manifested in areas other than the erotic. He is one who would rather find the golden age intact than attempt to create it anew. Morris indicates—as he does in the "Prologue" to *The Earthly Paradise*—that this drive seldom culminates in success or happiness. In *Jason*, the age of gold becomes a reiterated symbol of the past that cannot be recaptured and of an earthly paradise that men may glimpse but cannot enter. The Argonauts see its remnants as they approach the Garden of the Hesperides; they nostalgically recall it in song, "Alas for Saturn's days of gold" (2:150); they even glimpse it on their river journey through the forests of prehistoric Europe.[5] But the "fair forests, . . . / Where, innocent of craft, with joyous feasts/ The wise folk live as in the golden age" (2:140) are either illusory or inaccessible to the Argonauts. Their mission is to restore the spirit of Saturn's age to their own kingdoms, not to retreat from them. Jason's failure to do so, his lack of desire to make the land to which he returns an excellent earthly kingdom, is another indication of his inner flaw. He fails both to maintain the constancy in love natural to the people of the golden age and to repeatedly choose the "hard life and deathless praise" (2:130) of one who would quest for the ideal. Ironically, his discovery that he has cast away his honor, kingdom, and rightful love comes only as his life draws to an end. As he sits musing on the woman he has betrayed, he is crushed by the rotting prow of the Argo—a correlative to the decay of his life.

Morris's Medea, on the other hand, is a powerful, dynamic figure. Like Guenevere, she is a woman first enlivened then destroyed by passion. Blind to personal advantage, she relinquishes for love her chance of godlike power, her personal pride, and her loyalty to kin. Giving and losing all, she dedicates her self and life to Jason. Sacrificing her father and brother, she saves Jason's life and enables him to obtain the golden fleece. She helps Jason and his men escape the temptations offered by Circe and the Sirens. Aware, even in the first throes of her passion, that her lover may tire of her and seek a new woman, she is, nonetheless, "the fool of love" (2:108). She believes herself fated to adore him, and her very adoration, when combined with her strength of character, turns him against her. Creon's criticisms of her, that she is too powerful, too controlling, more king than queen, wound Jason's vanity and lessen his love. When he decides to reject Medea, he destroys her.

That in so doing he destroys himself is obvious. What is less apparent is that from the moment Medea recognizes that Jason does not love her, she behaves as one already dead. Even her vengeance is the sterile malignity of the dead-alive. Medea feels neither anger at Glauce nor remorse at killing her. She sees herself as her rival's savior, granting a swift demise as opposed to the death in life she herself is doomed to. The murder of the children she has borne to Jason is, to her, the gift of release from earth: "this lovely bier/ Of youth and love, and joy and happiness" (2:286). Because the death of the body is a reward, she denies it to both Jason and herself. Medea, like Guenevere before her, becomes both the victim of destructive erotic passion and its embodiment. Slayer and slain, victim and victimizer, it is her fate that moves the reader as Jason's does not. She remains, through all, the center of interest and sympathy.

Yet, while *Jason* focuses on Medea's tragic passion—foreshadowing its complications in the tale of King Athamas and his two queens, Nephele and Ino, which begins Book II, predicting its crisis through repeated images of the heat and fire of passion, and indicating its tensions in the antithesis set up between pleasure and knowledge—the themes of love, fate, and death are explored in other ways as well.

Jason is studded with episodes that examine the impulse to escape from the limitations of human life through passion, death, or both. Again, Morris's dialectical turn of mind is evident, for incidents illustrate the perils of such escape but present the drive for it in most provocative forms. In three such episodes—the Argonauts' encounters with Circe, the meeting with the Sirens, and the entrapment of Hylas by the nymph—enchanted men are drawn to fatal women who represent the beautiful and deadly experience of escape from the normal world.

Circe and her handmaids are shown as the least attractive of the perils to be overcome. Clearly, almost crudely representative of escape through indulgence in the lusts of the flesh, they present no real challenge. Circe's realm is a dreamlike land filled with drugged, heavy-eyed maidens and sorrowful male beasts. The women are harlots, "weary images of sin" (2:185), as much enslaved by sexuality as the men they have transformed. All are trapped in joyless passion, a merely temporary gratification which corrupts them, and Circe recognizes the similarity between their plight and Medea's love for Jason.

More alluringly described are the provocative Sirens whose temptation is more complex. Their offer of rest and calm, of a changeless life and land, and an end to "burning love unsatisfied" (2:198) is difficult even for Orpheus to oppose. As the singing contest between Orpheus and the Sirens develops, their promises of release from the turning of fortune and of peace, wisdom, and "calm, unwavering Godlike love,/ No lapse of time can turn or move" (2:203) are revealed as appeals to man's "deadly love of death" (2:192). Their realm is a "land of lies" (2:193), and they themselves are death figures, "Fair as the lightning thwart the sky" and "fair as the doomed victim's wreath" (2:199). Yet their attractiveness is never negated, and the desire they represent is not fully conquered.

The most powerful temptation, however, is described in the episode of Hylas and the nymph and the song it contains, later revised and titled "A Garden by the Sea."[6] Hylas is seduced by a mysterious nymph on "the chiefest day" (2:67) of summer: Midsummer's Day—the time of natural and erotic magic. When, in the prelude to dalliance, his shield strap breaks, Hylas removes his armor, symbolically relinquishing his duty and his defenses. As he woos the nymph, she withdraws, luring him away from the world of men and into her power. Like Keats's belle dame sans merci, she lulls her knight to sleep with a song breathing all the enchantment she offers. Her description of the garden-close

serves both to complete the seduction of Hylas and to summon
her sisters to bear him off. It exquisitely promises the enchanted
lover an entrance to a paradise of love:

> 'I know a little garden-close
> Set thick with lily and red rose,
> Where I would wander if I might
> From dewy morn to dewy night,
> And have one with me wandering.
>
> 'And though within it no birds sing,
> And though no pillared house is there,
> And though the apple boughs are bare
> Of fruit and blossom, would to God,
> Her feet upon the green grass trod,
> And I beheld them as before.
>
> 'There comes a murmur from the shore,
> And in the place two fair streams are,
> Drawn from the purple hills afar,
> Drawn down unto the restless sea;
> The hills whose flowers ne'er fed the bee,
> The shore no ship has ever seen,
> Still beaten by the billows green,
> Whose murmur comes unceasingly
> Unto the place for which I cry.
>
> 'For which I cry both day and night,
> For which I let slip all delight,
> That maketh me both deaf and blind,
> Careless to win, unskilled to find,
> And quick to lose what all men seek.
>
> 'Yet tottering as I am and weak,
> Still have I left a little breath
> To seek within the jaws of death
> An entrance to that happy place,
> To seek the unforgotten face
> Once seen, once kissed, once reft from me
> Anigh the murmuring of the sea.'

(2:69–70)

Though it may appear to be an earthly paradise, the land of
the close is a strangely hollow land. Perfect in beauty, it is, nonetheless, a place where "no birds sing," and where "flowers ne'er
fed the bee"—a land without life. On the shore that "no ship has

ever seen," there is no sound but the rest-provoking murmur of a strangely "restless" sea and the sound of two streams entering it. Still and silent, the land is simultaneously dreamlike and death-like. Like Tennyson's Lotos Land, it is a realm removed from the pains of reality but also from the activities of life. Yet, in lines that Maude Bodkin has described as vibrating "with longing for the imaged beauty of the garden," the singer of the lyric announces his intention: "To seek within the jaws of death/ An entrance to that happy place." And "the note of longing, mystic, exorbitant . . . finally dissolves the sensuous reality of the garden." The reader sees through the images to what the close really is—"the symbol of a Paradise to be sought only in death."[7]

Thus, in the Hylas episode, the yearning for love is inter-twined with the desire for death in one of Morris's most striking psychological configurations. Even single, apparently simple, images encapsulate the dualities in the poem. The lilies and roses, symbols of the height of summer, are strangely funereal. The apple boughs, though rich with the green leaves of summer, are without spring blossoms or the fruits of autumn and are thus described as "bare." The enclosed womblike garden of love is also the tomb of death. Alluding to Tennyson and Keats, Morris uti-lizes their images in his own vision. Indeed, the predicament of Keats's dying knight, conjured up by Morris's echo of "no birds sing," is the predicament of Hylas. Borne away to the world of the stream, Hylas remains: "Not dead, nor living, among faces fair,/ White limbs and wonders of the watery world" (2:73). In all, the seduction of Hylas suggests most poignantly the larger tension in *Jason* and the conflict within Morris himself—a tension between an acceptance of the realities of existence and a yearning to dis-miss them in an escape beyond the ordinary world.

Thus, *Jason* presents in microcosm many of the motifs Morris was to utilize in the larger *Earthly Paradise*. Intensifying his treatments of escape and of the quest for the golden age, he was to make of them a framework for a compendium of tales which would interweave his recurrent themes in new ways. Doubling and tripling his treatments of given subjects, writing tales which are mirror images of each other, interspersing them with poi-gnant personal lyrics, and binding all together with a series of underlying images, he created a poem of considerable richness and complexity. Yet, both his era and our own have misunder-stood his simplification of style and complexity of meaning. His own public liked his poem because they partially misread it; ours has chosen to ignore the work that earned him his fame.

II

While the publication of *Jason* in 1867 made Morris a popular poet, the publication in 1868–70 of the three volume *Earthly Paradise* made him a famous one. He was praised by aesthetes for his artistic purity, by contemporary positivists for liberating art from theology, and by critics weary of "obscurity" for his simplicity, health, and objectivity. Most important, the great middle-class public and those who guided its taste admired the "suitability" and readability of his tales in verse.[8] In our era, however, the poem has been largely ignored, and Morris's half-serious comment that "the title is the best part of it and will have a meaning for men when the rest is forgotten"[9] has been sadly prophetic. Paul Thompson speaks for the majority of contemporary scholars in suggesting that "*The Earthly Paradise* is an excellent way of passing a train journey, but it is not always easy at the end of the journey to remember what was in it."[10] The poem has been censured for pallor, diffuseness, and dullness or dismissed as the empty song of an idle singer. It has been attacked for representing an escapist tendency in Morris who, unable to confront either his marital crisis or the problems of his era, turned his back on the world and retreated into the simplistic retelling of worn-out legends.[11]

One of the obvious reasons for the eclipse of a poem once considered Morris's major work is the change in literary taste and critical theory in the past century. Our era no longer enjoys long, verse narratives or the genre of poetic romance, nor does it consider pathos and sweetness the vital tones in poetry. Diffuseness and occasional monotony, considered minor flaws by Morris's contemporaries, are cardinal sins to modern formalist critics, and lack of overt social and ethical relevance are anathema to critics of the neo-humanist and social schools. Readers of today favor brief, intense, and highly concentrated poetic experiences; they prefer the irony, paradox, and tension of *The Defence* volume to the lucid and harmonious verse narrative of *The Earthly Paradise*. Equipped to handle complexities of image or symbol, they are unable to deal with its transparent surfaces and simple effects.

Another less obvious reason for the neglect of *The Earthly Paradise* is a lack of awareness of the poem's purpose, theme, and structure and, equally important, of its central role in its creator's life and thought. *The Earthly Paradise* reveals Morris's brilliance in using pre-existent materials, as well as his way of reshaping them—symbolically or mythically—to emphasize his themes. It demonstrates his architectonic power, for it is structured with a

complex and impressive design in mind. Most important, its
themes are Morris's basic and abiding concerns, ones essential to
the understanding of his total body of work; the seeds of the
volumes to follow are found in the rich soil of *The Earthly
Paradise*.

The "Apology" which begins the poem has often been removed from its context and consequently misunderstood.
Labeled a document of the escapist tradition in literature, the
"Apology" has been cited as proof that Morris took neither his
times nor his poetry with sufficient seriousness.[12] Although it
may appear to announce Morris's avoidance of the problems
most important to his generation, it persuades the reader of his
full awareness of them. For example, when Morris says:

> Of Heaven or Hell I have no power to sing,
> I cannot ease the burden of your fears,
> Or make quick-coming death a little thing,
> Or bring again the pleasure of past years,
>
> (3:1)

he is not suggesting a lack of concern, but rather that neither he
nor any "singer" can ease the Victorian condition. He has no
answer to the problem of religious faith, nor can he solve the
problem of mutability. He is unable to alleviate "The heavy
trouble, the bewildering care/ That weighs us down who live and
earn our bread" (3:1), the economic questions of his times. Without the "knowledge for which words he may not find,/ Nor love
of things as vague as autumn wind" (6:332), he cannot authorita-
tively write of scientific inquiry or abstract speculation. Instead,
speaking as a "Dreamer of dreams, born out of . . . [his] due
time," he asks, "Why should I strive to set the crooked straight?"
(3:1). His question is a deliberate echo of the cry of Ecclesiastes in
another iron age: "Consider the work of God: for who can make
that straight which He hath made crooked?" (Eccles. 102:13). Not
only is Morris voicing his social despair, his belief that much
around him is vanity, but he is revealing his recognition that only
through the coming of a new Messiah shall "the crooked . . . be
made straight" (Isa. 40:4). Cure, the work of the hero is beyond the
powers of the singer, but the singer can point the way by showing
his generation models among the legendary figures of the past, as
Carlyle had done in his study, *On Heroes, Hero-Worship, and the
Heroic in History*. Thus, Morris will sing of "the mighty men" of
the past who can slay the "ravening monsters" in the "steely sea"
of life (3:2), and, by showing how they redeemed themselves and

their worlds, can remind his audience that heroism has existed and still may be restored.

As Morris's "Apology" suggests Carlyle's concept of hero-worship, so the opening of *The Earthly Paradise* contains Ruskin's social and aesthetic ideals. When Morris asks his readers to

> Forget six counties overhung with smoke,
> Forget the snorting steam and piston stroke,
> Forget the spreading of the hideous town;
>
> (3:3)

he is actually reminding them of the industrial blight of England and the growth of the urban Wen. In contrast to Victorian London and its ugliness they are to think of Chaucer's London, "small and white and clean" (3:3) and to regret its loss. They are to compare to the squalid cities of the present the smaller townships of the fourteenth century and the rural lands "where few were poor, if none were lordly rich" (5:209). In these peaceable kingdoms where injustice and class strife were rarely seen are found the remnants of the ideal state and the models for a better future.

Morris's title itself suggests the search for lost perfection: a terrestrial realm where the age of gold survives untouched by fate or death and an internal realm of thought and feeling that provides a paradise within. Well aware of history, Morris knew that the Greeks had dreamt of the Fortunate Isles and the Islands of the Blest, and had imaged perfect earthly life existing among the Scythians or Ethiopians. He knew the medieval visions of unfallen life among the Camerini, in the lands of Cockaigne and of Prester John, upon the Island of Saint Brendan, and in the Edens, Avalons, and Asgards of medieval lore. However, Morris's use of the idea of perfect lives and perfect lands is tinged with irony, for he stresses the destructive aspects of man's quests for them. To strive to build the age of gold in one's own land is right; to seek escape from home and duty is to be doomed to waste and failure.

Morris's first and discarded version of "The Wanderers' Prologue" which begins the poem, pointedly titled "The Fools' Paradise" (3:xiii), almost sermonizes on these points. Its characters, pirates led by their captain's fantasy of a deathless land, find only false paradises. One seemingly idyllic land is populated by invisible inhabitants who decapitate several of the pirates; another is the home of Stone Age savages who ambush the party; a third, a paradise in all externals, is inhabited by the dead, frozen into the postures of life. Even the captain's dreams of Eden become nightmares: in one, he arrives at an earthly paradise to discover that it is a land of the unhappy dead; in another, he finds a deathless land whose inhabitants yearn only for release from life. Gradually he realizes that he and his men have "sinned Adam's sin,/ To make us Gods who are but men,/ To find a heaven and dwell therein" (24:110) and, more important, have wasted their lives in a foolish quest.

While the earlier version of the prologue exposes the futility of the search, the published prologue probes its tragedy. Probably inspired by a passage from one of his favorite books, Paul Henri Mallet's *Northern Antiquities*, Morris visualizes the Wanderers' voyage as an unrecorded Norse exploration of the New World:

Had the sea-kings and their hardy followers been aware that beyond the regions of vines and forests there lay another, abounding in gold and silver and costly commodities, we should probably have seen at the present day a Norman dynasty reigning in Mexico. It is, in fact, obvious that the merest accident might in that age have led some enterprising adventurer a few degrees further south, and given rise to a series of events resulting in the final conquest of the tropical regions of America by the sea-faring Scandinavians.[13]

Following Mallet's hypothesis, Morris has his Wanderers embark for "the landless waters of the west" (3:13) in search of a world without old age or death. Although they are given a powerful motive for flight—the Black Death has invaded Norway—they are also given an attractive alternative to it, for they meet the fleet of Edward III of England, and the King invites them to join his crusade against France.[14] The world of Froissart is offered to them, but rejecting the chance of action, love, and glory in the known world, they chose to seek another, symbolized by the Tree of the Hesperides emblazoned on their sail.

Their quest becomes "a tale of woe . . . of folly, and of wasted life" (3:6) as they go from one false paradise to another. Knowing of Leif Erikson's voyages, they steer south of Vineland and are carried by Mallet's "accident" (a tempest) to the southern tip of North America. They reach a "flowery shore," but cannot penetrate the "dragon-guarded woods" (3:30) beyond it. Traveling north, they find a shrine surrounded by the bones of sacrificial victims and filled with the mummies of kings, and, at the summit of the mountain, they discover dead slaves embalmed to look alive and an aged king who dies of fear at their approach.[15] They are told by a group of Aztecs that the paradise they seek is eastward and seaward, ironically in the home which they have left.

Another Mexican tribe they encounter tells them of a godlike people beyond the mountains, but they turn out to be a brutal race of savage cannibals. Returning to the center of tribal civilization, the Wanderers live contentedly for almost thirty years, until they are again struck by their foolish desire. Tricked into voyaging to a remote island, fooled by a stranger who assures them that it is the abode of eternal youth, they find themselves in a gorgeously decorated hall, where they are kept as captive gods. In the confusion of war they manage to escape, finally reaching a peaceful Western Isle where, old and disillusioned, they may wait for death.[16]

Thus, Morris begins *The Earthly Paradise* by demonstrating that the search for a terrestrial Eden is a tragic waste of life. The Wanderers have sacrificed rightful action and human love only to learn that the lands east of the sun and west of the moon, the Avalons and Asgards of which they dream, cannot be found within the world of men. "Too fair for those / Who needs must die" (6:9), they elude those who seek them.

Accepting the failure of their quest, Morris's Wanderers join the Greek Elders of the island in telling of the heroes of the Greek and medieval worlds who have found the earthly paradise and of the many who have not. The narrators' bitter past and melancholy mood are reflected in the way in which they tell their tales. Living amid memory and regret, dead to the ardent hopes and fears of their lost youth, they "sing of names remembered / Because they, living not, can ne'er be dead, / Or long time take their memory quite away" (3:1). The names they remember are those of the great heroes of their past; the stories they relate are from their own national treasure houses.[17]

The Wanderers tell tales extant in 1349, the time of their embarkation, and Morris, striving for verisimilitude, accounts for their knowledge of the sources they utilize. Laurence, the Swabian priest, narrates stories from medieval Latin chronicles and Nicholas, another Wanderer, is described as a Breton to account for his knowledge of the French romance of Ogier the Dane. The one tale borrowed from *The Arabian Nights* is explained by having Ralph, the Norseman who has led the party, speak of his childhood in Byzantium, where his father was one of the Emperor's Varangian Guards. Although the stories do not consistently reveal the characters of their narrators, they do attempt to recapture the qualities of the sources from which they are derived. Those drawn from Mandeville's *Voyages*, "The Lady of the Land" and "The Watching of the Falcon," are described as being told to the Wanderers by Flemings (since the author was thought to have been Flemish) and recreate Mandeville's combination of fantastic events and factual tone. The moral and anecdotal quality of the *Gesta Romanorum* is transmitted when a Wanderer relates a legend he first heard in the guesthouse of Peterborough Cathedral. The tale, "The Proud King," reflects its source, for it too is a colorful sermon on the pride that goes before a fall. Other Wanderers' tales resemble those a traveler might have heard en route to Canterbury; still others bear the universal marks of fairy tale and Indo-European folklore.

The legends told by the Greek Elders are not differentiated from one another—their main source is Lemprière's *Classical Dictionary*—and Morris makes no attempt to preserve their Hellenistic background and spirit. However, the narrative tone they share with the tales told by the Wanderers, a reflection of their age, fatigue, and nostalgia, contributes to the tonal unity of the total work, as well as to the presentation of its major themes. For all tell tales not only of the search for an external golden age but of the quest for the paradise within, an experience or state of mind that will bring joy and fulfillment. Although Graham Hough suggests that Morris (and his narrators) seek paradise in art,[18] the book itself and its author's comments on it do not support this thesis. At best, art can be a temporary catharsis for the suffering caused by life; it may serve as a balm for the despairing, but not as a cure for their woes.

Instead, Morris seeks a nostrum in the experience of romantic love, only to conclude that love too fails to make a heaven of earth. The subject of twenty of the twenty-four tales that comprise the work is erotic love,[19] achieved or failed, triumphant over or destroyed by fate, saving men from destruction or condemning them to death. It is on these patterns rather than the physical quest for a terrestrial Eden that *The Earthly Paradise* is really centered. Morris underscored his themes for May and Jenny, the daughters he adored, in a poem dated 25 December 1870, which he inscribed in their copy of the book. His poem tells them that *The Earthly Paradise* is to teach them to turn their "eyes toward very Love . . . / And all the pain it bringeth meet / As nothing strange amid the sweet." It reminds his daughters that

> Those that struggled sore, and failed
> Had one thing left them, that availed
> When all things else were naught—
> > E'en Love—
>
> > > (24:343)

and explains ironically that since happy fulfilled lives leave no records, his stories have been heavy with "trouble" and "woe" (24:343).

Even without this explicit statement of purpose, Morris's point is clear. Personal laments on the demise of love, the cruelty of fate and her companion change, and the wish for death that results from the failure of passion dominate the poems on the months which head each pair of tales. The opening and end-links between tales portray the varied responses of the listeners to these concepts. Within the tales themselves, Morris creates worlds where the central duty is faith to passion and the punishment for failure is the death of the body or soul. He delineates characters whose triumphs stem from love's success and whose destruction arises from its failure. The total structure of the poem, the thematic images used throughout it, and the complex relationship among the tales—pairings and triplings of parallel or opposite situations and characters—are all shaped to illuminate Morris's conceptions of love, fate, and death.

Creating structural and thematic parallelism, Morris traces both the birth, growth, and death of the natural year and the course of human love. Although the pattern is incomplete, perhaps because he abandoned several stories originally planned for inclusion as too personally revealing, Morris's year of love moves from accounts of the birth of passion, through tales of its fruition and decline, to the tragedies of winter and the death of love.[20] The ten tales he places in the Spring and Summer sections are lighter in tone and more joyous in content than those for Fall and Winter; yet they foreshadow the darkening world portrayed in the final sections.

A similar account of a year of love is presented within the poems to the months which frame each pair of tales. These personal lyrics, in which Mackail found "an autobiography so delicate and so outspoken that it must needs be left to speak for itself,"[21] reveal much about Morris's pain at his rejection by his wife, his struggle for a reconciliation, and his despair at its failure. Replacing earlier and more objective lyrics, they form a rime royal sonnet sequence akin in tone, if not in form, to George Meredith's "Modern Love." They are of more than biographical importance, for they contribute to the overall structure of *The Earthly Paradise*. Correlating emotion and external landscape, they link human passion to the cycle of the seasons and to the recurrent pattern of the life of nature. Protesting mutability in love and the power of change—the agent of fate—they explore the tension between a yearning for death and a struggle to accept the bitterness of reality. Thus they foreshadow several of the major themes found within the tales and establish the tone of the total work.

Morris's calendar begins in March and the month that is the "first redresser of the winter's wrong" brings both the "hope of life" and the thought of death to the poet.[22] The birds who sing of birth and joy are in ironic contrast to the poet who knows that the source of "all this storm of bliss" is Death. Unable to enjoy "sweet forgetfulness," he is haunted by the brevity of life. His resolution—to live while he may, accepting "all the gifts that Death and Life may give" (3:82)—heartens him only temporarily. His consciousness of death is ironically reasserted in April, the "life of all the year." April, herself undying, leads him to muse on the decay inherent in the blossoming of the lilies and roses of summer, as well as on his own frustrated passion. Longing for a love which "never draweth nigh," the poet hears church bells echoing his plea: "Come again, Come back, past years! why will ye pass in vain?" (3:169). As he laments the triumph of time and the transiency of human passion, he yearns to recapture the relationship which, like his dream of summer, is touched with the signs of death.

May, the month of love, brings the poet a further intimation of the demise of passion and its consequences. Awake beside his sleeping lady, he witnesses a bitter pageant of love. In the grey of dawn, the Lord of Love appears and then quickly vanishes; the morning sun illuminates Old Age and Death, those whom Love has left behind. The shuddering poet must face his new companions and the unpleasant realities they represent. But he attempts to evade the message brought by May and seeks, in "June," a mood of pensive relaxation. The "rare happy dream" (4:87) of June does not last, and July brings the first of the confrontations between the poet and his lady.

On a rainy July afternoon the poet reminds his beloved of the fairness of the earlier part of the day, a correlative to their happy relationship of earlier years. His plea to her, "be happy now"— an echo of Morris's letters to Jane in these years[23]—is in vain. The movement from sunlight to storm in the natural world reflects the bitter change in the lovers' relationship: "foolish sin, / And nameless pride" have alienated the couple and now prevent their reunion. While the poet knows that the sun will return, he sadly questions if he and his lady can "regain what . . . [they] have lost meanwhile" (4:143).

"August" indicates that their old love is irretrievable. Wasting even the few good moments they still share "craving for the best," the couple mourn "Like lovers o'er the painted images / Of those who once their yearning hearts have blessed" (4:187). Each muses on a former affair or another love. Again, the poet asks his lady if she is happy. Although he receives an affirmative gesture, his realization that the brief moment of closeness may not come again leads him to despair.

"September" chronicles an intensification of the poet's un-happiness. Frustrated and anguished, he asks September for a vision. Receiving none, he is left with his longing for a vanished love. Knowing that the past is gone forever, he cries:

> Look long, O longing eyes, and look in vain!
> Strain idly, aching heart, and yet be wise,
> And hope no more for things to come again
> That thou beheldest once with careless eyes!
>
> (5:1)

Lonely and alienated, he compares himself to a man thrust out of a peaceful sleep who tries "To dream again the dream that made him glad / When in his arms his loving love he had" (5:1).

October, the beginning of the year's decline, leads him to thoughts of death. Asking his lady to gaze at the dying year, listening again to bells that toll the triumph of time, the poet indicates that he is more than half in love with death. It will be "soft and kind," he says, a "rest from bliss we know not when we find" and from frustrated love "which ne'er the end can gain." But, like Keats, he turns away from death; his desire for oblivion is submerged in the swelling tune of the bells, now symbolizing hope. As he seeks reunion, asking "May not our hands still meet / Since still we live to-day?" (5:122), he is not rejected. Thus, he forgets his pain in a moment of reconciliation.

The moment is transient, and the urge to live fades with its passing. In the powerful verses on November, the poet questions his ability to struggle with the thoughts that torment him. As he attempts to find solace in the external world beyond his "four walls, hung with pain and dreams," he gazes out at a full moon which "turns the dread midnight into dreamy noon, / Silent and full of wonders." Though he finds the sight beautiful and awe-some, it offers him no hope of life renewed. Instead it becomes a sign of his alienation, a symbol of love's mutability and of the finality of death:

> Yea, I have looked, and seen November there;
> The changeless seal of change it seemed to be,
> Fair death of things that, living once, were fair;

Bright sign of loneliness too great for me,
Strange image of the dread eternity,
In whose void patience how can these have part,
These outstretched feverish hands, this restless heart?

(5:206)

His acceptance of the inevitability of change seems to permit the poet to temporarily shake off his despair. On a snowy night in December, the bells toll out "the year foredone." They remind him of the sorrows the old year has brought—"Change, kindness lost, love left unloved alone;"—but they remind him, as well, that he was "once . . . loved if but amidst a dream." With the birth of the new year comes his resolution to endure:

Though nought of good, no God thou mayst discern,
Nor nought that is, thine utmost woe can move,
Though no soul knows wherewith thine heart doth yearn.

(6:1)

Without faith or the belief that his pain can be exorcised, he nonetheless resolves to cling to life in the hope of better days to come.

At the "murky ending of a leaden day" in January, the poet again receives a moment of reward. Yet again he must suffer the anguish caused by its transiency. In the "gathering night," his beloved turns to him, "silent, but with . . . [a] scarce-seen kindly smile." As sudden darkness falls outside the window— suggesting the bleakness of the natural world—a flash of light reveals a light in the lady's eyes, signaling the momentary warmth of love. The poet pleads with his beloved to:

. . . look, love, look again! the veil of doubt
Just for one flash, past counting, then was raised!
O eyes of heaven, as clear thy sweet soul blazed
On mine a moment! O come back again
Strange rest and dear amid the long dull pain!

But the moment of contact cannot be held:

Nay, nay, gone by! though there she sitteth still,
With wide grey eyes so frank and fathomless—
Be patient, heart, thy days they yet shall fill
With utter rest—Yea, now thy pain they bless,
And feed thy last hope of the world's redress.

(6:65)

Yet his "last hope" is undercut by the final bitter images of the poem, the "unseen hurrying rack," and the "wailing wind," which, like the poet, must seek their peace and rest elsewhere. All that remains to him is the wish for some future union, re-echoed in "February," the last of the seasonal poems. As the rain falls on a lonely and lifeless landscape, the poet reflects on the hollow spring to come. Even amid the joys of May he will relive "The useless hope, the useless craving pain" that made his face wet with more than raindrops. While he faintly hopes "for joy new born again," his final gesture is to accept the death in life of his present existence, one in which, shut off from all that matters, he can merely watch "the changeless change of seasons passing by" (6:175).

As in the poems on the months, contrasting moods of hope and despair are reflected by images of the changing lights, colors, and forms of nature, so in the twenty-four tales of *The Earthly Paradise*, images of color and its absence, and of places and landscapes, illuminate contrasting aspects of Morris's central themes. As in *The Defence* volume, Morris plays images of color—connoting life and love—against images of greyness—indicating despair or death. Again, sympathetic landscapes—natural settings which mirror the emotional states of the characters who inhabit them—reveal passion, joyfulness, or grief.[24] As in the early prose tales, Morris mingles vivid pictorial elements with vague or dreamlike backgrounds. He freezes a set of images into a *tableau vivant* (often resembling a Pre-Raphaelite painting), and then moves rapidly through a dreamlike background to another heightened depiction of a moment of intense passion or anguish. Through repetition, images become symbolic. Terrestrial paradises without decay or death, marked by the presence of single trees which bear both fruit and flower, are the symbols for perfect love. These, along with the haunts of earthly love, walled gardens and enclosed and sheltered valleys, are in contrast to the realms of love gone wrong. The silence and stillness of grey underworlds, barren wastelands, blighted gardens, and the desolation of ruined palaces reflect the failure of passion and the death of the heart.

The tales themselves parallel or reverse each other as they interweave the themes of love, fate, and death in multiple patterns. The successful quest for love which ends in the union of mortal and immortal in a perfect realm beyond the world is the subject of three tales: "Ogier the Dane," "The Land East of the Sun and West of the Moon," and "Cupid and Psyche." Morris's treatment in these three tales of the search for the anima—the soul in the form of a woman—is counterbalanced by three others: "The Watching of the Falcon," "The Man Who Never Laughed Again," and "The Hill of Venus," which deal with the failure of the quest for self or the discovery that a paradise of love is hell disguised. The love triangle in which two men are involved with same fated and fatal woman is explored in "The Lovers of Gudrun" and "Bellerophon at Argos"; two other tales, "The Land East of the Sun" and "Ogier the Dane," reverse the triangle of passion as they compare the love of two women for a single man. The kindly fate which brings love out of anticipated death is explored in "Atalanta's Race" and "The Man Born to Be King," while its thematic opposite, the malevolent fate that brings destructive passion and death in life, is examined in "The Death of Paris" and "The Watching of the Falcon."

Even archetypal characters gain impact as they are paired and repeated. The restless, discontented male unable to commit himself to love, like Bharam in "The Man Who Never Laughed Again," is echoed in the discontented, restless central figure in "The Story of Rhodope," a woman who cannot love or be attained. Woman as the pure anima, the preserver of man whose love brings life, is manifested in the Alcestis of "The Love of Alcestis," and in the Cecily of "The Man Born to Be King," while woman as the dark anima, the fatal force who drives men to doom, is shown in the immortals of "The Watching of the Falcon" and "The Death of Paris," as well as in the mortal figures of Sthenoboea in "Bellerophon at Argos" and of Gudrun in the tale which bears her name. Sometimes the benign and malign animas are figured in a single woman, as in the Lady of the Land, but they are more often shown as alter-egos, as with Sthenoboea and Philonoë, the twin sisters of the two tales of Bellerophon. Sthenoboea symbolizes the selfish, egocentric passion that seeks to victimize its object, Philonoë, the altruistic spirit that yearns to give and to preserve. The pure anima, as manifested in "Pygmalion and the Image," is a statue of Galatea which when humanized becomes benign and full of love. Its mirror image is seen in "The Ring Given to Venus," where the statue of the goddess comes to life as a demonic force. Many tales are dominated by the figure of Venus herself, but she is either *Generatrix* or *Petulantia*, never both. In "Atalanta's Race," "Pygmalion and the Image," and "Acontius and Cydippe," Venus is the mother of life, the benevolent power of love and delight. In "Cupid and Psyche," "The Ring Given to Venus," and "The Hill of Venus," she is the cruel force who brings barren lust and the threat of death.

Ten tales of *The Earthly Paradise* are dominated by the *Venus Generatrix*, the pure anima, and the fairy maiden or the human virgin in her benign aspect. "Atalanta's Race," "The Man Born to Be King," "The Doom of King Acrisius," "Cupid and Psyche," "Pygmalion and the Image," "Ogier the Dane," "The Land East of the Sun," "Acontius and Cydippe," "The Fostering of Aslaug," and "Bellerophon in Lycia" demonstrate love's triumph over fate and death. Their subject is the perfect love of mortal and immortal or the blissful hour of human love achieved; their pattern is of the successful journey or the passing of the test; their controlling image is of the sheltered valley or the flowering garden of delights. Yet, even these tales of "happy" love are undercut by veiled fears of change or of the threat of death, for Morris clearly indicates that perfect love is neither of nor for the earth. Three of his tales, "Ogier the Dane," "Cupid and Psyche," and "The Land East of the Sun" treat the successful quest for a terrestrial Eden and the triumphant escape from earth. The lovers in each case are chosen by immortals, but must undergo substantial trials before they may be deified by love. Ogier the Dane, borne off to Avalon by Morgan La Fay, experiences both the perfect love of an immortal and the flawed and earthly love of the Queen of France. When he must finally choose, he selects rightly, rejecting the mutable and destructive earthly queen for the eternal, constant love of the fairy maiden.

In Morris's rendition of "Cupid and Psyche," a version derived from Apuleius's *Golden Ass*, Psyche is depicted as the suffering anima in search of the love that will make her whole. Painting what Apuleius merely sketches, adding motivations and justifications for Psyche's behavior, Morris emphasizes her marriage of death, her fall (through a failure in patience and trust), and the pain and difficulty of her journey to redemption. When Psyche breaks the prohibition that forbids her to see and know the nature of her love, she almost dooms herself to the loss of paradise. Only through a complex process of painful maturation can she regain it. Despite her despair and wish for death, she must accomplish four tasks of increasing difficulty; in the process, she becomes a female hero, performing memorable deeds. She must order nature and her own chaotic self in the sorting of the seeds; she must calm the forces of destruction in the gathering of the golden fleeces from the Sun-Rams; she must acquire freedom and strength in seeking and containing the deadly waters of the Styx. Only after her last labor, a journey to the underworld and a confrontation with death itself, is she ready to abandon her old self and life.

After near failure and a deathlike sleep, she is redeemed by Love and prepared for divinity. Yet Morris stops short of painting the bliss of the apotheosis of Psyche; mortals, after all, cannot know divine and perfect love. Instead, his Psyche enters immortality thinking of the change and death on earth and feeling "godlike pity . . . / For her old self, for sons of men that die" (4:73).

"The Land East of the Sun," a later, darker draft of "The Palace East of the Sun," one of Morris's earliest written *Earthly Paradise* tales, is developed as a mirror image of Psyche's quest. Like Psyche, John, the lover, betrays his love and must suffer greatly for his fall. After gaining the woman who is his soul, he chooses to leave her terrestrial paradise and return to an imperfect earth. Though warned by his fairy bride of "lovers who outlived the love / That once they deemed the world would move" (5:46), he breaks his vow and summons her to him because he fears temptation by his brother's wife. Through his failure in patience and trust, he dooms himself, his fairy wife, and her entire land to death in life. Only after an arduous quest and purification by suffering does he regain his perfect lady and her land. Yet again, a tale of "happy" love, of "how twain grew one and came to bliss" is undercut by its narrator's comment on the chances of such ideal passion: "Woe's me! an idle dream it is!" (5:120).

Thus, Morris warns that to come to bliss is almost an impossibility. For all, except rare mortals loved by beings of another order and carried to a realm beyond the ordinary world, fulfilled passion is imperfect, changed by fate and time, threatened by mortality. For most mortals, trapped in their selfhood, the momentary blending of two souls into one is the highest human bliss. Such figures as Perseus and Andromeda in "The Doom of King Acrisius," Admetus and Alcestis in "The Love of Alcestis," and Acontius and Cydippe in the tale of the same name, can forget in perfect moments of human passion that love may change and that they themselves must die. Even this love is rare and Morris reminds us of the shortness of the perfect moment when he interrupts a tale of joy to comment:

> Love while ye may; if twain grow into one
> 'Tis for a little while; the time goes by,
> No hatred 'twixt the pair of friends doth lie,
> No troubles break their hearts—and yet, and yet—
> How could it be? we strove not to forget;
> Rather in vain to that old time we clung,
> Its hopes and wishes round our hearts we hung,

We played old parts, we used old names—in vain,
We go our ways, and twain once more are twain;
Let pass: at latest when we come to die
Thus shall the fashion of the world go by.

(3:229–230)

In a fallen world, "all love fails to see / Desire grow into perfect joy" (6:295), for, like the earthly gardens and verdant valleys in which it blossoms, human love is perishable. Most mortals are doomed to "snatch at love with eager hands, / And gather death that grows thereby" (5:153). Something in the universe forbids the lasting union of two mortal souls; and "all has sworn / That those shall ever be forlorn / Who strive to bring this thing to pass" (5:154). Ultimately, even the joyful face of love, presented in Morris's ten "happy" tales, is faintly stained with tears.

In analyzing the reasons for the imperfection of earthly passion, Morris does not indicate that its greatest enemy is death. All lives must fade "to twilight and dark night at last" (3:51), and, as the Wanderers note with resignation, all tales must end in the same way:

'He died, and in his place was set his son;
He died, and in a few days every one
Went on their way as though he had not been.'

(3:239)

Though, like King Admetus, mortals may protest that the gods are cruel to destroy the only creature who knows and fears his end, they know their protest is in vain. For the most part, Morris's characters look to no afterlife of reward and punishment and do not expect the heavenly reunion of lovers. Even Laurence, the Wanderer who is a Swabian priest and, thus, the spokesman for the occasional Christian views in the poem, sees death primarily as a gift of God, who uses it to end the pains of life and burning love. Less a terror than an end to woe, death is desired by many lovers; the yearning to be cut off before fate can destroy their bliss is echoed throughout the tales. Those who outlive passion like Medusa or the Florentine in "The Lady of the Land" welcome death as a kindness. It is to be preferred to death in life, the demise of the heart that results from passion's failure. Bellerophon's cry—"Life or death, / But never death in life for me" (6:238)—is an accurate reflection of the attitude of his creator.

The variety of death which Morris makes a major theme in *The Earthly Paradise* is the condition of emotional paralysis

which results in a dead soul in a living body. It is caused more by
malevolent fate than by individual flaws or failures, and fate,
imaged as a massive net which traps and drags men down to
doom, is the worst foe of earthly love. Its agencies are time and
change, and only terrestrial paradises are safe from their effects.
Only in an Eden may love "still be happiness / Unmixed with
change and ill distress" (5:45). The fallen world is doomed to

> great pain,
> And death of days that shall not be again;
> And yearning life within us, and desire
> That changes hearts as fire will quench the fire.
>
> (6:200–201)

Time and change, Morris notes bitterly, "are the engines of the
Gods, lest we / Through constant love, Gods too should come to
be" (6:201). Since fate decrees the unnatural changes that ruin life
and love, all man can ask is to be spared the pains of change until
the pains of death come with them:

> O Death-in-life, O sure pursuer, Change,
> Be kind, be kind, and touch me not, till strange,
> Changed too, thy face shows, when thy fellow Death
> Delays no more to freeze my faltering breath!
>
> (6:277)

Morris's cry is seldom heeded; therefore, those who suffer from
the signs of living-death are legion. The motif, announced in the
first volume through the figures of Medusa and the Lady of the
Land, is almost obsessively repeated in the later volumes. Death
in life is the malady of the King in "The Watching of the Falcon,"
OEnone in "Death of Paris," John, his bride, and her entire land
in "The Land East of the Sun," of Cydippe doomed to maiden-
hood, of Rhodope, of Gudrun and her lovers, of Laurence in
"The Ring Given to Venus," and of Walter in "The Hill of
Venus." All, because of passion's pain, lose their hopes and fears,
the signs of normal human life. All are spellbound, frozen into
inaction, incapable even of suicide though they yearn for death.
All show that they are ruined by their changeless eyes and faces,
Morris's recurrent symbols for "the soul wherein all hope is
dead" (5:162).

In "The Man Who Never Laughed Again," Morris's most
detailed study of the symptoms and results of living-death,
Bharam, the central figure, is transported to an earthly paradise

of perfect love. When, in a variation on the Bluebeard motif, he violates the sanctity of the closed room, he loses his immortal bride and is expelled from Eden. His fate is prefigured in the unchanging despair of the six mysterious men he waits upon and buries, as well as in the changeless eyes and visage of his friend, Firuz, another who has failed the test. When Bharam falls, he too enters death in life:

> And now no more he moaned, his eyes were dry;
> Shut in his body's bonds, his soul would wait,
> The utmost term of all its misery,
> Nor hope for any ease, nor pray to die.
>
> (5:204)

His "dreamy eyes distraught" and "changeless face drawn with . . . hidden pain" gain him the name he will bear until death frees him: "THE MAN WHO NE'ER SHALL LAUGH AGAIN" (5:204).

Paradoxically, in the ten dark tales of *The Earthly Paradise*, the very changelessness that has been the hallmark of the terrestrial Eden and the perfect love found only in it becomes the symbol of a hell on earth. The images of unchanging perfection in the "happy" tales find their ironic counterparts in the images of staring, sightless eyes and faces rigid with despair, as well as in descriptions of the dead embalmed to look alive. All are nightmare images of dead souls, travesties of life, as life devoid of love becomes a mimicry of death. Dominating the dark tales of *The Earthly Paradise*, legends of "bitter loves and clouded lives" (17:xvi), they help reveal what May Morris called the introspective side of her father's mind, exposing a mood he would seldom allow to surface in his mature works. Beginning in the tales of Summer with "The Love of Alcestis," "The Lady of the Land," and "The Watching of the Falcon," and moving to the tales of Fall and Winter, "The Death of Paris," "The Man Who Never Laughed Again," "The Ring Given to Venus," and "The Hill of Venus," Morris paints a darkened world of lust and change and death. His eye is on the canker rather than the rose. Even in the few among these tales which do not end in death, the memorable figures are those destroyed by passion, the frustrated and rejected, the questers who have failed. All the tales suggest the grimace of the Witch in the excluded tale of "Orpheus"[25] who laughs sardonically at the idea of a relationship in which "each loves each in sweet and equal wise" (24:245). Instead, love is revealed as a cruel trick of the indifferent gods; mortals are allowed a bit of

"sullied bliss" (6:279) before fate brings them pain. The way of
the world is that:

> . . . oftenest the well-beloved
> Shall pay the kiss back with a blow,
> Shall smile to see the hot tears flow,
> Shall answer with scarce-hidden scorn
> The bitter words by anguish torn
> From such a heart, as fain would rest
> Silent until death brings the best.
>
> (5:145)

The correlatives to destructive earthly passion are the barren
wasteland or the ruined palace, powerful images which first
appear in "The Lady of the Land" and gain in impact in the tales
that follow. The Lady, both goddess and monster—benign and
malign anima in one—lives in a land that parallels her death in
life. Her realm, silent but for the howl of beasts, is a wasteland;
her palace contains the glories of the ancient world, but like her
past love, they are shattered relics. Medusa in "The Doom of King
Acrisius" is another monster-goddess whose land reflects her
emotional paralysis. Her barren passion is symbolized by her
treeless realm of grey cliffs and a steely sea; the landscape without
color, growth or life mirrors her sterile soul.

The image of the wasteland is intensified in the tales of Fall
and Winter. Laurence, the protagonist of "The Ring Given to
Venus," meets his demon-mistress on a ruined shore where the
sea "sucks the pasture's blood" (6:163) as she has sucked his potency and life. Bharam in "The Man Who Never Laughed
Again," Walter in "The Hill of Venus," and Bellerophon in
"Bellerophon in Lycia" return to earthly worlds deformed to
wastelands. If, like Bellerophon and Laurence, they ultimately
gain rewards, their suffering far exceeds their joy. For the most
part, their failures in the quest for love leave Morris's characters
in barren hells, still yearning for the Edens they have sought and
lost. Internally, they suffer the void left by the death of passion,
the state in which they

> . . . find nought real except ourselves, and find
> All care for all things scattered to the wind,
> Scarce in our hearts the very pain alive.
> Compelled to breathe indeed, compelled to strive,
> Compelled to fear, yet not allowed to hope.
>
> (5:205)

Morris's anguish over the emotional void left by the demise of passion was intensified, if not caused, by what he considered his personal "failure,"[26] his alienation from his wife. His own pain adds another dimension to four tales written or revised in 1869 and 1870, the years in which the crisis became intense. In "Bellerophon at Argos," "The Lovers of Gudrun," "The Ring Given to Venus," and "The Hill of Venus," Morris presents his grimmest vision of fate and death triumphant over love. His intricate analysis of emotional death, the prominence he gives the feelings and dilemmas of two husbands who learn they are unloved, and the dominant roles played by fatal women—projections of the dark anima—contribute to the power of these fictions. While the four tales do not supplant art with biography or go beyond the limits of Morris's design, they are marked by an intensity that others of the stories lack.

The alienation from the self and the world as well as the wish for death that rejection by a loved one brings are explored in two tales, "Bellerophon at Argos" and "The Lovers of Gudrun." In these treatments of the tragic loves of two men involved with the same woman, unlike those (such as "Ogier the Dane" and "The Land East of the Sun") which deal with two women who compete for the same man, the participant who loses is a center of concern. The two tales are mirror images: both husbands, developed from minor figures in Morris's sources, are treated with great sympathy, though one is ultimately innocent and the other guilty. Both wives, though destructive, are victims who suffer death in life, though one is painted as corrupt and the other as beyond judgment.[27]

Proetus, King of Argos, is painted in Morris's own image, as a lover of life who is "not made for heaven or hell, / But simply for the earth" (6:102). His admiration of Bellerophon, the superior man, is not destroyed even when Sthenoboea, his cold and egocentric queen, swears falsely that Bellerophon has raped her. Alienated from the wife he knows does not love him, unable to condemn but forced to punish his friend, Proetus responds less with anger than with sorrow. He refuses to kill Bellerophon not because—as in Morris's source—the hero is a suppliant, but because he still cares for him. Sending Bellerophon to Lycia to be executed by Sthenoboea's father, Proetus still can hope the gods will save his friend. Yet, although he can forgive with magnanimity, Proetus himself is weary of his life and yearns for death. Proetus becomes a figure who is dead-alive, a spellbound victim lacking even the will to gain release through suicide.

On the other hand, Bodli, the rejected husband in "The Lovers of Gudrun," is not an entirely innocent victim. In the *Laxdale Saga*, he is merely one of Gudrun's string of men, a minor figure who kills Kiartan, his friend, as much in retaliation for an insult as for Gudrun's love. In Morris's version of the tale, he is the most fully realized and sympathetic character, the tool of his mad passion, tormented by his separation from a cold and passive wife. Like Proetus, Bodli feels himself the lesser man forced to destroy the friend superior to him; like Proetus, he desires his own annihilation. But Bodli is fated to act, and in killing Kiartan, he dooms himself and Gudrun to living-death. Morris centers this tale of "the seed and fruit of bitter love" (5:250) on Bodli. Again, softening the brutalities of his source and developing and explaining motivations absent from it, Morris makes Bodli half believe that Gudrun is deserted by her lover, Kiartan. The glimmerings of recognition come to Bodli on the night he weds Gudrun; realizing he has merely won possession of a body, knowing now that Gudrun does not love him, Bodli becomes a soul in whom all hope and fear are dead. Incapable of action, spellbound with despair, he hopes Kiartan will slay him. Ironically, Bodli becomes Kiartan's murderer, and his plea to the corpse of his dead rival reveals the tragic nature of his plight:

> O friend, O friend, when thee I meet in bliss,
> Will thou not give my love Gudrun to me,
> Since now indeed thine eyes made clear can see
> That I of all the world must love her most?
>
> (5:381)

Bodli loses more than his friend, for his cry to his half-mad wife after the murder to "Speak one word to me / Before my bitter shame and misery / Crushes my heart to death" (5:383) is never answered. We and Bodli never know whether the hand Gudrun then stretches out holds pity or rejection. Bodli's final torment is to live marked by a changeless face—unforgiving of himself, not knowing if his wife forgives him—until he is hunted down and killed. Gudrun, on the other hand, remains as Jack Lindsay notes, "a dead figure of female power, conceived in passive terms."[28] Yet the very deficiencies of Morris's portrait are thematically effective. Gudrun, like Sthenoboea, is painted less as a living woman than as a powerful force which destroys all who desire her. Cold and passive in their relations with their husbands, ambivalent and egocentric in their passions for their lovers, Gudrun and Sthenoboea are, like Jane Morris, types of fatal beauty who personify the destructive aspects of earthly love.[29] They are fated to be fatal, causing love even when they do not share it, causing destruction even when they do not intend it, and suffering the pains of bitter passions in their own souls.

All Morris's fatal women resemble the demonic Venus whom Morris draws most fully in "The Ring Given to Venus" and "The Hill of Venus," tales so haunted and tormented that his daughter felt obliged to comment on them, saying: "Both are stories of wild, barren passion and are built up in an atmosphere of such an unquenchable melancholy that if my Father had written little else of note . . . you would say, here is an inward-looking being with scarcely a hope in his life, cursed with a sense of the futilities of the world."[30] These visions of the dark goddess are foreshadowed in the earlier sections of *The Earthly Paradise* by her cruelty in "Cupid and Psyche" and by the Venus-Circe tapestries described in detail in "The Watching of the Falcon." Deriving his figure from the *Venus Petulantia* of ancient philosophy, the evil force who destroys men in search of pleasure, from the *Venus Verticordia*, whom Morris, like Rossetti, saw as the turner of hearts to lust, and from the demon of the Christian Middle Ages, Morris creates a figure still more deadly than her prototypes. Devoid of heart and soul, she is incapable of truly loving. To those ensnared by her, she brings contact without communication and desire without fulfillment. Utterly alluring in her eternal beauty, she is sterile, creating nothing and destroying all external values. The escape from mortal love she seems to offer is to hell disguised as paradise.

In "The Ring Given to Venus," Morris reveals the grotesque nature of the goddess through his hero's nightmare and the "Triumph of Love" which he must witness. In Laurence's waking dream, a synecdoche for his entanglement with Venus, the images of love which have adorned the "happy" tales of *The Earthly Paradise* are ironically reversed. The wine that has flowed for past lovers becomes poison; the garland that has crowned the golden head of the beloved rests upon a skull; the lute's sound is the tolling of a funeral bell, and the "golden door" (6:163), the entrance to a lovers' paradise, now leads to hell. The perversity of the love that the dark Venus brings is depicted in the strange procession in which she, Cupid, and Satan participate along with groups of lovers who illustrate the stages of romantic passion and the fates of those controlled by it. In an image reflecting in microcosm the progression of the total *Earthly Paradise*, Morris symbolizes the first group of happy lovers by a maiden who drops "a fresh red rose," and the last group—the sufferers of passion's bitter pain—by a woman who casts down a "black-bound

wreath / Of bitter herbs long come to death" (6:167). Although
the tale ends with Laurence's release from Venus (through the
offices of a tormented priest who gives his life to gain it), Morris
implies that Laurence has been partially destroyed. His involvement with the demon-mistress has been a nightmare he will never
quite forget.

In "The Hill of Venus," Morris's version of the Tannhäuser
legend, another hero finds a love that blights and kills. Unlike
Swinburne's protagonist in "Laus Veneris," Morris's Walter is
not tormented by the conflict between God and Venus; God
barely enters the tale. Instead, Walter escapes from a loveless
world to seek the goddess "Born to give peace to souls that strive"
(6:290). Yet even in a terrestrial Eden, surrounded by the famous
lovers of the Greek and medieval worlds, he cannot find peace.
His cry of exaltation upon finding his beloved in the sheltered
valley of the Venusberg: "For this, for this / God made the world,
that I might feel thy kiss!" (6:294) yields to the silence of his
living-death. When, unable to accept or to be reconciled to the
external world, he chooses to return to Venus, he knows that his
love clings to "the false heart of an evil thing" (6:321). Alive in
body, but with a soul that knows "No ignorance, no wonder, and
no hope" (6:323), he never sees the flowering staff, a symbol of
God's mercy, which ironically contrasts with his dead soul.

In placing "The Hill of Venus" last among the tales and in
closing *The Earthly Paradise* with an epilogue that indicates the
coming demise of the aged Wanderers, as well as with a farewell
to the book itself, Morris stresses the finalities of life. The abiding
impression of *The Earthly Paradise* is of the vanity of human
desires. The dream implicit in the early tales of the work, of a
world beyond this world in which charmed lovers may conquer
trials and gain true union, is slowly cancelled by the contrasting
vision of the tales of Fall and Winter. That the year of nature will
be reborn in spring becomes a bitter contrast to and not a consolation for the grievous fact of human mutability. The poem
ironically persuades its readers that the quest for love must always
end in failure, that one path back to Eden has been lost.

In all, the works of the 1860s are elegiac: sustained laments for
the loss of human love and life as well as for the passing of the age
of gold. Yet, though Morris stands within a personal wilderness,
he neither abandons the external world nor evades the questioning of self. Rather, "Scenes from the Fall of Troy," *Jason*, and
The Earthly Paradise are the testaments of a period of necessary, if
painful, reflection. In their exploration and ultimate rejection of
traditional answers to the human plight, they are the first steps

toward more adventurous personal and social quests. In the despair and negation they voice lies the goad that will move Morris to embrace the stoic ethic of the North and to assert that men—through fellowship—must build their Eden in the ordinary world, the only paradise that they will ever find.

FOUR

THE "STORMY YEARS":
AN INTERLUDE

THE YEARS from 1868 to 1875 marked a crucial turning point in Morris's career as a poet and writer of prose romances. The period of transition in his creative life coincided with an era of pain and crisis in his personal life, a time so fraught with problems that Mackail sought to suppress its events. Calling the period "those stormy years of *The Earthly Paradise* time and the time following it," Mackail noted that his biographical account "must be excessively flat owing to the amount of tact that had to be exercised right and left . . . [tact] unpleasantly near untruthfulness often."[1] Recent biographers Philip Henderson and Jack Lindsay have supplied some new information and offered many new conjectures about the dilemmas, marital and psychological, confronting Morris.[2] Although the full extent of the poet's awareness of and response to his wife's involvement with Rossetti and of his own desire for a love relationship with Georgiana Burne-Jones, the wife of his closest friend, can probably never be determined, it is evident that Morris responded with conflict to a series of painful personal situations. These circumstances were to initiate an intense depression, but they ultimately led to a new understanding of self and to new paths of literary growth and social action.

The "stormy years" had considerable effects on the form and content of Morris's literary works, as he began to subject his established beliefs to intense and painful re-examination. Depressed by the problems of romantic love, tormented by his experiences of rejection and frustration, he expressed, through poetry, his hopes and fears about passion. In despair, he sought to deal with the question of how much fate or its agent, the force of change, intervened in the lives of men and to ascertain how men could best endure it. More than half in love with easeful death, he confronted his desire for and fear of it, directly, through his journeys to Iceland, and—symbolically—by exorcising his emotions through the writing of poetry.

The poems Morris wrote between 1868 and 1875 consist of lyrics and tales intended for, but not used in *The Earthly Paradise*; a group of medievalized ballads, lyrics, and narrative fragments, often northern in source or inspiration; and an important—if aesthetically unsatisfactory—group of personal lyrics reiterating the poet's agony over unrequited love, the power of fate and change, and the desire for death—themes he had detailed in *The Earthly Paradise*.[3] The dating of many of these poems is conjectural, but most were written between 1868 and 1872. Some were published in *Poems by the Way* in 1891, others were collected by May Morris in volume twenty-four of the *Works* and in the first volume of her *William Morris, Artist, Writer, Socialist*. These poems have been supplemented by additional poems and fragments published by R. C. Ellison and K. L. Goodwin, who, in his essay on the "Unpublished Lyrics of William Morris,"[4] has dealt with the drafts and histories of works excluded from the Morris canon, published a number of previously unpublished poems, and offered convincing explanations of the textual and biographical reasons for their exclusion. Morris's one long published poem of the period, *Love is Enough: or the Freeing of Pharamond*, written in 1871 and published in 1873, further develops the themes of the personal lyrics, but has been dismissed by most critics as an aesthetic failure or avoided as an unfathomable mystery.

Critical approaches to these works have been chiefly biographical[5] and even the important prose documents of the era, the *Icelandic Journals* of 1871 and 1873 and the fragment of a novel Morris wrote in 1872, have been examined primarily in terms of how they illuminate Morris's relationship with his wife and with Georgiana Burne-Jones. Therefore, this chapter will not deal principally with these questions or replicate the efforts of those who have already done so. Instead, it will focus on Morris's gradually shifting attitudes to the themes of love, fate, and death—utilizing the *Icelandic Journals* of 1871 and 1873—which mark a transition to new attitudes and which engender new literary experiments. What Iceland and the materials Morris drew from it did for him was to help him re-establish the stance of objectivity which had broken down during the years of his most intense distress, 1868 to 1871. His movement away from despair was not, of course, a clear upward progression; to make it appear so is an oversimplification. However, by 1873 the process of recovery, clearly apparent in the *Journal* of that year, was beginning.

Prior to the summer of 1871, Morris's preoccupation with failure in love was almost obsessive. The plaintive poems to the months in *The Earthly Paradise* are supplemented by others, personal poems which suggest similar themes and tones. They too must be read as comments on the impossibility of fulfillment in love and lamentations on the loss of the hope of reciprocation. "May Grown A-Cold" (24:358), for example, deals with a man's rude awakening from a dream of satisfied passion and with the alienation such awareness brings; "Pain and Time Strive Not" mourns a similar waking and reflects the poet's nostalgia for the time "before farewell" (9:187). The lovely sonnet, "Sad-Eyed and Soft and Grey" (24:356), an *aube*, accuses the morning, despite its beauty, of breaking the dream of love. "Song," with its refrain, *"half forgotten, unforgiven and alone,"* again utilizes the theme of "bitter waking" from the dream of passion, but adds a note of anger directed against both the "well-beloved" and the self:

> Yea, it pleased her to behold me
> Mocked by tales that love had told me,
> Mocked by tales and mocked by eyes
> Wells of loving mysteries;
> Mocked by eyes and mocked by speech
> Till I deemed I might beseech
> For one word, that scarcely speaking
> She would snatch me from that waking,
> *Half forgotten, unforgiven and alone.*
>
> (24:360)

The same tone of anger at the loss of hope and love is evident in "Guileful Love," but it is now directed not against the human participants but against the force of passion itself:

> LOVE set me in a flowery garden fair
> Love showed me many marvels moving there
> Love said, Take these, if nought thy soul doth dare
> To feel my fiery hand upon thine heart,
> Take these, and live, and lose the better part.
>
> Love showed me Death, and said, Make no delay;
> Love showed me Change, and said, Joy ebbs away;
> Love showed me Eld amid regrets grown grey—

I laughed for joy, and round his heart I clung,
Sickened and swooned by bitter-sweetness stung.

But I awoke at last, and born again,
Laid eager hands upon unrest and pain
And wrapped myself about with longing vain:
Ah, better still and better all things grew,
As more the root and heart of Love I knew.

O Love Love Love, what is it thou hast done?
All pains, all fears I knew, save only one;
Where is the fair earth now, where is the sun?
Thou didst not say my Love might never move
Her eyes, her hands, her lips to bless my love.[6]

In "Guileful Love," written for *A Book of Verse*, the hand illuminated manuscript Morris designed and executed for Georgie in
1870,[7] the poet echoes such poems as "May" in *The Earthly
Paradise*.[8] In this poem, however, the Lord of Love is fiercer and
more destructive than the Greek diety of the earlier lyric. Indeed,
Love is seen as fraudulent; his garden of delights is proved a false
paradise. Even after the poet has shown his willingness to accept
and endure the pains and fears of passion, Love denies his appeal.
Love is finally indicted for directing the poet's yearnings to an
unattainable lady and for creating a situation in which consummation will always be impossible. The beloved will remain, as
Morris addresses her in a sonnet, "Near But Far Away";[9] she will
be, in the words of "Lonely Love and Loveless Death," "never
lost, never nigh."[10] When the truth of her inaccessibility strikes
the poet, he often responds with the wish for death. More interestingly, he twice attempts to analyze the causes of and reasons for
his pain.

Two poems of the "stormy years" attempt catharsis through
self-examination. Significantly, both are incomplete. In "Why
Dost Thou Struggle," the poet tries to emphathize with the lady
who rejects him, seeking to understand her reasons for her emotions. The lady speaks in a way reminiscent of Guenevere as she
tries to explain why she first accepted and then discarded a man's
love. When she states that she has let a "childish heart" adore her
because his passion soothed her sorrow over someone else's lack
of it, the reader recognizes that, like Guenevere, the lady had erred
in permitting a loveless misalliance. Like the Queen, she too
must both live a lie and rationalize in her own defense:

Dante Gabriel Rossetti: *Proserpine*. Oil painting of 1874 of Jane Burden Morris. (Courtesy of The Tate Gallery, London.)

I wore a mask, because though certainly
I loved him not, yet there was something soft
And sweet to have him ever loving me:
Belike it is I well-nigh loved him oft—

Nigh loved him oft, and needs must grant to him
Some kindness out of all he asked of me
And hoped his love would still hang vague and dim
About my life like half-heard melody.

(24:362)

But, while she pities the man who comes: "Thinking to gain yet one more golden step / Toward love's shrine" (24:363), she has given her heart and faith to another, for whom she will wait.

The second poetic fragment, "Alone unhappy by the fire I sat," has been cited by Morris's recent biographers as offering the clearest autobiographical statement of his plight.[11] But this verse epistle, written to Georgie, is thematically significant in that, while discussing specific problems and individuals, it blames the inevitable force of change for the poet's sorrow. Pain is caused by the impossibility of maintaining constancy in love relationships and by the human inability to recapture the past:

Alone unhappy by the fire I sat
And pondered o'er the changing of the days
And of the death of this good hope and that
That time agone our hearts to heaven would raise
But now lie buried 'neath the stony ways
Where change and folly lead our wearied feet
Till face to face this verse and sorrow meet.

I strove to think what like the days would be
If ere we die we should grow glad again
But yet no image of felicity
From out such twice-changed days my heart could gain
For still on pain I thought, and still on pain
Of shifts from grief to joy we poets sing
And of the long days make a little thing.

But grief meseems is like eternity
While our hearts ache and far-off seems the rest
If we are not content that all should die
That we so fondly once unto us pressed
Unless our love for folly be confessed
And we stare back with cold and wondering eyes
On the burnt rags of our fool's paradise.

So I when of the happy days to come
I strove to think no whit would all avail,
Rather my thoughts went back to that changed home
And in mine ears there rang some piteous tale
And all my heart for very pain did fail
To think of thine; I cannot bridge the space
'Twixt what may be and thy sad weary face.[12]

Again, as in *The Earthly Paradise*, the faces of change are multiple. While the emphasis in most of the poems is on unaltering, thus deadly, grief or on the shift from joy to woe, a few indicate the hope for a change for the better or chronicle its actual occurrence. "Love Fulfilled," for example, originally included in *A Book of Verse*, reflects upon a time of frustration and the consequent yearning for "sleep and death," but indicates that change has come and "Now unrest, pain, bliss are one, / Love, unhidden and alone" (9:139). The beautiful "Thunder in the Garden" centers on the change that brings about the unanticipated moment of love's consummation. As in "January" in *The Earthly Paradise*, a variation in the external weather provokes a new response in the heart of the beloved.[13] However, in "January," the wintry storm and the change in the beloved's eyes bring only a moment of hope; in "Thunder in the Garden," the summer storm and the change in the beloved's smile bring about an actual alteration of the relationship:

For her smile was of longing, no longer of glee,
And her fingers, entwined with mine own,
With caresses unquiet sought kindness of me
For the gift that I never had known.

Fertilizing and renewing the garden, the life-giving rain simultaneously frees the lady to reciprocate the poet's love:

That she craved for my lips that had craved her so often,
And the hand that had trembled to touch,
That the tears filled her eyes I had hoped not to soften
In this world was a marvel too much.

It was dusk 'mid the thunder, dusk e'en as the night,
When first brake out our love like the storm,
But no night-hour was it, and back came the light
While our hands with each other were warm.

(9:154)

Thus, although moments of despair at love's loss predominate and pessimism far outweighs optimism in the personal poems, Morris suggests occasional positive moments. He often deals with the two possibilities by alternating or juxtaposing them. *Love is Enough* is his lengthiest and perhaps least successful attempt to do so. But one brief poem, "Echoes of Love's House," connected in theme and image with the longer work, effectively summarizes the two opposing views. It may be read as a dialogue of the mind with itself in which the positive view of passion expressed in the first line of each couplet is answered by the ironic, negative view in the second:

> Love gives every gift whereby we long to live:
> 'Love takes every gift, and nothing back doth give.'
>
> Love unlocks the lips that else were ever dumb:
> 'Love locks up the lips whence all things good might come.'
>
> Love makes clear the eyes that else would never see:
> 'Love makes blind the eyes to all but me and thee.'
>
> Love turns life to joy till nought is left to gain:
> 'Love turns life to woe till hope is nought and vain.'
>
> Love, who changest all, change me nevermore!
> 'Love, who changest all, change my sorrow sore!'
>
> Love burns up the world to changeless heaven and blest:
> 'Love burns up the world to a void of all unrest.'
>
> And there we twain are left, and no more work we need:
> 'And I am left alone, and who my work shall heed?'
>
> Ah! I praise thee, Love, for utter joyance won!
> 'And is my praise nought worth for all my life undone?'
>
> (9:103)

"Echoes of Love's House" depicts, in miniature, the main subject of *Love is Enough*: love's ability to grant joy and pain and to create heaven and hell. The dual attitudes toward passion which are apparent in this poem create much of its richness and difficulty. The poem is complicated by the intricate structural use of love as subject matter. The quest for eros is the subject of the masque, "The Freeing of Pharamond," which is the central event of the poem. The masque itself is given to celebrate the wedding of an emperor and empress, whose union is based on their mutual passion. It is witnessed by a pair of married peasant lovers, and, even the wandering actors who play the masque figures of Pharamond and Azalais, are shown to be in love. All comment, directly or indirectly, on their own romantic experience and that of others. Moreover, Love, played by an actor, is both a character in the masque and a commentator on it. Finally, the "Music," a group of lyric interludes which intersperse the poem and separate the scenes of the masque, is an important thematic and personal treatment of erotic passion.[14]

The masque within the poem, "The Freeing of Pharamond," ostensibly "showeth of a King whom nothing but love might satisfy, who left all to seek love, and having found it, found this also, that he had enough, though he lacked all else" (9:3). In reality, the quest for love described in the six scenes of the masque is incomplete and paradoxical. Basing the masque on "The Dream of Maxem Wledig," one of the tales translated in Lady Charlotte Guest's *Mabinogion*, Morris turns the story of an emperor of Rome who does not give all for love but successfully gains his desire and his kingdom into the tale of Pharamond, who, giving all for passion's sake, is left without both his throne and the lasting consummation of his love.

Morris retains the deliberate archaism and poetic quality of Lady Charlotte Guest's translation, alluding initially to his source rather than recapitulating it. In "The Dream of Maxem Wledig," the Emperor of Rome falls asleep on a hunt and has a vision of "a maiden sitting before him in a chair of ruddy gold"[15] from which he is awakened by the clash of shields and the sound of horns. Pharamond's first dream of his beloved occurs as he lies on a battle field and is awakened by the clash of arms. "Unkingly, unhappy" (9:15), Pharamond, like Maxem, suffers the death in life in which "nor spirit nor existence was left him, because of the maiden whom he had seen in his sleep, for . . . love . . . pervaded his whole frame."[16] Both kings, unable to resume their former lives of valor and action, are first encouraged and then reviled by their subjects. Both decide to seek the women who, they believe, will restore them. But while Maxem's adventures involve the medieval conventions of the sending of messengers and the display of royal state, Pharamond's take the form of the romantic quest of the individual in search of the soul in the form of a woman. By the third scene of the masque, Morris has discarded a source that no longer fits his theme and has created his own plot line.

Before Pharamond's initial vision of love, he has been a Morrisian hero, looking backward to the men who *act* rather than wander in *The Earthly Paradise* and forward to the northern heroes of the late 1870s. He has been a type of Sigurd: "Rough hand in the field, ready righter of wrong, / Reckless of danger, but recking of pity" (9:19), who has fought courageously against overwhelming odds and accepted defeat and his father's death with stoic courage. A heroic soul whose actions have leavened the "waning world," he has first saved his kingdom from external enemies and then ruled "a dull folk, who deemed all . . . [his] kingship / A thing due and easy" (9:33). Like Tennyson's Ulysses, he is endowed with contradictory traits which are "unmeet . . . for rulers of the earth" (9:22), and the dream of love which initially makes him joyous almost immediately renders him spellbound. Dead-alive, with "no change in the eyes" (9:14), he becomes like one of the haunted figures who dominate the final tales of *The Earthly Paradise*. Obsessed by "the unknown desire / of . . . [his] soul . . . wrought in [the] shape of a woman" (9:29), he becomes alienated from his world, his people, and himself. His quest for the woman, significantly called his "twin sister" (9:29), becomes a quest for the missing part of himself.

Pharamond, "now grown wise in love" (9:37), as Morris had said of himself in the "Envoi" to *The Earthly Paradise*, must undergo a lengthy and difficult journey. Its events, related rather than dramatized, include the traditional romance and folklore trials of peril, imprisonment, and slavery. Sustained by "the hope that endureth" (9:42), Pharamond and Oliver, his loving foster father, cross threatening mountains, a "desert of horror" (9:43), and turbulent oceans. They experience battle, plague, and famine; they are captured by a queen who wishes to keep Pharamond as her slave and lover; they are kidnapped by pirates, sold as thralls, forced to labor in the mines and to beg in the streets for their bread. In all, Pharamond undergoes in microcosm many of the adventures of the questing heroes of Morris's last prose romances.

Alone and near death, Pharamond finally meets Azalais. A male sleeping beauty, he is awakened by her kiss and restored to life by her magical love. Without courtship or conventional impediments, he enjoys a brief idyllic union with her. However, he leaves his beloved's rural cottage to return to the people of his kingdom whom he mistakenly believes must "yearn / To see his face, and hear his voice once more" (9:65). His attempt to return to duty and action is ironic, for his good rule has been forgotten and his personal heroism has been maligned. Renouncing power and glory, Pharamond finds himself "freed" from the bondage of rule.[17] His former kingdom seems a mere shadow; its new king, a man who is dead-alive, locked in a changeless existence. Persuaded that love is enough, Pharamond decides to return to "the poor land and kingless of the shepherding people" (9:70) where his beloved abides.

Yet, while he hopes for a permanent reunion with his beloved: for "fresh dawn, and fresh noon, and fresh night of desire / Still following and changing with nothing forgotten" (9:75), he is far away from it. He must face an arduous repetition of the physical and psychic trials of his journey. He must cope with weariness, sorrow, and his sense of inner weakness. As he says in the last line he speaks: "Love were enough if thy lips were not lacking" (9:75), but the "if" is the point. The love object is far away and the lover, though hopeful, cannot be fully certain of his ability to reunite with her. The end of the masque leaves him in mid-quest. He is not yet reunited with the woman who is soul, and both the process of union and the spiritual regeneration which accompanies it are far from complete.

The fragmented quest—thematically and structurally akin to the unfinished personal poems of the "stormy years"—does not ignore love's cruelty and kinship with emotional and physical death. These themes are developed more fully in the ambiguous figure of Love who serves as a character-commentator of the masque. Omniscient, omnipotent, implacable, Love speaks in Biblical language, in accord with medieval tradition and the Pre-Raphaelite convention of describing profane sexuality in religious terminology. Clearly the ruler of the world of the poem, Love is alternately depicted as a guide and redeemer and as a cruel and fearsome lord. While Love protests that he is ultimately kind, that the scourgings and penances he administers are for man's true good, it is his destructive aspect, most aptly symbolized by his appearance before the audience "with a cup of bitter drink and his hands bloody" (9:48), which echoes through the poem. Even his final appearance before the curtain of the masque, in which he utters his promise of reward for faithful lovers, shows his essential duality:

> . . . from these hands reward ye shall receive.
> —Reward of what?—Life springing fresh again.—
> Life of delight?—I say it not—Of pain?
> It may be—Pain eternal?—Who may tell?

(9:77)

Love can only promise that the pain will be heavenly rather than hellish in nature. Offering his faithful worshippers a sign that the agony he causes will be constructive, he points to the process of the world of nature:

> The sign of Earth, its sorrow and its bliss,
> Waxing and waning, steadfastness and change;
>
> . . . .
>
> —In what wise, ah, in what wise shall it be?
> How shall the bark that girds the winter tree
> Babble about the sap that sleeps beneath,
> And tell the fashion of its life and death?
>
> (9:77–78)

Yet, while he protests that even painful change is better than that changelessness which is death, his promise of eventual happiness—in some cases, of reunion through death or the ending of the finite world—seems insufficient consolation. His dual nature remains constant; his underlying statement is that his waxing and waning, however cruel, must be accepted. He and his ways are as mysterious as the changes in the world of nature and equally as inevitable.

The themes of the changing nature of love and the changing process of nature are further interwoven in the lyrical interludes in the poem, each of which Morris entitles "Music." Like the poems to the months in *The Earthly Paradise*, these sections of "Music" serve as philosophical and thematic comments on events in and beyond those of the work of which they are part. Although the progression of emotions they depict is partially dictated by the events occurring in the masque, they contain elements not directly related to it. They most clearly describe the poet's personal feelings about erotic passion.

The first "Music" pictures a waning world of nature, but protesting that "love is enough," the poet announces that true lovers can transcend external and internal decline:

> . . . *their hands shall not tremble, their feet shall not falter,*
> *The Void shall not weary, the fear shall not alter*
> *These lips and these eyes of the loved and the lover.*
>
> (9:5)

The second "Music" amplifies the themes and images introduced in the first. "Love is enough," though the worlds of nature and eros alternate between joy and misery, though one cries out for death amid the agony of unrequited passion. The hope that is to sustain those presently unloved is the hope of requital. As with the coming of spring, so in love *"the dry seed shall quicken, the hard earth shall soften"* and *"earth's garden may bloom round my love's feet and me"* (9:10).

The third "Music" celebrates such a seasonal and emotional rebirth, a momentary fulfillment of love which, unknown and measureless, *"sprang without sowing,"* and *"grew without heeding."* Although there has been *"pain in its blossom, despair in its seeding"* (9:21), these have now been almost obliterated in the joy of a time of happy union. It is noteworthy that both the second and third parts of the "Music" are linked in theme and image with the last two stanzas of Morris's fine lyric of the same period, "Love's Gleaning-Tide."

> Ah, when the summer comes again
> How shall we say, we sowed in vain?
> The root was joy, the stem was pain,
>   The ear a nameless blending.
>
> The root is dead and gone, my love,
> The stem's a rod our truth to prove;
> The ear is stored for nought to move
>   Till heaven and earth have ending.
>
> (9:120)

Yet, while "Love's Gleaning-Tide" sternly preaches an acceptance of love's cruelty, the third "Music" celebrates the *"harvest and the garnering season"* (9:21) in the language of triumphant joy.

This tone alters in the fourth "Music," as the power of change again affects the poet. The lyric is a cry to the world of men to leave the poet alone. Alienated from his friends, he wishes neither their pity nor their help in his erotic problems. He informs the Job's comforters around him, that he has moments of union with his beloved or (the phrasing is ambiguous) the dream of them:

> *There is soft speech between us and words of forgiving*
>   *Till in dead of the midnight, her kisses thrill through me*
> *—Pass by me and hearken, and waken me not!*
>
> (9:36)

But the union is revealed as merely temporary or as an idle dream, and the fifth "Music," the most complex of the series, describes the poet's confrontation with despair.

In a version of the tale of Jacob and the Angel, the poet speaks of a dream vision in which, *"wearied and bleeding,"* he met, wrestled with, and overcame the sinister figure of *"a Shadow of the Night."* In the middle of a dead landscape, he vanquishes his foe and forces him to crown him victor. Awaking, he finds himself *"alone—and yet not forsaken."* The "Shadow of the Night," an image of false passion and a projection of his depression, has departed. *"Love lived to seek"*; thus, continuing his quest, the poet is rewarded by a second dream, this time of a lovers' heaven: *"A land wherein Love is the light and the lord, / Where my tale shall be heard, and my wounds gain a glory"* (9:47).

The second dream is also broken and the seventh "Music" does not show the lover arriving at his promised land. Instead, the poet pleads with lovers who yearn for death to cherish life even when hope is or appears dead.[18] Love, he insists, will finally be rewarded, even if it must wait until the resurrection of the dead or the reborn world to follow.

Again change comes, and, in the eighth "Music," a lyric celebrating the union of Pharamond and Azalais, the reader is told that Love has finally arrived:

> *Change is come, and past over, no more strife, no more learning:*
> *Now your lips and your forehead are sealed with his seal,*
>   *Look backward and smile at the thorns and the burning.*
> *—Sweet rest, O my soul, and no fear of returning!*
>
> (9:63)

With his arrival has come the promise of changeless bliss, the suggestion of perfect life and love within a realm other than the ordinary world. The last "Music" serves to close the masque while restating its ostensible theme. In it the poet promises that those who strive sufficiently shall reach the *"House of Fulfillment of Craving"* and announces that Love has led the lover home. However, what is most striking in the last lyric is the description of the difficult path which awaits those who choose to seek erotic passion:

> *'Come—pain ye shall have, and be blind to the ending!*
>   *Come—fear ye shall have, mid the sky's overcasting!*
>   *Come—change ye shall have, for far are ye wending!*
>   *Come—no crown ye shall have for your thirst and your fasting,*
>   *But the kissed lips of Love and fair life everlasting!'*
>
> (9:76)

The final lyric and the poem as a whole suggest the poet's

preoccupation with the thorny paths and the uncertain destinies of those who aspire to passion. The quest for love may be man's noblest search—far better than the seeking of power or gold—but there is no certainty of its successful outcome. The force of love may be all-powerful, but it is as uncontrollable and amoral as a storm or an earthquake. The moments of joy in love are to be cherished, but they are inevitably intermingled with the moments of pain which must be stoically endured.

Morris's other literary experiment of the period, his unpublished novel, begun in 1872 and never completed,[19] raises, in different form, the same issues of love's power, amorality, and inevitability. Similar to the early prose tale, "Frank's Sealed Letter," in subject, contemporary setting, and the utilization of a letter as a crucial element in the plot,[20] it is built upon a love triangle. It describes the passion of two brothers, John and Arthur, for the same woman, Clara, and her love for John and marriage to Arthur. Both the brothers in the tale resemble Morris and Ned Burne-Jones in appearance, behavior, and taste. Both are similar in character and bear the hallmarks of the old Oxford brotherhood: they love history and romance, admire and empathize with nature, especially with the river; both are idealists, concerned with righting social injustice but simultaneously in love with the world of imagination. Arthur, whose eyes have "a far away and dreamy look," is well versed in archaeological lore and "a book worm" who can tell "scraps of stories from old chronicles and the like."[21] He is fascinated by ancient armor, furniture, and painting. However, it is John, the protagonist, who bears Morris's essential characteristics. John rebels openly against becoming a clergyman, loves fishing and boating (Morris's favorite recreations), and even resembles the poet physically.[22] Most important, it is John who expresses Morris's youthful attitudes towards love, recapturing their absolutism and somewhat hysterical tone:

If you feel real love you must know that you really think the whole world exists only to minister to your passion— . . . ; it is worth passing through all the pain that clings about it—and if you do not feel this, you are not in love: and the desire you have will pass away into something else—into friendship, or into disgust or hatred . . . all is either love or not love; there is nothing between—everything else; friendship kindness goodness, is a shadow and a lie![23]

Like Leuchnar in "Gertha's Lovers"—the early prose tale which deals with the love of two men as close as brothers for the same woman—John is a chivalrous idealizer of passion, though shy and humble in his expression of it. Indeed, John echoes the epigraph affixed to "Gertha's Lovers" as well as Leuchnar's and Morris's view that "the love of man and woman should go before everything" (1:189).[24]

Clara, the object of both brothers' love, represents a new image of woman in Morris's work. In Arthur's adolescent dream of her, she is revealed as a figure of the pure anima, living and loving in an earthly paradise:

. . . he was walking with Clara through meadows not at all like the Leaser meads which yet they both agreed to think were none other it seemed; they were thickly studded with apple trees in bloom, and it was moonlight, yet the birds were singing in full chorus; and Clara herself was clad in fluttering raiment like he had seen on angels in old pictures instead of her usual dress, and she spoke to him in verse in the rhythm of some fragment of old poetry that he had forgotten awake, . . .[25]

This aspect of Clara, a variation of Pharamond's vision of Azalais and a reiteration of an image present in Morris's works from "The Hollow Land" on, is not new. But, in her physical appearance and behavior, Clara is a prototype of Ellen in *News from Nowhere* and of the pure animas of the last romances. She is, like them, a child of the rural world, living in harmony with it. With her tanned hands and feet, grey eyes, and brown hair full of light, she shares their vigorous health, energetic gaiety, and constant activity. Her interest in all events and people around her, her disregard for rigid conventional behavior, and her wise innocence mark her as a new symbol of the woman who is soul. She is the first of the intelligent, companionable, sympathetic women who would be ideal beloveds, but who are unattainable.[26]

The conflict inadvertantly caused by her desirability was to be the pivot of Morris's plot. The fragment extant, the separate pages that constitute John's letter, and a note on the back of a page indicate that John and Clara fall in love. Their passion is interrupted by the necessity of John's leaving the pastoral world to earn his living, while Arthur, without knowing of his brother's feelings, also comes to love Clara. The reader learns from John's letter that Arthur woos Clara and wins her hand—though not her full heart—and that John yields up the woman he loves to the brother he cannot bear to hurt. John's return to the countryside was to occur only after many years had passed, when Clara and Arthur have had a child. This return was to trigger a series of conflicts between love and loyalty as the three struggled with their senses of kinship, friendship, and duty. That the conflict was to have resulted in a violent crisis seems indicated in Arthur's dream of Clara, clearly meant as a foreshadowing, and apocalyptic in imagery and tone:

. . . as it happens in dreams the landscape changed and there were big blue mountains all about the mead and a rushing stream through it, and suddenly his heart seemed to stop beating for fear and she stopped him & faced him, with fear in her eyes too, and as he tried to speak & could not, she had turned into his brother and they were both quite children again and he thought they had lost themselves & were to die, and the rush of the stream seemed to get louder & louder, and the wind to rise & howl about the hollows of the mountainside, and presently a horse came galloping past, and then a herd of cows rushed up and then a great flock of sheep seemed to fill up all the valley their endless backs all moving like a sea, and the sound of the bell wethers filling all the air, and then with a sense of something dreadful going to happen he woke panting & gasping with an unuttered cry, and the horror of the dream was so strong on him that at first he seemed to wake into a world of white flame.[27]

There is no indication that Morris had actually worked out the end of his novel. Indeed, it is probable that he could not. Discouragement by Georgiana Burne-Jones and the painfulness of working on something that did not "come easily" were only partial reasons for abandoning it.[28] Morris's reticence, his conviction that he must not wear his heart on his sleeve, was another. Perhaps, most important, Morris was too much engrossed in his private experience of painful love to transmute it into seemingly objective form. It is possible that he could not determine how the conflict of loves—a problem he was unable to deal with fully in his own life—could be successfully resolved in the novel. The work, however, hints at a road not taken, for after 1875, Morris chose to become increasingly less "realistic" in his choice of literary forms and less overtly biographical in his selection of content. Still deeply troubled by the problems of romantic love, he moved toward objectifying his intense pain.

It is evident that Morris's attitude toward passion remains highly ambivalent in the "stormy years" and that, because of love's pain, the world—though occasionally lit by hope—is essentially viewed as a place

> Of gainless eld & restless youth
> Of love well trusted turned to shame;
> And then the change we may not name;

The change the end, And thou dost wend
Unto the dark whence all things came.[29]

But Morris's beliefs about "the end" and the passage to the "dark" so bitterly expressed in "What All Men Long For & What None Shall Have," gradually began to alter in the years from 1871 to 1875. Forced to explore his feelings about death in his Icelandic journey of 1871, re-examining and changing them in his second journey of 1873, Morris moved from a mingled fear of and desire for oblivion to a firm, but essentially untroubled, acceptance of death's reality, and a turn away from his preoccupation with it.

Prior to 1873, Morris's attitudes towards mortality were chiefly "romantic" ones, darkened and intensified by his personal unhappiness. The poems of the "stormy years" retain patterns and motives present in his earliest works and richly expressed in *The Earthly Paradise*. In the personal poems of the period and in *Love is Enough*, Morris continues to utilize the convention of the hope for reunion through death and to yearn for permanent happiness in an earthly or unearthly lovers' paradise. He continues to indicate his belief that the death of the heart is a worse fate than the death of the body and to stress his conviction that the loss of love begets the wish to die.

The wish for a lovers' reunion through death is strongly expressed in a number of the personal poems. In the envoi-sonnet, "Rhyme Slayeth Shame," the poem is told to sing to the lady the words the poet cannot speak to her because of the psychological separation between them. The sonnet, though traditional in theme, is unusual in the closing lines of its sestet. The envoi is to tell the poet's beloved that he will "follow where her footsteps lead, / Until the veil of speech death draws away" (24:357). Although he may avow his love in this world, the consummation of passion must await the world beyond. The same theme is reiterated in a similar sonnet, "As This Thin Thread," in which the poet pleads that his passion, itself undying, be tolerated by his lady until death. "Keep what I give till Death our eyes shall clear" (24:359), he begs, indicating that only the demise of the lovers will permit them to see face to face, allowing the lady to reciprocate his passion. The need and hope for reunion after earthly life is over is sounded in "Love Alone" (first written for *A Book of Verse*)[30] with its prayer for "A never-ending day / Wherein we twain may sit, parted undying still / With thoughts of the old story, our sundered hearts to fill."[31]

The most extended exploration of the yearning for union in a paradise for lovers occurs in "Everlasting Spring." As K. L. Goodwin indicates, the poem looks forward "to a paradisal period when love will be fully reciprocated and fulfilled."[32] But this will not occur on earth. Instead, the poet and his beloved will wander through an "endless day" in a "far-off country": "Those fair meads of the old painter with their blossoms red and white."[33] They will become spirits in paradise as painted by a medieval or renaissance master. Only in a realm beyond the ordinary world will they share mutual love, changeless in rapture and constancy. Only there will they experience a reunion unbroken by the ordinary morning which ruptures the lover's dream of happy passion.

"Everlasting Spring" is Morris's most explicit paradisacal fantasy, but it is undercut by his own lack of faith. Like other poems which postulate a heavenly reunion, a faint hope and deep lack of conviction underlie its lines. The poet's very statement of belief in consummation in an afterlife: "*I long to trust* the story of that innocent sweet home"[34]—reveals his lack of faith in it.

If the hope for reunion through death is faint, the preference for physical death over death in life is strong. Several of the personal poems deal with the death of the heart leading to the desire for a physical end. As Morris writes in "Lonely Love and Loveless Death" and places in *A Book of Verse*: when "No love standeth by / Death sickeneth and blindeth."[35] The end of desire creates a darkened world and a yearning for oblivion. In a fragment published by Goodwin, "Dead and gone is all desire / Gone and left me cold and bare," the poet questions, "Oh my heart! How mayst thou bear it?"[36] His prevailing answer is that he and his heart cannot. The tone of despair permeates some of the most powerful lyrics of the period. In the sonnet, "The Doomed Ship," it is transmuted into fine poetry—in part because Morris draws on the tradition of such poems as Cowper's "The Castaway."

> The doomed ship drives on helpless through the sea,
> All that the mariners may do is done
> And death is left for men to gaze upon,
> While side by side two friends sit silently;
> Friends once, foes once, and now by death made free
> Of Love and Hate, of all things lost or won;
> Yet still the wonder of that strife bygone
> Clouds all the hope or horror that may be.

Thus, Sorrow, are we sitting side by side
Amid this welter of the grey despair,
Nor have we images of foul or fair
To vex, save of thy kissed face of a bride,
Thy scornful face of tears when I was tried,
And failed 'neath pain I was not made to bear.[37]

The analogy of the two doomed mariners, spellbound by their impending death, is more than a simile for the poet's relation to his depression. Failing "'neath pain . . . [he] was not made to bear," the poet wishes to perish, hoping that death will bring him release from the death in life of his destructive sorrow.

Just as the conflict between optimism and pessimism about the fruits of love is most fully realized in *Love is Enough,* so too the yearning for physical death as a release from frustrated passion reaches its zenith in the same work. As E. P. Thompson has noticed, "toward the end of the narrative the longing for death and the yearning for 'Love' become so confused as to be indistinguishable. . . . The superficial subject [of the narrative] may be 'Love,' but the underlying theme is the desire for unconsciousness and death."[38] But, as Frederick Kirchhoff has indicated, the problem is not one of confusion. Instead, *Love is Enough* is significant because it brings Morris's death wish into the open.[39] The poet is fully aware that, in his own life and in the lives of his fictional characters, the frustration of passion brings about the urge to die. When, in the crisis of the masque, Pharamond meets Love face to face, the relationship between love and death is made explicit. The scene begins with Love stating that Pharamond is "near to death" because of his unfulfilled passion and that, for the same reason, Azalais "sickeneth past all help or cure" (9:53). Both lovers—both parts of the self—are in search of physical death as a cure for the agony their separation has induced. Pharamond, dead-alive, believes that the figure he sees, that of Love, is an embodiment of death and expresses his desire for oblivion:

Love:
Hearken, O Pharamond, why camest thou hither?

King Pharamond:
I came seeking Death; I have found him belike.

Love:
In what land of the world art thou lying, O Pharamond?

King Pharamond:
In a land 'twixt two worlds: nor long shall I dwell there.

Love:
Who am I, Pharamond, that stand here beside thee?

King Pharamond:
The Death I have sought—thou art welcome; I greet thee.

(9:54)

Azalais too, suffering from "Love turned to abasement, and
rest gone forever," has willingly sought death:

. . . last night I awoke with a pain piercing through me,
And a cry in my ears, and Death passed on before,
As one pointing the way, and I rose up sore trembling,
And by cloud and by night went before the sun's coming,
As one goeth to death,—

(9:59)

Both lovers believe that Love is Death. In both, the desire for an
end to pain takes the form of the deadly love of death. Pharamond
first identifies the force of passion as a form of death, telling Love:
"Sooth didst thou say when thou call'dst thyself Death" (9:55).
Pharamond then goes on to request his demise ("Be thou God, be
thou Death, yet I love thee and dread not" [9:55]) and to confess
his yearning for oblivion. Only after he has admitted that he has
adored "A dream and a lie—and my death" (9:55) and that he
continues to love them is he free to meet his beloved. He sees her as
the figure of an angel waking him "into death and deliverance"
(9:61). Only after Azalais confronts the specter of her own annihilation is she free to initiate her passion for Pharamond by kissing him. Not until the end of the scene do the lovers realize that
though their "first words were of dreaming and death . . . we
die not!" (9:62).

Although the scene with its series of ironies, disguises, and
misdirected responses is ostensibly an illustration of Love's point
that he brings the necessary death of the old self and the birth of
the new, it is not an effective proof of the argument. Instead, the
undermeaning dominates, and Pharamond and Azalais find each
other only after each has faced—but not triumphed over—the
yearning for oblivion. The separation that follows their temporary union is perhaps caused by the fact that neither can move
beyond death to love; both are still too involved with change and

mortality. Even their place of meeting is significant, for it occurs beneath the "mountain-wall the earth-fires rent of old" (9:53), a spent volcano common to the landscape of Iceland.

The source of the imagery of the spent volcano was Morris's 1871 journey to Iceland, an experience which embodied his conflicts and was the partial cause of major changes in his life and work. Maude Bodkin observed long ago that Morris's Icelandic journey represented his "confrontation with death."[40] What has not been clearly recognized, but what is revealed by Love is Enough, written upon his return, is that the journey and the Journal of 1871, which is its record, chronicles only the beginning of a lengthy process. Love is Enough, like the 1871 Journal, does not show Morris's conquest of his desire for death but expresses instead his awareness of the fact that he feels such a drive.

The Journal of 1871, incomplete until the summer of 1873 (a month before Morris's second journey to Iceland), is the record of a battle with despair rather than a diary of a quest for adventure. Although Morris openly admits that he is "homesick" and depressed, he avoids overt analysis of his emotions. Instead, in this deliberately impersonal autobiography, he projects his feelings into passages of landscape description of the place he called the "terrible shore": "beyond that we saw the mainland, a terrible shore indeed: a great mass of dark grey mountains worked into pyramids and shelves, looking as if they had been built and half-ruined; they were striped with snow high up, and wreaths of cloud dragged across them here and there, and above them were two peaks and a jagged ridge of pure white snow" (8:19).

The descriptive words and colors that are insistently repeated throughout the Journal indicate Morris's predisposition to see Iceland as a place of death. Absent are green tuns and brightly colored flowers, while the blacks and dark grays of mountains and the equally brooding grayness of cloudy skies and rough seas dominate the account. The "grey and uncheerful" sky and "the desolate grey sea" (8:18) are further darkened by his associations between grayness and despair. The stark whites and blacks and the burnt red and rust of extinct volcanoes, tones that he sees as the basic colors of the landscape, suggest to him a dead or dying land. Even the swift running, glacier-born "white rivers" are perceived as "dismal white stream[s] running through a waste of black sand" (8:42). Though not without some beauty and sublime excitement, Iceland, at first, appears to him a composite of "dreadful wastes" and "grisly desolation" (8:42), "a doleful land . . . with its great rubbish heaps of sand" (8:28). The Icelandic deserts are clearly his symbol of the wasteland; the high peaks which surround and penetrate them become his emblem of fear in the face of death.

Even water is not seen as life-giving and, noting that he has always thought lakes melancholy spots, Morris depicts the gloom of an Icelandic tarn:

> . . . just think of an Icelandic one! the great spiky hills on two sides of it, the black rift and heavy grey Armansfell behind us, and on the other side the grey lava going up in one long slope, . . . and three separate hills thrusting up out of the lava-sea: the spiky hills were very dark in spite of the sunny day and the deep water (how deep it must be) green like a cold sea.
>
> (8:172)

The places of saga he has come to visit are personally experienced as scenes of past anguish and death. "What a mournful place this is," he comments on Herdholt, scene of the bitter love triangle he had depicted in "The Lovers of Gudrun": "how every place and name marks the death of its short-lived eagerness and glory" (8:108). In all, the bareness of the mountains, the emptiness of valleys, the memories of the saga past, make the poet recognize "how far away I was and shut in" (8:150). The land itself both whispers and screams of sorrow and death.

However, in the course of the *Journal*, it becomes evident that Morris begins to see more than projections of his desire and fear. Repeating—in a variation of the line he had used in his poignant poem, "Iceland First Seen"—the question, "What came I out for to see?" (9:125), he becomes aware that in Iceland there is little that is mean and prosaic. Even if the land speaks of painful emotion and of death, it is connected to that which—because it moves him so overwhelmingly—is alive and pregnant with imaginative possibilities. Moreover, he begins to recognize that while he is attracted to death, he is also afraid of it. He notes his upset in fording the "white rivers" and his fright at the possibility of drowning, his terror in crossing the steep mountain passes and his fear in looking down at their threatening ravines.

Gradually testing his courage, he begins to conquer part of his fear of death. Always nervous about it, he repeatedly forces himself to ford the rivers. Ostensibly accusing himself of laziness, he registers his shame and grief that he has not gone all the way into a cave (another activity he finds somewhat perilous) and, thus, has failed to see "a pillar of ice . . . that rises from floor to roof, and a frozen waterfall." His question to himself—"why didn't I try it?'' (8:84)—suggests his sense of having failed a symbolic and a literal test.

When he undertakes a visit to an Icelandic wasteland and must pass through "the gate of the wilderness," "a particularly solemn place" (8:75) which is the portal to a three-day trek across the desert, he registers his awareness that the journey is both a physical and a spiritual trial of his strength:

we make for a part of the wall that is broken down into a ruin of black stones and begin to scale it in spite of its most impassable look, and somehow stumble up to the top of the pass (Hellisskarð) and there we are in the wilderness: a great plain of black and grey sand, grey rocks sticking up out of it; tufts of sea-pink, and bladder campion scattered about here and there, and a strange plant, a dwarf willow, that grows in these wastes only, a few sprays of long green leaves wreathing about as it were a tangle of bare roots, white and blanched like bones: that is the near detail of the waste, but further on, on all sides rise cliffs and mountains, whose local colour is dark grey or black (except now and then a red place burnt by old volcanic fires) and which show through the atmosphere of this cloudy and showery day various shades of inky purple. As we ride on, we see ahead and to our left, the wide spreading cone of Skialdbreið (Broad-shield) . . . on our right and closer to us than these, is an enormous wall-sided mountain with a regular roof like a house called Hlöðufell (Barn-fell). It stands quite isolated, is some four miles long I should think, and has never been scaled by any one: over its shoulder we can see now the waste of Long-Jokul, that looks as if it ended the world, green-white and gleaming in the doubtful sun; . . . .

Meanwhile we have put Hlöðufell behind us, but Skialdbreið is still unchanged on our left: on our right is a mass of jagged bare mountains, all beset with clouds, that, drifting away now and then show dreadful inaccessible ravines and closed up valleys with no trace of grass about them among the toothed peaks and rent walls; I think it was the most horrible sight of mountains I had the whole journey long.

(8:75–77)

When the terrifying mountains have been viewed and the waste-land successfully crossed, Morris announces with triumph: "Certainly, this is what I came out for to see, . . . nor indeed to-day did it depress me at all" (8:77).

But of all the aspects of the Icelandic terrain, it is the mountains and the passes through them which frighten Morris most. To him, they represent vast "presences," indifferent to humanity, even actively malign to life. To climb a peak or to traverse a narrow pass is to be forced, bodily and spiritually, to confront the fear of death. The sight of the "jagged bare mountains" referred to in the passage above may have been Morris's most terrifying sight, but the crossing of other peaks emerges as his most awful and symbol-laden experience. Crossing the pass of Thorsmark becomes a journey to death and an entrance to hell itself:

. . . the cliffs were much higher especially on this side and most unimaginably strange: they overhung in some places much more than seemed possible; they had caves in them just like the hell-mouths in 13th century illuminations; or great straight pillars were rent from them. . . . The great mountain-wall which closes up the valley, with its jagged outlying teeth, was right before us now, looking quite impassable, though the map marks a pass, leading up into one of the main roads north and east.

(8:52–53)

His experience at Thorsmark leaves him "downhearted with the savagery of the place," and the area is etched in his memory as a realm of "distortion and disruption" (8:54). The necessity of traversing the steep pass of Búlandshöftői haunts him for several days prior to his actual journey through it and, momentarily, he thinks he will "go round by another way" (8:123). His anxiety is assuaged only after he has confronted his fear and realized "that the [actual] danger was little or nothing" (8:134).

Gradually, through Morris's testing of himself and the subsequent realization that he—and others—can survive amid Iceland's physical savagery, he begins to develop a new perspective. Morris comes to understand that in Iceland, which represents "a material order ultimately indifferent to human fate,"[41] "whatever solace your life is to have . . . must come out of yourself" (8:108). Recognizing the relationship between literature and life, he sees how saga and one of its values—stoic endurance in living and dying—arises out of existence in Iceland. He begins "to understand how people under all disadvantages should find their imaginations kindle amid such scenes" (8:54). He begins to recover his own imagination: at the sight of the Thing or communal court, both the democratic heart of Iceland and its place of trial by combat, he finds "that the thin thread of insight and imagination, which comes so seldom to us, and is such a joy when it comes, did not fail me" (8:168).

Moreover, he begins to recognize that he needs the resolution and independence depicted in saga tales, the "old stories, not over hopeful themselves" (8:108), which speak of reticence, heroic endurance, and courage in the face of death. Both the place and the tales linked to it gradually help Morris to see himself sharing in an age old drama of suffering and, therefore, as having to play his role well. His growing identification with those made and unmade by Iceland, the heroes of saga, coupled with his physical and spiritual progress in combating his personal fears, began to make him feel the resurgence of inner heroism.

In all, the *Journal* of 1871 records the beginning but not the completion of a quest for new values and inner resources. Like Pharamond's incomplete psychic journey, however, Morris's first Icelandic voyage did not immediately reward him with wholeness or rebirth,[42] nor was his process of recovery rapid and complete.

Instead, in the two year interval between the Icelandic voyages, Morris records in his poetry and fiction his only partially successful attempts to deal with his problems and rekindle his imagination. Both the matter of *Love is Enough* and the unpublished novel and the literary experimentation within them are evidences of this endeavor. However, one other poem, written in 1872 or early 1873, directly deals with Morris's preoccupation with death and continued ambivalence about it. Called "O fair gold goddess," it is a "translation" of an eddic lay ostensibly written by Vilhjálmr the Vandraeðaskáld or William the Troublous Skald—none other than William Morris himself.[43]

Cynically noting his beloved's cruel wish to have him gone, the poet describes his own strong desire to return to Iceland:

> To live a life there
> Too short for sorrow,
> Too loud with sword-clash
> For any weeping.

Equating himself with the heroes of saga who struggled and failed, the poet yearns to fare:

> Along the way
> That leads to Valhall
> Long rest before me,
> And my right hand holding
> A story maybe
> To give to Odin.[44]

The poem is significant, for, while it describes the desire for oblivion, it indicates a new perspective on death. Death is now to be sought in heroic life and action. However, the poem demonstrates as well how strongly Morris felt the need to test himself a second time by making another visit to Iceland. It was a journey Morris decided to take, and, in the fragmentary *Journal* of 1873 where he records it, the process of change and recovery fully manifests itself. As Morris wrote to Aglaia Coronio on his return from traveling: "I have gained a great deal and it was no idle whim that drew me there, but a true instinct for what I needed."[45]

Despite its incompleteness, the 1873 *Journal* clarifies the fact that Morris perceives and reacts to Iceland in ways different from those of 1871. Consciously measuring himself, he notes that he no longer fears "white rivers" and climbing expeditions; his accounts of them ring with a sense of adventure rather than an obsession with death. He proudly announces that he has lost his nervousness in fording rivers; he finds awe and wonder more powerful than fear in his climbs up mountains and crossings of ravines. The Armansfell—the same mountain range he had seen even on a sunny day as "heavy grey" and filled with sorrow and foreboding[46]—becomes a source of joy early in the second journey. After a heavy rain, he witnesses "the great ridges and peaks of the Armansfell range with broken lights striking among the widest and most aweful of gorges among them . . . and then at last I remembered all I had come to see and the land conquered my misgivings once for all, I hope" (8:188).

The desert and the passage through a vast wasteland, so filled with portent in 1871, is no longer seen primarily as a confrontation with death. Instead, Morris is surprised when he finds that he has passed the last living creatures that he and his friends will see for a number of days. While the desert is still seen as barren and somewhat ghastly, the poet emphasizes the effect of sunlight on its dark sands; he describes a summer shower and the glorious rainbow following it rather than stressing the deathlike qualities of the volcanic sands and lava fields. Even Icelandic lakes no longer speak primarily of melancholy. Rowing on Grimmtaþir, he does not concentrate upon the cold, dark waters or the grim mountains which border the lake. Instead, he expounds upon its small and varied islands, one "a curious collection of small cinder hills and lava, grown about with sweet grass, on which it was pleasant to lie in the sun," another, "very pretty, all grown over with birch and willow . . . a little deep round pond in the middle . . . angelical all round the borders" (8:228).

Icelandic mountains are as formidable as ever but, in the 1873 *Journal*, Morris stresses the beauty of mountain fields and Icelandic valleys as if he were really seeing them for the first time. He begins to enjoy and differentiate lovingly among Iceland's mountain wildflowers. The sight of a field full of blossoms: "Loki's purse (money-rattle), buttercups, milkwort, white clover, cranesbill, one or two alpine flowers I can't name, and a most lovely little dark blue gentian" leads him directly to the comment that "it was a very happy morning" (8:189). An "ordinary" valley filled with sheep and green turf makes him again recognize the miraculous in the commonplace. "There was something beautiful about . . . [it]," he comments, "long green-sided, shut in at either end" (8:223). The valley does not make him feel "shut in," a common experience alluded to in the 1871 *Journal*, but instead becomes an emblem of his recovered and renewed desire for life:

moreover, there was something eminently touching about the valley and its nearness to the waste that gave me that momentary insight into what the whole thing means that blesses us sometimes and is gone again.

(8:225)

In his simple, eloquent epiphany, he sees the valley and the waste juxtaposed against each other, each to be dealt with and accepted for what it is, as an embodiment of the nature of human life. The experiences of the valley—love and joy—and the traumas of the wasteland—despair and death—are viewed as interwoven patterns. They must be dealt with in the best human ways possible, but without the refusal to see them or the attempt to evade them.

Morris called his determination not to revisit Iceland a third time "a hole in my life."[47] But he had found what he "came . . . out for to see" (9:125), and the land was to be visited constantly in his memory. Its impact upon him was to be enduring and its effects were soon clearly visible in both his creative and personal life.

Iceland resounds in the new literature Morris begins to write, deepening and intensifying his fascination with Northern materials and endowing both his translations and his original works derived from Scandinavian sources with a more truly Northern sensibility. Its more lasting importance in his work, however, was that it provided him with groups of fresh images which were to become significant keys to the symbolic prose romances of his last years.

To Morris, images derived from Iceland—especially those drawn from the *Journal* of 1871—came to embody states of heightened consciousness, to symbolize the wasteland experiences of emotional and physical death, and to shape the patterns of test and trial in the later works. In contrast, other images of Iceland—especially those which originated in the *Journal* of 1873—become part of the representation of the severe but healthy relationship between man and nature in the prose romances. The landscape of simple Icelandic valleys serves as a projection of desirable relationships in life and love; islands and rushing rivers symbolize the drive for exploration and adventure. Recognizing Iceland's importance to his art, the mythic quality of its landscape and the powerful aid it could give to the imagination, Morris recommends that good English painters utilize it for their romantic and visionary landscapes.[48]

At the personal and psychic level, Iceland's importance to Morris is most clearly visible in his new determination to "be self-made about myself."[49] As he wrote in the unpublished envoi to his translation of the *Eyrbyggja Saga*, he was determined to hope for a future change for the better in love and to work to bring about necessary changes in life:

> Who knows what out of all may grow;
> Who knows but I myself at last
> May face the truth, with all fear cast
> Clean forth of me; real Love and I
> Set side by side before I die.[50]

In 1875, he entered what Mackail describes as "a fresh and crowded period in his life."[51] His renewed energy began to expand in new directions; he began to forge a new personal ethic and to increase both his activities and his social activism. He became engrossed in the renovation and expansion of the firm of Morris and Company, in aesthetic and social issues such as those represented by the Society for the Protection of Ancient Buildings, and in the sphere of politics, first in liberalism and anti-imperialism, then in socialism. As he strove to transmute the glories of the *Volsunga Saga* into an epic of his own, his period of literary experimentation bore fruit. Devoting himself more fully to his Northern Muse, he reforged his style and began to transform his portrayals of the themes of love, fate, and death. Seeing all three less as foes and destroyers than as natural processes which were to be met with acceptance, and borne, when necessary, with fortitude, he began to write a new kind of literature.

FIVE

PARABLES FOR THE TIMES

I

MORRIS'S ICELANDIC journeys were clearly important to the process of personal recovery which he experienced after 1873, enabling him to deal with his death wish and marking the beginning of his new attitudes toward fate and chance. Moreover, Iceland became a symbol of the possibilities of egalitarian and communal life which would impel him toward an involvement in social action. He did not, of course, altogether relinquish his private preoccupations, and the major works of the mid-1870s and 1880s still manifest his battles with depression, as well as his search for a new variety of love and an answer to the problems caused by erotic passion. However, while these works illustrate his concentrated efforts to seek the roots of personal wholeness, they show him searching for it, less through a concern with the private self, and more through an interest in the communal and social selves.

The major works of the period, *The Story of Sigurd the Volsung, The Pilgrims of Hope, A Dream of John Ball, The House of the Wolfings,* and *The Roots of the Mountains,* show Morris integrating the themes of personal love and general benevolence, demonstrating the interactions between individuals and the groups of which they are part. Erotic problems and situations in these works reflect, and are reflected in, the nature of the realms in which they occur. In *Sigurd,* Morris depicts the destructive power of passion as a primary cause of the demise of an entire world; in *The Pilgrims of Hope,* he shows how passion is sacrificed to a cause more important than personal gratification. In *The House of the Wolfings,* he demonstrates how erotic love yields to social necessity and, thus, redeems both individuals and their society; while, in *The Roots of the Mountains,* he concentrates on how the conflict between the desire of the individual and the need of the group may be resolved. In *Sigurd,* the first work of this period, Morris again traces the connections among love, fate, and death. In the remaining works, he explores eros and/or his secularized concept of caritas, an ideal of fellowship and brotherly love.

Simultaneously, the works of this period reveal Morris's new social vision based, at first, on his concept of the life of the ancient Norsemen and, later, on his adherence to the Marxism or "scientific socialism" evolving in his own time. In the literary works of the mid-1870s and 1880s, Morris creates a set of parables for his era. Because he feels that ameliorating the evils of his society is not enough, but that his world must be entirely reconstructed, Morris does not propose concrete solutions to Victorian social problems or pragmatic alternatives to its way of life. Instead, drawing upon history and myth, he creates worlds that are criticisms of his own. Even those works based on history, like *A Dream of John Ball*, are intended to be mythic. Going beyond the realm of conscious ideology, they depict ideal worlds which appeal to the universal, nonrational desire for the rebuilding of a lost terrestrial Eden and the restoration of a golden age.

The ancient Norse world—particularly Iceland—seemed to Morris to represent a culture whose values and institutions were superior to those of Victorian England. Morris found, in the Iceland depicted in history and saga, an example of a hard and simple life accepted with courage and patience, an equality in personal rights (at least, in those of the freedmen), a sturdy independence and lack of servility, and, within the gens or tribe, a spirit of cooperation. His view of saga society unquestionably prepared him to accept Marxism, for he admired the ancient Icelanders' drive for freedom from kings, respect for manual labor, and, above all, their communal democracy represented by the procedures of the Althing.[1] In the 1870s, he saw these social patterns as productive of a good life; by the 1880s, he saw them as clearly proto-socialist. Thus, though his love for the ancient Norse world remained constant, the reasons for it changed in the course of his lifetime.

Indeed, his earliest interest in the North had been, chiefly, a romantic one. Scandinavian history and literature appealed to him as remote, exotic, and perfect for use in the Gothic tales he was writing. In the 1850s, he utilized materials from Benjamin Thorpe's *Northern Mythology* and *Yule-Tide Stories* in the tales he contributed to the *Oxford and Cambridge Magazine*;[2] he began to read the translations and summaries of Eddic poems and sagas available to him.[3] The same fascination with the romantic elements in Norse literature led, in the late 1860s, to his inclusion in *The Earthly Paradise* of "The Land East of the Sun and West of the Moon," derived from the tales told by Thorpe and Sir George

Dasent, as well as to his addition to the work of "The Fostering of Aslaug," chiefly drawn from Thorpe. He worked, as well, on an incomplete rendition of the story of Swanhild ("The Wooing of Swanhild"), derived from the end of the *Volsunga Saga*, and on "The Wooing of Hallbiorn," a poem whose source was the *Landnómabók*.[4] At the same time, he began his scholarly immersion in Icelandic primary sources, and this resulted in the great *Earthly Paradise* tale of "The Lovers of Gudrun," based on the *Laxdale Saga*.

Indeed, Morris's shift from a romantic view to an historical and linguistic study of Icelandic materials actually commenced in the autumn of 1868, when he began to learn the language with Eiríkr Magnússon. With Magnússon serving as coauthor and dictionary (the first English-Icelandic dictionary was not available until 1874), Morris began a series of studies and translations which affected both the style and the content of his later works. In 1869, he translated the *Volsunga Saga*, which seemed to him a document of great historical, social, and mythic significance: "the Great Story of the North, which should be to all our race what the Tale of Troy was to the Greeks" (7:286).[5] In the same year, he translated *Grettis Saga* ("The Story of Grettir the Strong") and "The Story of Gunnlaug the Worm-Tongue," the tale of a tragic love triangle. His prose translation of the *Volsunga Saga* was published in 1870, and, in 1871, he turned the stories of "Frithiof the Bold" and of "Kormak the Son of Ogmund," (*Kormáks Saga*) into English. In 1871, he also translated and calligraphed the first work he had studied with Magnússon, the *Eyrbyggja Saga* or "The Story of the Dwellers of Eyr," and began to work on the translations later published in the *Saga Library*.[6] In 1873, he prepared the collection of short sagas, published in 1875 as *Three Northern Love Stories*. Besides the already published tales of Gunnlaug and Frithiof, which had appeared in the *Dark Blue Magazine* in 1871, he included in this volume the tale of "Viglund the Fair," and the three brief tales of "Thorstein Staff-Smitten," "Hogni and Hedinn," and "Roi the Fool."[7]

Apparently still not satiated by the vast amount of translation and writing that occupied him, Morris found time to study his contemporaries' scholarly works and translations from the Norse, and to compose a number of original poems inspired by Northern literature and culture.[8] Most important, however, his immersion in Scandinavian literature influenced his literary style and choice of content—even in works not Northern in form or spirit. For, as he learned to translate saga effectively, he found a remedy for what he considered his stylistic problem, his tendency to write verse narrative which he thought "too long and flabby."[9] Admiring the restrained expression and sparsely ornamented beauty of his originals, increasingly valuing the Germanic elements in the English language, he began to develop a new diction. As Anthony Ugolnik demonstrates, Morris's translations, restrained and true to the spirit of their originals, show him learning to curtail his narrative impulse and to use economy in expression.[10]

The result of his work in translation was that he changed his mind about his ability to turn the *Volsunga Saga* into poetry and altered his earlier belief that "no verse could render the best parts of it."[11] In his 1870 preface to his prose translation of the *Volsunga*, he expressed the hope that an English audience would appreciate the Saga's greatness and find "amidst all its wildness and remoteness, . . . startling realism . . . subtilty [*sic*] . . . [and] close sympathy with all the passions that may move himself today" (7:286).[12] Hoping to bring the work still closer to the English, he began in 1875 the last of his long and important poems, *The Story of Sigurd the Volsung and The Fall of the Niblungs.*

Sigurd, published in 1876 and acclaimed by Bernard Shaw as "the greatest epic since Homer,"[13] transcends its sources and becomes an original poem. Although it is based mainly on the *Volsunga Saga* with an ending derived from the *Nibelungenlied*, *Sigurd* is a new and rich reinterpretation of medieval materials. But, in response to what Morris considered Richard Wagner's outrageous liberties with "the Great Story of the North," and because of his own reverence for his sources, he denied how fully he had altered and reshaped them. "I stick very closely to the *Volsunga* in my poem of Sigurd," he insists in a letter of 1876; "it is in fact the same story, modern amplification and sentiment excepted. I have invented nothing but detail."[14]

Morris is quite inaccurate, for to amplify, to add modern sentiment and new detail—much of it derived from his two Icelandic journeys—and to reshape and restructure his primary materials, is to create a new literary work. To unify his epic, he eliminates the saga account of the genesis of the House of the Volsungs and begins his poem with Sigurd's immediate ancestors, including only those who illustrate facets of the hero's character or whose adventures illuminate the epic's central themes. To insure continuity, he omits incidents such as those of the conflict between Sigmund's son, Helgi, and King Hunding and of Sigurd's revenge for the slaying of his father, Sigmund. To gain dramatic impact, he ends his poem with Gudrun's plunge into the sea and ignores her rescue by and marriage to Jonakr, and the dismal fates of their offspring. In all, he de-emphasizes the saga's concentration on the annihilation of "the whole root and stem of the Giukings" (7:396) to center his epic on key characters and to expand his treatment of cosmic, social, and personal issues.[15]

Modern sentiment causes him to make his epic palatable to a middle-class Victorian audience by not presenting what they might consider crude supernaturalism, grotesque horror, or indications of unworthy motivations on the parts of the heroic figures. Morris's Signy does not sew her children's gloves to their hands to test their courage, nor does she have Sigmund kill them when they prove cowardly. Brynhild, enraged, does not snort venom or flash fire, and Gudrun does not give Atli their children's hearts to eat. Ignoring the saga accounts of Sigurd's greed, Morris does not portray him as avaricious.[16] His Sigurd does not kill Fafnir primarily to gain his hoard, nor does he justify his action by stating that "every brave and true man will fain have his hand on wealth till that last day [of death]" (7:331).[17] He sincerely repents his broken troth to Brynhild and he neither attempts to seduce her nor proposes to her a *ménage à trois* with Gunnar.

Modern amplification permits him to add dimensions to lesser figures, often treating them as "typical" characters. Andvari becomes a personification of blind greed; Regin, portrayed as more than a malignant dwarf, becomes a complex Faust figure and a power-mad political tyrant. Sigurd slays him because Regin plans to become master of the world. Gunnar and Atli are made into symbols of the lust for gold and power; Gunnar's motivations for Sigurd's murder are both sexual jealousy and an overweening desire to become "sole King in the world-throne, unequalled, unconstrained" (12:216), and Atli is impelled to murder the Niblungs by the mere mention of the treasure they possess.

In general, therefore, Morris sharpens moral distinctions which had been either unstressed or simply intimated in the saga. Like Wagner, he heightens the contrasts between good and evil, between those heroes who are ideal warriors and social saviors and their base opponents. His purpose is to suggest the *Volsunga*'s broad cosmic and social implications and, thus, to note its relevance to his own era.

However, Morris's most significant alterations consist of his unification and repatterning of materials from his sources and his addition of thematic imagery to them. These result in a poem quite different from its sources. J. W. Blench has shown how

Morris adds symmetry to the events of the *Volsunga*, creating in "Sigmund" (Book I) a prologue in the form of a narrative genealogy and in "Gudrun" (Book IV), an epilogue, and thus placing the tragic story of Sigurd and Brynhild at the center of his poem.[18] Furthermore, Morris creates greater unity within the poem by developing parallel episodes and settings, by utilizing foreshadowings to connect the four separate books of the epic, and by developing a series of thematic images which help to amplify his major themes. Each of the four books, for example, begins with a descriptive passage emphasizing the qualities and values of the realm in which the actions will begin. In addition, each book, with the exception of "Regin" (Book II), which emphasizes hope and promise, culminates with a disaster to a society which has figured in it. As Dennis Balch comments, Morris stresses the "wavelike pattern of repeated catastrophe" that will end with Ragnarök and regeneration.[19]

Events and characters presented at the beginning of the poem skillfully foreshadow those which appear at the end. The first two books, centering on the dawn and the day of life, and on the truly heroic society, anticipate the tragedies of the third and fourth books, the accounts of the social twilight and night of the world. The figure of Signy, a psychic Valkyrie bound to a husband she hates and on whom she takes vengeance, anticipates the characters of Brynhild and Gudrun. When Signy and Sigmund join in passion, they blend her wisdom with his valor, much as Brynhild and Sigurd will do. When Signy stands before the burning hall of Siggeir, a hall she has destroyed, she anticipates Gudrun standing before the hall of Atli which she has set ablaze. The wicked Borghild handing the cup of poison to Sinfiotli (the son of Sigmund and Signy) and thus killing him, foreshadows Grimhild's psychological destruction of Sigurd through the magic cup of forgetfulness which she offers him. Two repetitions of Sigurd's approach to Hindfell, two meetings with Brynhild in her palace at Lymdale, and two parallel oaths of love, sworn ironically to two different women, serve to link the middle books of the poem.

Each book contains at least one account of a scop or hero singing and harping; the subject of their songs is cosmic process, the changes by which an earlier world has been born and destroyed, and the growth and decline of the world of the poem. At Signy's wedding, a scop sings of the Norse genesis and, at Sigurd's birth, of the deeds and heroic ancestry of Sigmund, his father. Heimir, the king of Lymdale, sings of the future and of Sigurd's own deeds before the hero goes to meet the Niblungs, while Sigurd, arriving at their hall, sings of the glory of his ancestors. The songs culminate in the two sung by Gunnar in the fourth book: his battle song in Atli's hall—which describes the Niblungs' deeds and predicts the coming of Ragnarök—and his death song in the pit of adders—a harping that concentrates less on death than on the beginning of the world—thus returning the reader to the song of genesis which has opened the epic.

The sustained and reiterated imagery of harping and singing, of ruined and deserted halls, of the tree and the flame, and, most important, of the process of the days and seasons moving the world toward Ragnarök further amplifies and unifies the poem. All the thematic imagery is directed, in various ways, to the exploration of one major concept—that of change and process.

Images of the building and destroying of halls, which Jessie Kocmonová indicates are symbols of the unity of the folk,[20] clearly represent the rise and fall of given clan or tribal cultures. The poem moves from the building of the Volsung hall, the "candle in the dark" (12:1) to the extinction by fire of the evil but magnificent hall of Atli. As power moves from the Volsungs to the Niblungs to Atli's people, the nature and values of each group are figured in descriptions of the halls they build. Subsequent images of the halls (transformed, deserted, or destroyed) show the process of the change or deterioration of given cultures.[21]

The tree and the fire[22] are also utilized to suggest the power of change. Images of a tree, which becomes both the hall and the torch that consumes it, are implied throughout the poem. Branstock, the tree that is the center of the Volsung hall and is akin to Yggdrasil, the tree of life, becomes the torch that sets the heroic world ablaze. Hiordis's epic simile comparing the "Volsung dwelling" (12:58) to a noble tree that is first laid low but then transformed into a great ship of conquest and glory almost epitomizes the first half of the poem. Images of fire not only link the first and fourth book of the poem to the central books which deal with Sigurd but also prefigure the conflagration and rebirth implicit in Ragnarök.

In all, the decline and death of the heroic world becomes an underlying theme of the poem. From the first page of *Sigurd*, images of the "last of the latter days" (12:1), the "Day of Doom" (12:7), proliferate. The flames of Ragnarök illuminate the burning of Siggeir's hall, the ring of fire surrounding Brynhild on Hyndfell, and the flaming pyre that consumes her body and Sigurd's. The Norse apocalypse is again prefigured in repeated images, those of the seasons moving to the three-year-long winter that precedes the end of the world and those of the dawn moving to the darkness of the night of death. Even the beasts who participate in the poem's events are visualized as prefigurations of the mythic monsters who will combat the gods and heroes in the last battle. Fafnir and the great serpent who kills Gunnar are types of the Midgard Serpent; the she-wolf who devours Sigmund's brothers is an embodiment of the wolf, Fenrir, who will swallow the sun.

Morris's symbolism is enriched by his knowledge of the work of Max Müller, the German mythologist popular in England. Müller had interpreted the legend of Sigurd as a solar myth, specifically as an explanation of the death of the sun either at the end of the day or at the close of the sunny season. To him, Sigurd was a sun deity, Brynhild represented either the spring or the fertile earth, and Gudrun personified the late summer or the earth at harvest time. Envisioning Gunnar as a symbol of darkness and winter, Müller interpreted his marriage to Brynhild as a rape of spring and his murder of Sigurd as the killing of the sun—specifically, the winter solstice.[23] That Morris knew Müller's thesis—at least in broad outline—seems clear,[24] and Morris's use of it helps him to create a cosmic myth that is also a warning to his own society.

Morris traces the movement from dawn to darkness in communities and in morality in the four books into which he divides his epic. He begins *Sigurd* in the bright world of the Volsungs, a realm of justice and equality which reflects his idea of the heroic age he had begun to prefer to the chivalric. In a society based on the gens or clan and on the concept of communal work, Morris found the highest values of saga life intact. The first book depicts the spring of the world. Thus, it moves from the season of spring—the May evening when Siggeir's emissary arrives to ask for Signy's hand, to her wedding on Midsummer Day, to the autumn when her father and brothers are murdered by Siggeir, to the winter when Sigmund and Sinfiotli are buried alive, to the promise of spring's return, when Hiordis, pregnant with Sigurd, is rescued by King Elf. Set in the earliest of the societies Morris describes, the first book of *Sigurd* centers on dawn and stresses the hope implicit in the beginning of day. The Volsung line appears destroyed, but is not; Sigmund, "the best of the trees of the garden" (12:8) is felled, but will blossom again through Sigurd, his last seed. Significantly, Sigmund waits until sunrise to die; his passing occurs as the first sunbeams bathe his eyes, and Sigurd is born at dawn, with his eyes looking straight at the sun of an April morning.

Sigurd, whose nativity begins the second book, brings daylight to his world. His birth, ending "the dark tide," is proclaimed as the "Dawn of the Day" (12:65, 66), and his name itself means "dawn" or "daylight." Although, like his father, he is called a "mighty tree" (12:73), he is repeatedly depicted as a figure representing the light and the summer sun. He is reared in the utopian world of Elf, but, when he reaches adolescence, he can no more be confined in the pastoral world which fostered him than "the hazel copse may hold / The sun of the earliest dawning" (12:70). Before embarking on his initiatory adventures, Sigurd appears to King Gripir shining like "the earliest sun's uprising" (12:98). Ruddy, bright-eyed, and golden-haired, arrayed in flashing armor, he is later seen by the people of Lymdale as Balder, the summer sun god, come to earth. He appears to Regin, who recognizes him as "the sun of summer" (12:158) with his presence blazing like "the heart of the sun" (12:103). At the end of the second book, his life-giving power arouses and wins the sleeping Brynhild. In an analogy to the sun's awakening of the earth from the slumber of night or winter, he woos her with the promise of love and fertility.

The second book of *Sigurd*, the book of day and summer, ends with a joyous love scene which stretches from dawn to night. But Sigurd and Brynhild must enter the shadowy vale of the Niblungs, where they will undergo the "dimming of the day" (12:306). At the center of the third book are the Niblungs, who are the "Cloudy People" (12:306) in more than name alone. Their dark hair, pale complexions, and somber coal-blue armor are the external evidences of their clouded moral nature; they are overcast by pride, jealousy, and greed. In the third book, a book of twilight and autumn, part of the action is set in the evening or in the grayness before dawn. Sigurd weds Gudrun in the autumn and joins the midwinter wars of the Niblung lords; his death comes as he closes his eyes at the first faint glimmer of dawn.

It is Atli, "the king that knows not ruth" (12:235), and his morally darkened land which Morris uses to depict the night and the winter of earth in the fourth book of the epic. In a series of scenes, now chiefly confined to artificially lit interiors or moonlit nights, the "Cloudy People," who have destroyed the daylight represented by Sigurd, are themselves destroyed by Atli's darkness. In turn, Atli and his land are consumed by the light of fire, for the poem culminates with a symbolic blaze. The flames with which Gudrun destroys Atli's palace symbolize those of Ragnarök, the final conflagration that will destroy the heroic world and the gods themselves.

To Morris, the *Volsunga Saga* was the world's great tale "Of utter love defeated utterly, / Of grief too strong to give Love time to die!''[25] and, in his own epic, he emphasizes the destruction wrought by the frustration of passion and by jealousy and self-ishness in love. While the first book concentrates on the familial and communal love of the Volsungs, the theme of the renunciation of erotic passion is introduced. Signy sacrifices her chance of love and marries King Siggeir to strengthen and aid her family. Her incestuous relationship with Sigmund is not at all motivated by passion, but is, instead, a rational act calculated to avenge her family and make way for Ragnarök, "the uttermost ending of earth, / And the day when death should be dead, and the new sun's nightless birth" (12:28). Hiordis's choice of the aged Sigmund over the young Lyngi is not impelled by love; instead, she chooses fame and praise over what, to her, seem the transient joys of desire. Through these sacrifices of personal desire, the Volsung line and the values it represents are preserved.

In contrast, the second book shows the beauty of erotic love through the relationship of Sigurd and Brynhild, and the third book demonstrates the destructive aspects of passion. The initial relationship of Sigurd and Brynhild represents the bond appropriate to loving friends and equals. It is symbolized by sunlight, and the hero swears his troth by the sun itself: "the sun shall die in the heavens and the day no more be fair, / If I seek not love in Lymdale and the house that fostered thee" (12:130). Brynhild replies with a similar oath, and the troth-swearing is repeated when the lovers meet in Lymdale. However, the oath becomes ironic when Sigurd swears it a third time, this time to Gudrun. The magic potion which Grimhild, the Niblung Queen, administers to him makes him not only forget Brynhild but also his own identity and the heroic values which are part of it. His drinking of it, described as the first death he dies, is a correlative to his new and less worthy attraction to Gudrun. This love is not the blending of wisdom and valor that characterizes the ideal relationship, but is based on Gudrun's mute adoration of Sigurd and on his pity for her and awareness of her pain. Their marriage, founded not on ignoble emotions but on less than ideal grounds, destroys not only themselves and Brynhild but the entire society of the Niblungs. Sigurd's death is actually precipitated by Andvari's ring, the stolen token which bears a "thrice-cursed burden of greed" (12:210). Given to Gudrun as a love gift by Sigurd, the ring forces Brynhild to recognize that she has been betrayed. Sigurd's death is hastened by the sexual jealousy between Gudrun and Brynhild which erupts when Gudrun, "her face yet dreamy with the love of yesternight" (12:206), encounters the frustrated and frigid Brynhild at the river. The death is cemented by Gunnar's greed and jealousy as his desire for the gold mingles with his rage at his sense of Brynhild's love and hate for Sigurd.

Indeed, Brynhild's great love and hatred for Sigurd sets blood brother against blood brother and makes Gunnar, Hogni, and Guttorm Sigurd's murderers. For Sigurd and Brynhild, death is a savior of love and a release from death in life. But, for the Niblungs, it is the destroyer of the sacred bond of kinship and the goad to vengeance. Gudrun's love for the dead Sigurd leads her to destroy her brothers and her own house. In turn, her love for them, which she can feel only when they too are slain, drives her to kill their murderer, her second husband, Atli. Finally, the destructive force of passion drives her to attempt her own destruction.

Thus, fatal and flawed passion is a partial cause of the break-down of personal, social, and cosmic order. Not only are the ties of kinship and blood brotherhood dissevered but also right relation-ship—social love in its broadest form—is destroyed. With the death of Sigurd, a great line of heroes ends; with the deaths of the Niblung lords, a society vanishes. Finally, with the destruction of Atli and his followers, power itself dissolves. Only lesser men remain on a disordered earth and they await a cosmic end. The failure of personal love and of fellowship leads from the morning of the world to the long night before Ragnarök.

Morris's epic is dominated by those who are fated to love and to suffer. Sigurd, Brynhild, Gunnar, and, above all, Gudrun bear the changeless eyes and faces and undergo the death in life that remain Morris's constant symbols. Yet, all are now depicted as strong and proud, silent and stoical in their pain.[26] Thus, the overall effect is different: Morris's emphasis is no longer on the pains of eros but on the courage to endure them. To Morris, Norse sagas demonstrate "the worship of Courage,"[27] and he extends this philosophy even to fatal disappointments in love. Man must "do the deed and abide it" (12:127), demonstrating his heroic endurance and bearing his pain with fortitude. Moreover, Morris insists that individuals must try to show an altruistic tenderness for all mankind—to blend their private desires with public benevolence. Linking erotic passion and an ideal of fellowship, Morris declares that the good days of earth are forged by "daring deeds . . . and the eager hearts of love" (12:126); in an indifferent cosmos, these are man's only weapons.

Similarly, Morris's attitude towards fate is focused upon courageous acceptance of what is destined and what is doomed to change rather than upon pessimism or the abandonment of will. Emphasizing confrontation rather than evasion, Morris explains that Signy foreknows the disaster her marriage will bring, but chooses heroically to fulfill the will of the Norns. Volsung and Sinfiotli, Hogni and Gunnar know of, but refuse to avoid, their destined deaths. Morris's Sigurd follows his saga prototype in nobly accepting his destiny, and even Regin, the questioning sceptic, recognizes and obeys the power of fate. Only Grimhild attempts to evade the Norns, and her *hubris* is a factor in the destruction of those around her.

In addition, Morris emphasizes the calm, unfrightened acceptance of the end of life. The heroic ethic, laughing death to scorn, is manifested by Sigurd, as well as by Gunnar and Hogni at Atli's court. Brynhild's suicide is as much a matter of choice as of despair; there is nothing weak in her decision to end her death in life. Yet death is no longer imbued with the sinister attractiveness it held in *The Earthly Paradise* and in *Love is Enough*. It is simply an end, one that even the gods must face, and as such it is neither to be unduly desired or to be unfittingly avoided. Life counts. The heroism with which one lives it, despite the pains of love and fate, is what gives man his only immortality, his remembrance in the minds of other men.

In all, Morris's new treatment of his themes in *Sigurd* demonstrates his ability to break through his personal problems and recommit himself to the world of men. Dorothy Hoare sees Morris's selection of saga as a choice of escape from life.[28] But, to those acquainted with the body of his works, it is obvious that Sigurd signals not escape but recommitment. Saga values, particularly those of courage, fellowship, and fortitude, suggest to him a way of approaching not only his own problems but also those of England. The "simple, straight-forward response to life in saga"[29] becomes his new personal and social ideal. His acceptance of the grimness of the saga world implies his growing willingness to face the darker aspects of man's life. Thus, *Sigurd* postulates an alternative to being an "idle singer," that of becoming, as Sigurd does, a champion of justice and equality, "a straightener of the crooked" (12:206). On a personal level, the poem marks Morris's turning from passivity to action: it announces the beginning of his personal crusade to set the crooked straight—through social and political activism and through the communism of Karl Marx.

II

Sigurd is the last major work written before Morris's conversion to "scientific socialism," and the important poems and prose romances that follow it are often profoundly influenced and always at least touched by the new ideology in which he came to believe. Morris's opposition to England's support of Turkey in the Russo-Turkish war of 1877 placed him squarely in the liberal and radical camp, and, in 1879, he became treasurer of the National Liberal League, a working-class group composed chiefly of radicals. The election of 1880, which brought Gladstone and the Liberals to power, made him realize that, as representatives of the people, the elected Liberals were little better than the Tories. Thus, he moved further to the left and, in 1883, became a member of Henry Hyndman's Democratic Federation (later called the Social Democratic Federation or SDF), the first Marxist-socialist organization in England. He began to work actively at proselytizing, lecturing, and writing for his new cause. In 1885, breaking with Hyndman after a conflict based on personalities rather than political differences, he spearheaded the creation of a Hammersmith Branch of the Socialist League and founded and edited a new paper, *Commonweal*, to promote the cause of socialism.

Meanwhile, reading the works of Marx and of contemporary historians who dealt with problems and events relevant to socialism—such as those of the Paris Commune of 1870—he began to apply his Marxist views to his literary works. Morris's socialism manifested itself not only in his choice of subject matter but also in his selection of themes and in his use of his old literary techniques to new ends. He became increasingly concerned with the concepts of fellowship and communal love, with the idea of survival through the continuation of the group, with the concept of a new Marxist apocalypse which would lead to the rebirth of a golden age—in all, with a materialist religion of humanity. Continuing to tighten the form and expression he had learned from translating saga, he further simplified his language to gain the response of a broader, less elite audience. Moreover, he began to utilize his recurrent images and motifs for new analogical purposes.

The first manifestations of these changes are to be found in *The Pilgrims of Hope* and *A Dream of John Ball*, two of Morris's most directly political works of fiction. The poem and the short prose romance, both written when Morris was deeply involved in socialism, are clearly didactic, attempting to inculcate in a proletarian audience the moral and social values important to Morris. Furthermore, both works serve as bridges between *Sigurd* and Morris's prose sequels to it, the romances called *The House of the Wolfings* and *The Roots of the Mountains*. Yet, at first glance, *The Pilgrims of Hope* appears atypical; like Morris's unfinished novel, it is one of the few works set in his own era and culture—England and France during the period of the Paris Commune.

Although *The Pilgrims of Hope* appeared in *Commonweal* between April 1885 and July 1886, the group of dramatic monologues and dramatic lyrics which comprise the total poem were not revised or republished in entirety during Morris's lifetime.[30] The poet's decision not to recast and repolish all of them was unfortunate, for, within a realistic framework which indicates how vividly and effectively he can utilize realism as a mode of presentation, Morris explores in a socialist context the problems of individual and communal love.

The hero of the tale which underlies the thirteen separate episodes of *The Pilgrims of Hope* is Richard, who, with the country girl he loves, is drawn by the "Message of the March Wind" (24:369) from an idyllic rural world to the grim and chartered streets of London. Influenced by a French radical he had known in his childhood, and moved in adulthood by an agitator at the London Radical Club—none other than William Morris, "thickset and short, and dressed in shabby blue" (24:383),—he finds a new birth in socialism. But his rebirth is not without pangs, for Arthur, a friend he has converted to socialism, falls in love with Richard's wife, who turns from her husband to her new lover. The three sacrifice their private desires to the cause in which they believe and go to Paris to aid the Commune. Richard, who hopes to die in the wake of a deed undertaken for the communards, survives the war-machine. His wife and her lover are killed, while Richard sadly but stoically returns to England to raise his son as a future revolutionary.

Richard's wife, "strong as the maidens of old, / Whose spears and whose swords were the warders of homestead, of field and of fold" (24:378) is a modern Valkyrie, reminiscent of Brynhild in her power and in her fatal beauty. She has truly loved her husband, and the child she has borne him, unlike most of the fruits of modern marriage, is born of their love:

Many and many an one of wont and use is born;
For a husband is taken to bed as a hat or a ribbon is worn.
Prudence begets her thousands: 'Good is a housekeeper's life,
So shall I sell my body that I may be matron and wife.'
'And I shall endure foul wedlock and bear the children of need.'
Some are there born of hate—many the children of greed.

(24:379)

Her marriage and childbearing have not been motivated by convenience or the desire for money and security, but despite this she rejects her husband and, by implication, her son. Her actions are never fully explained nor are the motivations for them clarified. The reader learns only what Richard himself discovers, that the wife he loves and the friend whom he thinks of as "a perfect knight of old time" (24:397) have betrayed him.

Richard's response to the betrayal is sorrowful rather than guilty or angry, and his wife's grief at no longer loving him is sympathetically depicted. The result, however, is the alienation of the couple and Richard's desire for death.

> But we sat apart again,
> Not speaking, while between us was the sharp and bitter pain
> As the sword 'twixt the lovers bewildered in the fruitless marriage bed.
> Yet a while, and we spoke together, and I scarce knew what I said,
> But it was not wrath or reproaching, or the chill of love-born hate;
>
> . . . .
>
> We were gentle and kind together, and if any had seen us so,
> They had said, 'These two are one in the face of all trouble and woe.'
> But indeed as a wedded couple we shrank from the eyes of men,
> As we dwelt together and pondered on the days that come not again.
>   (24:398–99)

Like Sigurd and Brynhild, Richard and his wife are permanently sundered by forces partially beyond their control; like Bodli and Proetus in *The Earthly Paradise*, Richard prefers death to death in life, but unlike them, he craves to do a noble deed before his demise. He finds it in fighting as part of the fellowship of the Paris communards, against capitalism.

Thus the simple story, clearly intended for a proletarian audience, traces the heroic action and endurance of an "ordinary" man. Yet Richard is depicted as something of a modern, if an unsung, Sigurd; he too leaves a peaceful pastoral world in quest of adventure. Drawn by a wind which, like Shelley's West Wind, is destroyer and preserver both, he comes to try to right wrongs and to destroy the evil force that corrupts song, art, beauty, and love for the sake of gold. As Sigurd strives to free and purify his folk, so Richard enters the flood of the city to help create "the eyes without blindness, the heart without guile" (24:373). He too believes his destiny is to speed the day of "the uttermost battle" (24:405), a Marxist apocalypse in which the gods and heroes of socialism will combat and vanquish the monsters of capitalism, thus bringing a new golden age to birth.

The images of diurnal, seasonal, and cosmic process that have shaped *Sigurd* are used for a new end, the promotion of Marxist socialism. "The seed of midwinter, unheeded, unperished" (24:371) which will blossom and bear fruit is no longer that of erotic love, as in the poems of the "stormy years,"[31] but of the people's hope for an era of communal fellowship. The spark and the flame, omnipresent images in *Sigurd*, are now those of revolution. Images of spring and autumn embody the hopes for the triumph of the proletariat and the harvest of joy in "the day to be" (24:408). The "day" is the revolution toward which the world inevitably moves, and Morris envisions its coming as improving and perfecting even the world of nature.

> . . . hope without a fear
> Shall speed us on through the story of the changes of the year.
> Now spring shall pluck the garland that summer weaves for all,
> And autumn spread the banquet and winter fill the hall.
>
> (24:403)

However, what E. P. Thompson aptly characterizes as "the poignancy of loss"[32] in the poem is not politically inspired. Morris did not consider the Paris Commune of 1870 a failure; instead, he believed that its mere existence would serve as "a rallying-point for all future revolutionists."[33] His grief is at the necessity of leaving the pastoral world to encounter the inevitable conflict; his sorrow is at the loss of personal love. Thus, Morris clearly embodies his own experiences in his account of Richard's rejection and endurance in the face of despair.

Richard refuses to dwell on or verbalize his pain and grief; instead, he bears them stoically. Even his last moment with his wife is a silent one. When she looks at him with the "lovely, friendly eyes / Of the days gone by and remembered" (24:407), he fights back tears and watches her run to Arthur, who has been felled by a mortar. While Richard is wounded, his wife and Arthur are killed; lying "dead on one litter together" (24:408), they are taken for husband and wife or a pair of lovers separated by the sword of death.

The tragic love triangle is ironically resolved by the deaths of the two participants who wished to live. Richard, who had yearned to die, gains the determination to live, and, reentering the pastoral world, learns to "cling to the love of the past and the love of the day to be" (24:408). Devoting his life to his cause and to raising his son, so that "two men there might be hereafter to battle against the wrong" (24:408), he finds the strength to endure in the barren present.

As Oswald Doughty has indicated, Morris seeks and finds catharsis by writing in *The Pilgrims of Hope* of the death of his wife and her lover.[34] Simultaneously, however, he is teaching himself and others how to cope with a painful life experience. Again preaching heroic values, he finds part of Richard's nobility in his honorable behavior in love: his refusal to punish his wife or his friend for their fated passion, his lack of concern for conventional notions of marital rights and duties, his selflessness in working side by side with the lovers for the Commune, and his ability to accept the pain of being unloved. Never bemoaning his fate, deciding to spend his life in a cause he finds more important than his personal passion, Richard reflects his creator while looking backward to Sigurd and forward to the heroes of Morris's historical prose romances.

Like *The Pilgrims of Hope*, *A Dream of John Ball*, which appeared in *Commonweal* from November 1886 through January 1887, centers on a historical moment important to socialists, utilizing it to highlight a drama of personal sacrifice for a cause and to further illuminate the concepts of fellowship and communality. Bringing his historical parable close to his English audience by selecting what many considered an important moment in their national development, Morris carefully bases his fictional versions of events on the medieval and contemporary works of English historians. Supplementing Froissart's account of the rebellion with such sources as Holinshed's *Chronicles* and *The Chronicle of John Hardying*, he turns to nineteenth-century historians for analysis and interpretation. He derives materials from Sir Henry Maine, Bishop Stubbs, Edward Freeman, John Richard Green, and Thorold Rogers, as well as from the more popular writings of Southey, Macaulay, and Cobbett.[35] As in his treatment of the Paris Commune, Morris's sketch of the Peasants' Revolt of 1381 stresses not its failure but the promise of hopeful struggle it should convey to contemporary adherents of revolutionary ideals. Reading history as Marxist myth, Morris looks to a moment in the national past as a prefiguration of an inevitable future confrontation.

Moreover, Morris incorporates in *A Dream of John Ball* elements from his own past and present. Again employing several of the literary techniques dominant in his earlier works, he uses them to enrich his statement of his new personal credo. His choice of the dream-vision form, for example, looks back to such early prose tales as "A Dream," "Lindenborg Pool," and "Svend and His Brethren."[36] But the dream-vision is no longer utilized primarily for its supernatural effect, and his reason for selecting the genre goes beyond its appropriateness to the medieval subject matter with which he deals. Instead, the dream-vision functions to bring together past, present, and future, and thus to create myth out of history. The very ambiguity of the title deliberately suggests that the tale is John Ball's dream of a fourteenth-century world of equality and fellowship as well as William Morris's dream of himself (as both medieval and Victorian man) and of a future beyond the Ragnarök of revolution. At times the two dreams coalesce; when John Ball makes his famous statement about fellowship, his remarks fuse his medieval concept of caritas and Morris's idea of secular communal brotherhood:

. . . fellowship is heaven, and lack of fellowship is hell: fellowship is life, and lack of fellowship is death: and the deeds that ye do upon the earth, it is for fellowship's sake that ye do them, and the life that is in it, that shall live on and on forever, and each one of you part of it, while many a man's life upon the earth from the earth shall wane.

(16:230)

Both men see the antagonists of fellowship as the same figures. The enemies are not only the rulers and tyrants of the earth but also the alienated egoist, "the proud man, the oppressor, who scorneth fellowship, and himself is a world to himself and needeth no helper nor helpeth any, but, heeding no law, layeth law on other men" (16:234). Despite the centuries between them, John Ball and William Morris share the same conception of the nature of a righteous life; it should be composed of "hopeful strife and blameless peace" (16:286).

At other moments, however, William Morris's vision diverges from John Ball's. Even in his medieval guise, as a scholar with "a tongue that can tell [and write] rhymes" (16:219), Morris expresses his unique sensibility in choosing to tell the men of Kent a tale of the brave men of Iceland. His nineteenth-century consciousness makes him question, and ask John Ball to question, the concept of heavenly fellowship under Christ, the King's son of heaven. For Morris thinks of fellowship as a product of earth and of earth as the only heaven man can know. Morris's belief that the paradise man must build lies in this world leads him to discuss, once again, the nature of death.

While John Ball sees death and resurrection—reflected in the painting of the "Doom of the last Day" (16:263) which adorns the chancel arch of the local church—in the religious terms of his period, William Morris rejects Ball's traditional views. Enunciating the ideas which had been germinating since the years of *The*

Earthly Paradise and which had begun to crystallize in Iceland, he denies the concept of otherworldly rewards or punishments and repudiates the ideas of the fear of death and the hope of personal immortality. His response to Ball's beliefs about the punishment of the souls of the evil is an agnostic's disclaimer: "Friend, I never saw a soul, save in the body; I cannot tell" (16:263). His reaction to the sight of the bodies of the slain is to find more vitality in their clothing and armor than in the waxen images their corpses become. He does not fear or sorrow at either their demise or the thought of his own, for, as he tells the astonished priest, he cannot truly imagine the reality of death. Although Ball momentarily thinks that he and his guest from the future agree about immortality, he finds that they do not. Morris believes not in personal survival but in human continuity which dictates "that though I die and end, yet mankind yet liveth, therefore I end not, since I am a man" (16:265). Thus, he argues that the only immortality is through the group and through the race of man, and that death itself is an unending sleep.

Heralding the end of his preoccupation with death, Morris insists that man's concern must be with life, with aiding in the struggle against those who wish to impose the death in life of injustice on others. The purpose of existence is to make both one's life and one's death bear fruit in a worthy cause. As moonlight gives way to the first glimmer of dawn, Morris reiterates his new convictions about the purpose of life. His final message of hope, his visionary legacy to John Ball and himself, is that "the Fellowship of Men shall endure, however many tribulations it may have to wear through" (16:284). Though neither John Ball nor he will be alive to witness it, Morris expresses his deeply felt belief in an inevitable socialist triumph and in the coming of a future golden age. Now convinced that there will be a reborn world after the Ragnarök of revolution, he pursues his attempt to educate his own generation and those which will come after by turning once more to a past which embodies the values that the world to come will need.

III

In *The House of the Wolfings* and *The Roots of the Mountains*, the first full-length prose romances of the 1880s, Morris uses the raw materials of *A Dream of John Ball* to new ends. Again stressing the concepts of fellowship, of life as "hopeful strife and blameless peace," and of survival after death through the continuity of the group, he returns to the North and to the heroic age in which he finds the communal and egalitarian roots of the Middle Ages. He integrates the world of *John Ball* with the worlds of *Sigurd* and ancient Icelandic saga by describing, in these prose romances, the Norse forebears of English society in the fourteenth century. The romances literally depict the ancestors of the noble men and women of Kent, the Gothic peoples from whom their hardy goodness, communal spirit, and strength of mind and body derive. Thus, Morris illustrates how traits useful to society can endure through periods of history.

Morris described the theme of *The House of the Wolfings*, which was published in December 1888, as "the melting of the individual into the society of the tribes."[37] In this romance, Morris continues the discussion of an issue he had raised in *The Pilgrims of Hope* and *A Dream of John Ball*, that of the sacrifice of individual desire for the sake of a group and a goal beyond self, now setting the problem in a world akin to that of *Sigurd*. The very title Morris selects, *The House of the Wolfings*, indicates the romance's relationship to *Sigurd*, for "Wolfings" (children of Wolf or Odin) is a name applied to the Volsungs.[38] The protagonists of *The House of the Wolfings*, however, are not specifically the Scandinavians, but their brother tribes, the primitive Gothic or Teutonic peoples whom Morris held in almost equal regard. To him, they were the groups whose "vigorous life . . . was once more to lead the world onwards," since they "had the fate decreed them of catching up the torch of progress from the dying hands of Rome."[39] Morris's vision of their life, derived in part from Caesar's *Commentaries*, Tacitus's *Germania*, and *Beowulf*, in part from nineteenth-century historiraphy, and in part from his own imagination, dominates his first late prose romance.

The spirit of saga pervades the work, for Morris writes a Teutonic equivalent of the Icelandic materials he so admired. Thus, he utilizes the catalogues, genealogies, prophecies, and digressions conventional in saga. As in his 1869 translation of the *Volsunga*, he mingles prose and verse. The prose of *The House of the Wolfings* imitates, in its use of quasi-Icelandic compounds and traditional kennings and images, that of Morris's earlier saga translations. Its poetry is modeled upon Morris's own renditions of sections of the *Elder Edda* and uses the compression, repetition, and alliteration characteristic of Icelandic poetry. Some of Morris's verse, such as

> Now, now, ye War-sons!
> Now the Wolf waketh!

> Lo how the Wood-beast
> Wendeth in onset
> E'en as his feet fare
> Fall on and follow!
>
> (14:180)

is stylistically similar to his translations from the *Edda*. Other verse, though less imitative in form, develops the conventional saga topics of heroism, death, and "the ways of Weird" (14:44). In all, the understatement and austere tone of the romance and the devices Morris employs within it are attempts to recapture the qualities of works of the heroic age.

But *The House of the Wolfings* imitates more than the stylistic characteristics of saga and folk epic; it recapitulates the values—courage, endurance, self-sacrifice, and loyalty to kin and group—of the heroic age. As John Goode says, Morris's "choice of a society resembling that of the early teutonic tribes demonstrates . . . a fine awareness of contemporary historiography. Maine, Freeman, Morgan and Engels himself had all given a good deal of attention to this epoch since it seemed to offer a point in time when the needs of the individual for private freedom were balanced with maximum equilibrium against the coherence of the community."[40]

Equally important, Morris and his socialist colleague, E. Belfort Bax, had themselves contributed to Victorian historiography, describing the Teutonic peoples in their joint work "Socialism from the Root Up," written for *Commonweal* in 1886 and republished in 1893 as *Socialism: Its Growth & Outcome*. Drawing their materials from the detailed analysis of the development of society made by Lewis H. Morgan in *Ancient Society* (1877) and copied at length by Friedrich Engels in *The Origins of the Family, Private Property and the State* (1884), Morris and Bax had written a brief socialist outline of history, including a praise of barbarism and an attack on ancient Rome. Tracing the three phases of barbaric society, "the Gens, the Tribe and the People," they contrasted barbarism's organic and vital nature with the mechanism of both the Roman world and the modern age. Happily announcing that modern civilization and its vices are "only a stage in the development of the human race, just as barbarism was,"[41] they look forward to its replacement by a socialist era which would incorporate in it the virtues of the heroic age.

The specific phase of social development that Morris and Bax praise in "Socialism from the Root Up" and that Morris writes of in *The House of the Wolfings* is the one which Morgan and Engels designate as "upper barbarism." Morgan and Engels had seen the history of man as an evolution through three stages of savagery to the crucial periods of lower, middle, and upper barbarism, and finally to civilization. They had envisioned "upper barbarism" as the era of the heroic peoples: the Homeric Greeks, the Vikings, and the German and Celtic tribes of the Roman period. They characterized the epoch as the age of iron tools and weapons and as the source of a rich oral tradition of mythology and epic. Both Morgan and Engels saw the people and the life they led as superior to their civilized equivalents; to them the upper barbarian was a noble, vigorous, and naturally moral human being, living in the heroic community of the gens or clan and dwelling in political, social, and economic cooperation with his fellows. To Morris, who loved the literary materials which had supposedly originated in the era, who looked forward to "barbarism once more flooding the world," and described the leading passion of his life as the "hatred of modern civilization,"[42] Morgan's and Engels's praise of heroic primitivism came as inspiration.

Morris saw in "upper barbarism" an escape from Victorian mechanism and from the ravages of the Industrial Revolution. Renewed and higher barbarism would, he felt, infuse new life into an effete world, providing a cure for the cold, meaningless world view proposed by modern scientific law and capitalist economic law; it would revivify human feeling and restore emotions tainted and weakened by civilization. Equating "upper barbarism" with ideal communism, seeing in the collective ownership and cultivation of the land by the gens the true spirit of the commune, Morris found in barbarian society a world in which human rights were not separated from human duties, a world without class exploitation in which the individual and his community were not automatically at odds. Like Morgan and Engels, he hoped that the future would bring *"a revival, in a higher form, of the liberty, equality and fraternity of the ancient gentes."*[43]

Thus, Morris makes the epoch of "upper barbarism" both the setting and a vital theme of *The House of the Wolfings*. The romance concentrates on a group of gentes living within a mark—the tract of land held in common by the community. Each gens, which Morris calls a House, is designated by an animal name, for its members believe themselves descended from a semi-animal, semi-human ancestor. All members of a gens are related by blood, and descent is matrilinear. They must take wives from outside their clan and wed the women of other friendly Houses. Members of a House owe each other aid, protection, and the avenging of injury, and all work communally in and for the central dwelling (or Roof). All own and work their land in common. The people of a gens are led, when necessary, by those among them they choose in free elections because they consider them the most worthy.

Morris describes Rome, the enemy facing the Teutonic gentes, in terms again drawn from Morgan and Engels. It represents "the rottenness of a decaying civilization," and Morris adheres to Engel's belief that the Germanic clans were victorious over the Romans because of their values and way of life. Barbarism gave them "their individual ability and courage, their sense of freedom, their democratic instinct . . . all the qualities which had been lost to the Romans and were alone capable of forming new states and making new nationalities grow out of the slime of the Roman world." Like Engels, Morris believes that "only barbarians are able to rejuvenate a world in the throes of collapsing civilization. And precisely that highest stage of barbarism, to which and in which the Germans worked their way upward before the migrations, was the most favorable for this process."[44] Thus, Morris concentrates on the heroism that assures the gentes' victory in their battle "for the life . . . [they] have made in the land . . . [they] have made" (14:161).

Moreover, linking the past with the present, Morris identifies the peoples with the English proletariat—an analogy he had already made in his 1884 lecture on "Art and Socialism"[45]—and the Roman exploiters with the entrepreneurs of his time. He sees urban Rome as analogous to Victorian London in its life and attitude toward labor:[46] "It may be said of them that they have forgotten kindred and have none . . . mighty men among them ordain where they shall dwell, and what shall be their meat, and how long they shall labour after they are weary, and in all wise what manner of life shall be amongst them; and though they be called free men who suffer this, yet may no house or kindred gainsay this rule and order. In sooth they are a people mighty but unhappy" (14:45). Like the English working-class, the Roman proletarians are "not so well entreated as . . . draught-beasts . . . and these thralls and those aforesaid unhappy freemen do all tilling and herding and all deeds of craftsmanship" (14:46). The wealthy, "men whom they call masters and lords who do nought" (14:46), like the Victorian capitalists, are the parasites in society,

The men that all folk fled from, the swift to drive the spoil,
The men that fashioned nothing but the trap to make men toil.

(14:79)

To Morris, the triumph of Gothic equality and communality over Roman exploitation and self-interest depicted in *The House of the Wolfings* is a foreshadowing of the triumph of the proletariat in the Marxist revolution to come, the victory that will result in a higher stage of social development.

Thus, the romance begins with a barely fictionalized summary of Morgan's and Engels's account of life in the gentes of "upper barbarism." Morris speaks of the mark and of how "the folk that now dwelt there had learned the craft of iron-founding, so that they had no lack of wares of iron and steel" (14:3). In depicting the Houses which inhabit the mark, Morris praises their way of life and their egalitarian spirit: "the men of one branch of kindred dwelt under one roof together, and had therein their place and dignity; nor were there many degrees amongst them . . . , but all they of one blood were brethren and of equal dignity" (14:5). Continuing the description, Morris comments on marriage customs in the gentes, how men "might not wed the women of their own House," but must wed with "such Houses of the Mark as were not so close akin . . . ; and this was a law that none dreamed of breaking" (14:5). As the romance progresses, he describes the barbarians' reverence for their totemic ancestors, the adoption of aliens into the gentes, and the democratic election of war-leaders. He illustrates the myths and folk-poetry of the Gothic tribesmen, portrays the way they wield their iron weapons, and demonstrates their pure communism in action.

In addition, Morris bases his central characters on figures associated with the heroic age of "upper barbarism." Thiodolf or Folk-Wolf, the hero, is partially modeled on the Sigurds of Norse saga and Morris's epic and on Beowulf. Like the saga Sigurd, Thiodolf is "the king-leek in the garden" (14:17), the finest and strongest of men. Like Morris's epic hero he is the ideal leader, a "helper of the folk" who thrives on "the praise of the people" (14:170). His death and funeral rites resemble those of Beowulf, while the promise that he will come again is based on the legends of Barbarossa and King Arthur. Like Brynhild before her, Thiodolf's beloved, Wood-Sun, is a Valkyrie; like many women of heroic legend, she is not wholly mortal. Even the dwarf who makes Thiodolf's enchanted armor has his counterpart in such Norse figures as that of Regin. The central characters of *The*

House of the Wolfings, Thiodolf, Wood-Sun, and their daughter Hall-Sun, further illustrate its main theme of "the melting of the individual into the society of the tribes," for all must sacrifice their individual desires to the general good. Within the framework of ancient history and myth, Morris once again deals with the tension between romantic love and the needs and duties of fellowship.

The symbol of fellowship is the Roof or communal hall which, like Heorot or the House of the Volsungs, holds "the memories of the generations and the very life of the Wolfings and their hopes for the days to be" (14:30). Shining within it is a second symbol, that of the Hall-Sun, the eternal light that signifies the sun and represents the strength and spirit of the united folk. The Roof itself is "the seat of a communal life that flows from Nature,"[47] and the groups which live and celebrate within it feel a kinship not only with each other but also with the cycles of the world of nature.

Thus, the people of the gens worship "the kind acres—which they themselves and their fathers had made fruitful, wedding them to the seasons of seed-time and harvest, that the birth that came from them might become a part of the kindred of the Wolf, and the joy and might of past springs and summers might run in the blood of the Wolfing children" (14:30). They envision their personal identities as part of the continuity of the group and the world of nature. Thiodolf, musing on his existence, sees himself in terms of the commune and the changing seasonal life of his people:

There he was between the plough-stilts in the acres of the kindred when the west wind was blowing over the promise of early spring; or smiting down the ripe wheat in the hot afternoon amidst the laughter and merry talk of man and maid . . . ; or wending the windless woods in the first frosts before the snow came, the hunter's bow or javelin in hand: or coming back from the wood with the quarry on the sledge across the snow, when winter was deep, through the biting icy wind and whirl of the drifting snow, to the lights and music of the Great Roof, and the merry talk therein and the smiling of the faces glad to see the hunting-carles come back; and the full draughts of mead, and the sweet rest a night-tide when the north wind was moaning round the ancient home.

(14:105–6)

Imbued with a sense of their existence as a part of process, finding their full gratification within the community, most of the kindred of the Wolf are willing, even eager, to relinquish their individual lives to assure the continuing life of the group. A leader's daughter offers herself as a human sacrifice to lead other victims to the house of the gods. Two women slay themselves to avoid aiding the Romans and betraying their people. A war-duke sacrifices himself and his forces to insure the victory of the majority of the tribesmen. The most striking sacrifices, however, are those of personal love. Hall-Sun, the child of Thiodolf and Wood-Sun, chooses fellowship over eros, renouncing marriage "to be the soul of the Wolfings" (14:176) and to guard the lamp that signifies her people's destiny. Becoming the priestess and hearth goddess of the folk, she dedicates her beauty to her people and her gift of prophecy to foretelling the destiny of her race.

It is more difficult for her mother, Wood-Sun, and her father, Thiodolf, to sacrifice their private passion for the sake of the folk. Thiodolf, adopted rather than born into the House of the Wolfings, has, in youth, fallen in love with a woman who is not of a House with which he may wed, who is not, indeed, entirely mortal. In one of the most clearly symbolic incidents in the romance, Morris allows Thiodolf to tell the story of his union with his anima and the integration of the personality which has resulted from it. It is his successful relationship with Wood-Sun, a spirit of nature in the form of a woman, that has made him the Folk-Wolf, the might of his people. Undergoing with Wood-Sun the central experience of transformation, he has become a man reborn to a new world of altruistic love. His detachment from slavery to his ego manifests itself in his siring of a daughter who is the perfected spirit of both himself and his consort, in his ability to love frankly and fully, and in his dedication to a life of fellowship.

His temptation and fall occur when he is middle-aged. When, out of love for Wood-Sun, he dons a magic hauberk wrought by dwarves, he forgets his oath "To live for the House of the Wolfings, and at last to die for their need" (14:112). The armor that Wood-Sun gives him to render him invincible (perhaps suggested by the armor Venus gives to Aeneas in Morris's 1875 translation of *The Aeneids*),[48] alienates him from himself and his gens. In wearing it, he unknowingly chooses "death in life" rather than "life in death victorious" (14:165). Temporarily seduced by the egoistical individualism and selfishness that the hauberk represents, he loses his love for the kindred and feels, instead, only the wish for self-preservation and the desire to escape responsibility: "I loved them [the Wolfings] not, and was not of them, and outside myself there was nothing: within me was the world and nought without me!" (14:169), he reports. When Wood-Sun, sacrificing her desire to save Thiodolf's life, reveals to him the secret of the hauberk, he casts it aside. He dies on the dais of the Roof he has saved, his fame assured, his life a legacy to his tribe.[49] It is through deeds such as Thiodolf's, Morris makes plain, that Europe will be reborn; it is through his group that he will become immortal, "ever reborn and yet reborn" (14:109). Like Barbarossa or King Arthur, his people envision him not dead but merely sleeping, certain to return to aid them at the moment of their greatest need. Even the passion of Thiodolf and Wood-Sun will be immortalized. It will live not in a Pre-Raphaelite lovers' heaven but in the abiding consciousness of the race. Incorporated into fellowship, it will abide with the soul of the Wolfings and, when they are gone, "with the Kindreds of the Earth" (14:166).

Thus, while the plot of *The House of the Wolfings* deals with the conflict between the individual libido and the needs of the community, the ending of the romance reconciles the two forces. The book demonstrates how passion generates fellowship and how erotic love is perpetuated in the love of the folk. In celebrating the triumph of fellowship, the merging of the gens into the tribe, Morris now defines the concept as subsuming and preserving erotic love, as well. Moreover, in the writing of heroic legend, Morris is again measuring himself. He obliquely reveals his own emotional condition and his new movement towards action. Suggesting a mysterious rebirth through erotic love, he hints at least at temporary union with his anima. Choosing a middle-aged hero who must face his aging process and first premonitions of death, he suggests his own acceptance of these forces. Furthermore, in describing his protagonist's self-involvement and attraction to escape, Morris depicts and judges his own. As he analyzes himself before his conversion to socialism, he indicates his wearing of the armor of egoism and alienation and his renunciation of it—his turning outward to fellowship. Above all, however, he affirms his continuing preoccupation with the relationship between eros and caritas, his continuing search for an answer to the problem of love.

In his next prose romance, *The Roots of the Mountains*, written and published in 1889, Morris depicts the fortunes of the House of the Wolf three centuries after the events chronicled in *The House of the Wolfings*. Having traced the evolution of a group from gens to tribe, he continues the historical paradigm he had outlined in "Socialism from the Root Up" by describing how the tribe joins with others to become one people. Set in the fifth century, the era of the Huns' invasion of western Europe, the book is no longer an imitation of saga but a romance.

Its tone differs from that of its predecessor. Although poems containing kennings and alliterations are interspersed throughout *The Roots of the Mountains,* they no longer imitate heroic or Icelandic poetry. The stark prose of *The House of the Wolfings* vanishes, and Morris begins to slip into the ornamented quasi-medieval style of the final romances. As he attempts to show the close relationship between the heroic and early chivalric eras, Morris describes the blending of heroic and chivalric values and customs. Moving from a legend of sacrifice to a tale of reconciliation, he depicts a world that has not yet suffered the antagonism between individual and social interests which, according to Marxist theory, civilization must cause.

Morris is writing socialist myth rather than Marxist history, and he sets *The Roots of the Mountains* in a land so good that it seems an earthly paradise "wherein people die not, but live forever, without growing any older than when they first came thither" (15:232). In reality, the land is subject to both change and death, but its spirit is that of the age of gold. "Thus then lived this folk in much plenty and ease of life, though not delicately nor desiring things out of measure. They wrought with their hands and wearied themselves; and they rested from their toil and feasted and were merry: tomorrow was not a burden to them, nor yesterday a thing which they would fain forget: life shamed them not, nor did death make them afraid" (15:11).

Deviating from Marxist theory, Morris shows the gens system coexisting with early medieval institutions. As in *The House of the Wolfings,* the gentes are strong and pure; exogamous marriage with Houses with which one has "kinship, affinity, and friendship" (15:7) is the rule, and the Roof still holds within it all kinfolk and those joined to them. In Burgdale, the most advanced of the communities in the romance, gentes government has been supplemented with an alderman and an informal council of the heads of the most prominent families. Yet the democratic institutions of the Folk-Mote and of the election of war-leaders still prevail. Aristocrats by merit, the tribal chiefs dedicate themselves to lives of service. The alderman swears "to set right above law and mercy above custom" (15:71) and his son, the hero, Face-of-god, explains what the tribal concept of leadership means to him:

When I drive the herds it shall be at the neighbours' bidding whereso they will; not necks of men shall I smite, but the stalks of the tall wheat, and the boles of the timber-tree which the woodreeve hath marked for felling; the stilts of the plow rather than the hilts of the sword shall harden my hands; my shafts shall be for the deer, and my spears for the wood-boar, till war and sorrow fall upon us, and I fight for the ceasing of war and trouble. And though I be called a chief and of the blood of chiefs, yet shall I not be masterful to the goodman of the Dale, but rather to my hound; for my chieftainship shall be that I shall be well beloved and trusted, and that no man shall grudge against me.

(15:140)

Both Face-of-god and his father, as well as Folk-might, the head of Silverdale and a descendant of the House of the Wolf, live the values they espouse, aware that failure to do so will result in the destruction of their tribes.

The tyrannical oppressors who threaten to destroy them are no longer the Romans, whose corrupt civilization has contracted and decayed, but the swarthy, dwarflike Huns who threaten both Rome and Germania. The hunnish master-slave culture is again seen as a prototype of Victorian capitalism.[50] The Huns treat their thralls as machines, tormenting and dehumanizing them; in an early system of division of labor, they utilize them for a variety of occupations, ranging from prostitution to mining.

Again, as in *The House of the Wolfings*, Morris deals with the tensions between the desires of individuals and the needs of the community. While not ignoring the obstacles to fellowship posed by sexual jealousy and frustrated eroticism, he concentrates on showing how these may be overcome. His main theme is union and he demonstrates how, through the love relationships between various leaders and the cooperation between several different social groups, the Gothic tribes unite to defeat the Huns and to form a people who will "increase and multiply, till . . . valiant men and clean maidens make the bitter sweet and purify the earth" (15:235). Morris's myth of reconciliation takes many forms as he describes forgiveness and marriage among individuals, union among political and social units, and the wedding of cosmic forces, all of which will result in the creation of a golden age on the ordinary earth.

The main characters of *The Roots of the Mountains* are men and women who simultaneously develop themselves as individuals and participate fully in the collective life of their tribes. The romance is a *Bildungsroman*, and the process of self-discovery and maturation is seen in both personal and social terms. Face-of-god or Gold-mane, as he is sometimes called, refuses the chance to explore the "civilized" Roman cities of the plain and turns, instead, to the woods which represent his tribal past. Embarking on a quest for an unknown goal, he feels as if he "were seeking something, I know not what, that should fill up something lacking to me, I know not what" (15:19). His goal is not the acquisition of treasure or immortality, but a love which will both grant him personal satisfaction and assure the good of his people. Love is not enough, however, and his discovery of his passion for Sun-beam or the Friend merely initiates him into the journey to manhood. By facing a series of problems, he painfully learns what Sun-beam instantly apprehends—that "there are more folk in the world than thou and I only" (15:108)—and grows from egoist to altruist. As he matures, he gains the wisdom necessary to come to terms with his rejection of the Bride, his childhood sweetheart, to overcome his guilt at breaking his troth to her, and to help her conquer her anger and desire for death.

The Bride also learns and grows. At first, bitterly hurt, she angrily repudiates love as "a wasting folly, that should but beguile me, and wound me, and depart, leaving me empty of joy and heedless of life" (15:272). Rejecting men, she chooses to become a virgin Valkyrie and hopes to die fighting for her people. But, though wounded, she is not killed.[51] Gradually, she comes to accept her sundering from Face: "Belike . . . [it] came because we were so sure, and had no defence against the wearing of the days; even as it fareth with a folk that hath no foes" (15:385)—and to permit Folk-might, her rival's brother and the leader of the House of the Wolf in Silverdale, to love her.

Though alluding to the triangle formed by Sigurd, Brynhild, and Gudrun, the three-cornered situation in *The Roots of the Mountains* does not culminate in tragedy. Sun-beam expresses kindness and compassion for her rival; the Bride restrains her jealousy and anger. A ring, the symbol in *Sigurd* of the forces that bring destruction, is used here as the symbol of reconciliation. Given by Sun-beam to Face-of-god to be presented to the Bride, the ring is a token of Face's oath to let the Bride rear his second male offspring. The oath is kept, and Folk-might is not goaded to behave like Gunnar. He too separates private anger from public duty and fights side by side with Face-of-god against the Huns. Because antisocial drives are controlled, the promise of love can be fulfilled. The Bride learns to accept change in feeling as a part of the inevitable process of change in life. She finds in the promise of eventual union with Folk-might "both the seed of hope, and the sun of desire that shall quicken it" (15:272). Morris depicts the Bride and Folk-might forming a marriage based on her "friendly love" for him and on her acceptance of his passion for her. Like the conventional romantic union between Face-of-god and Sun-beam, their marriage will be beneficial to the participants and to the kindreds at large.

Interestingly, marriage is viewed as an arrangement which must conform to and promote communal needs. Face-of-god, though passionately in love, does not bring Sun-beam into his House until she has been adopted by a kindred whom the men of his gens are supposed to wed. Even before Sun-beam meets and falls in love with Face-of-god, she has decided to wed him for the sake of her weakened House. The Bride accepts the suit of Folkmight, in part, for the sake of the kindred. In all, Morris is as much concerned with marriage as a metaphor for social union as he is with its role in binding individuals. The alliances he depicts are designed to promote the making of a people, through whom "the lost way . . . shall be found and the crooked made straight" (15:233). In the epilogue to the romance, the Bride's cherishing of Face-of-god's child along with her own represents both personal reconciliation and the sacred bonds between Burgdale and Silverdale which will bring forth a new people and an age of fellowship.

The union and fertility resulting from love and fellowship is suggested through the imagery, symbolism, and structure of *The Roots of the Mountains*. The romance is circular; itself a ring, it begins with the bringing home of a woman to lie in with her child and closes with the bringing of another infant to its new home. It begins in the autumn and closes with the promise of a harvest soon to come. The people of the romance feel their kinship with the processes of the natural world. As Blue Calhoun observes, "the most important quality of life in Burgstead is its participation in the seasonal cycle, the 'eternal recurrence of lovely changes'" (22:11).[52] Thus, the Burgdalers make "offerings to the Gods for the Fruitfulness of the Year, [and for] the Ingathering of the Increase" (15:9). Worshipping the gods of earth, they celebrate human and natural fertility by selecting Midsummer Day as the communal day of marriage. They accept death without fear, for, as they believe in the continuous life of the earth, so they believe in the continuous life of the world of men.

The folk of Burgdale and Silverdale do not separate the divine from the personal and natural worlds. They believe that all, except the Huns, are descendants of the gods, and they feel themselves close to cosmic forces which love and protect them. For example, the House of the Face, the gens to which Face-of-god belongs, is totemically related to the sun god. A carved head "with a ring of rays about it" (15:9) is its sign; the head of the House is the priest and avatar of his deity, a god depicted as shooting evil and slaying the dragon of night. In accordance with Max Müller's solar theory, Morris names his central hero "Face-of-god" to stress his affinity with the sun. Like Sigurd, Face-of-god is golden-haired and beautiful, Burgdale's embodiment of light and power. Rising before dawn, he turns his face "toward the Face of the Sun" (15:260) and prays to him; many of his important insights and major tests occur at sunrise.

As a sun symbol, Face-of-god represents creation and increase through love and fertility. The names "the Friend" and "Sun-beam," selected for Face's beloved, are equally symbolic. Friendship, as Morris makes clear in *News from Nowhere*, is the true basis of lasting love, and Sun-beam, an emanation of the solar force, is clearly Face-of-god's pure anima and rightful cosmic mate. Although the Bride's name may appear ironic, since she is not the bride of the expected groom, it indicates her function as the human representative of the spirit of vegetation. As such, she symbolizes the fertile earth ultimately wedded to the strength of the folk. The result of the union of two sun figures and of the earth and a mighty people is the promise of a reborn world.

Yet, despite Morris's skillful use of the metaphors of personal, social, and cosmic union, his romance lacks conviction. E. P. Thompson is correct in attacking the triumphant ending with its multiple marriages and simply-won victory over the Huns as too easily achieved.[53] The plot—completed halfway through the romance—is poorly contrived and proportioned. The characters are somewhat unrealized. Even Face-of-god cannot always differentiate between Sun-beam and the Bride, and the reader may wonder why he chooses one of the two women, almost identical in beauty and behavior, over the other. Morris does not adequately depict his new ideal of friendly love, nor does he portray the process of personal reconciliation effectively. He seems unable to show convincingly the forgiveness that may grow between two lovers who have found that they must separate.

Perhaps recognizing the partial failure of *The Roots of the Mountains*, he re-examines the same problems in his next romance, *News from Nowhere*. Again exploring the relationship between private passion and the public weal, again dealing with friendly love and with the sundering of those who no longer are in love, Morris rejects the more simplistic of the solutions he had proposed in *The Roots of the Mountains*.

Despite the occasional awkwardness of *The House of the Wolfings* and the more serious flaws of *The Roots of the Mountains*, both these romances and *A Dream of John Ball* are important as contributions to the literature of social protest. Beginning with *Sigurd*, the works of the 1870s and 1880s show

Morris increasingly employing not formal allegories but para-bolic fictions with subtle didactic intentions and implicit secondary meanings in order to comment on himself and his own era. As he designs literature to show alienated modern man the world of harmony and unity his modern civilization had led him to forfeit, he reveals his new vision of his world, his fellows, and himself. Through the creation of historical myths, he richly ex-plores the tensions and connections between the individual and the society of which he is a part. Through psychological mythopoeia, he deals simultaneously with himself as representa-tive of humankind, of race, and of culture, and explores the drives and conflicts of his unique inner being.

Thus, Morris begins to build the method and the mythic constructs which will dominate the romances of his last years. Further utilizing the myth of heroism, he will describe the regen-eration of the individual and link the reborn man with the forces of social salvation. Developing the myth of friendly love, he will envision a new ideal and weigh its possibilities. Expanding the myth of fellowship, he will postulate a way of life valuable both to the individual and to the world in which he dwells. Moving from the world of the past, he will enter, first, the world of the future and, finally, the realm of pure imagination.

SIX

NEWS FROM NOWHERE:
A SECOND INTERLUDE

To ENTER the world of Morris's last prose romances is to enter a land east of the sun and west of the moon. No longer set in the historical past as were *A Dream of John Ball, The House of the Wolfings,* and *The Roots of the Mountains, News from Nowhere,* the first of Morris's final group of romances shows past, present, and future converging in the timeless, ageless realm of dream. The shift away from an historic base is significant, for Morris has moved from the irretrievable to the possible and from the creation of historical legend to the engendering of psychological and sociological myth.

News from Nowhere; or, An Epoch of Rest, published in *Commonweal* in 1890 and in book form the following year, fuses Morris's dreams, hopes, and fears for himself and his society with his vision of a new and higher golden age, an age based on Marxist views of the future, aspects of fourteenth century English society, and concepts of utopia current in his own era. The book, a Marxist utopian romance, is an account of Morris's and all men's quest for love and fellowship, their desire to see the restoration of human harmony with nature, and their acceptance of the processes of change and fate and death. Although Morris does not depict the resolution of all his inner conflicts or present the solutions to all problems that the future world may have to face, he creates, in *News from Nowhere,* a moving study of the human aspects of utopia.

Morris partially explained how *News from Nowhere* should be read when he remarked that "the only safe way of reading a Utopia is to consider it as the expression of the temperament of its author."[1] He reveals much of his essential nature in the romance, objectifying and transmuting into images his needs and aspirations as well as their connections to the drives that motivate the human race in general. The nostalgic turn of Morris's temperament, a nostalgia both for his personal past and for the childhood of the world he had portrayed in *The House of the Wolfings* and *The Roots of the Mountains,* is etched on its pages. Transporting these feelings to a future world, *News from Nowhere* celebrates a vanished England, a vanished state of nature, and a vanished personal childhood. Even the garden of Kelmscott House at Hammersmith where Morris, the romance character, begins his sojourn in utopia does not grow modern hybrid roses, but, instead, those "very like the produce of an old country garden" (16:15). The bread he eats in Nowhere is the home-baked "big, rather close, dark-coloured, sweet-tasting farmhouse loaf" (16:15) of his childhood. Nowherian children love to swim or ride on little forest ponies as he did as a child, and most of them replicate his experience in reading at an early age but writing only when they are much older. In an incident which Proust might well have borrowed, the scent of a Nowherian herb brings back to Morris "early days in the kitchen-garden at Woodford" (his childhood home) and the memory of "the large blue plums which grew on the wall beyond the sweet-herb patch" (16:17).

Morris also deposits in the world of Nowhere the loves and deeds of his maturer years. Nowherians relish the fishing, tenting, and camping he so enjoyed; they love to journey up the Thames on holiday as he had often done. His own verses adorn the walls of a Nowherian sleeping chamber, while the "Anti-Scrape Society," which he helped found, preserves, in the future, the best Victorian architecture. Even his unsuccessful campaign to remove the incongruous monuments in Westminster Abbey achieves its end in Nowhere. He is remembered as he wished to be, for Old Hammond, ostensibly his grandson, recalls him as "a genuine artist, a man of genius, and a revolutionist" (16:97).

Yet, although it is autobiographical, *News from Nowhere* does not derive all of its power or even the greater part of its matter from what is entirely personal to Morris. Instead, much of its inspiration is literary and political, drawn from the utopian romances authored by Morris's contemporaries and the economic and social documents of Karl Marx and Friedrich Engels. Morris had always been an omnivorous reader of all varieties of romance. Disliking many of the realistic novels of the "great tradition," he preferred medieval romances, the historical romances of Sir Walter Scott and Dumas père, and works of the same kind written by his own contemporaries.[2] He seems to have been particularly partial to the fantasies and utopian fictions proliferating in the 1870s and 1880s, and *News from Nowhere* is influenced by such books as Samuel Butler's *Erewhon,* Richard Jefferies' *After London,* and W. H. Hudson's *A Crystal Age.*

Indeed, *News from Nowhere* is often described as a reaction against a utopian work Morris did not like, Edward Bellamy's *Looking Backward*. Although Morris had begun to think about creating a romance of the future at least as early as 1887, when he had John Ball wonder whether to wish his guest, William Morris, "some dream of the days beyond thine to tell what shall be, as thou hast told me" (16:286), he was clearly spurred on to write it by the appearance of *Looking Backward*, which he reviewed for *Commonweal* in 1889. Morris's concept of the time "when men shall have the fruits of the earth and the fruits of their toil thereon, without money and without price" (16:285) reflects his antipathy to what he considered Bellamy's "Cockney paradise" (16:xx). Morris disliked Bellamy's "unhistoric and unartistic" modern temperament[3] and the mechanistic world he saw as its consequence. He hated Bellamy's idea of a world of state socialism in which labor is painless but joyless. Yet Morris's basic antipathy to Bellamy arose chiefly from his disagreement with Bellamy's social values and aesthetic convictions. While Bellamy favored the urban, Morris preferred the pastoral; while Bellamy lauded the Industrial Revolution and the power of the machine, Morris yearned for the restoration of an organic way of life which utilized the mechanical only to alleviate the burdens which humans might find "irksome" (16:97); while Bellamy sought salvation through the omnipotent state, Morris wished for the time when it would have withered away. And, while Bellamy conceived of the future as in itself a novel, presenting a structured "realistic" picture of a society, Morris envisioned the future as containing what to him were the timeless, universal truths of the genre of romance.

The complete subtitle of *News from Nowhere—An Epoch of Rest, Being Some Chapters from a Utopian Romance*—establishes Morris's intentions about genre. Thus, he carefully employs materials that fit his definition of utopian romance, i.e., as the depiction of a world with as few flaws as human nature will permit. For example, though he utilizes elements derived from *Erewhon*, a book he loved, he avoids using Butler's satiric incidents or imitating his dryly comic tone. Instead, he is influenced by Butler's initial description of the charm of Erewhon's landscape and the beauty, health, and courtesy of its people. He may also have found support for his own views in the Erewhonian renunciation of machinery and lack of belief in personal immortality.[4] Again, Morris may have been affected by "the atmosphere of heightened reality blended with fantasy,"[5] characteristic of Richard Jefferies' *After London*; he does not adopt either

Jefferies' anti-utopian vision of England or pessimistic tone. Unlike the England of *After London*, Morris's England does not relapse "into a wild state of nature";[6] it becomes a pastoral arcadia, a trim and tidy garden. London has not been obliterated in Morris's romance; it has been decentralized into the communities from which it originally came. In general, the society Morris paints is the opposite of the feudal, hierarchical tyranny depicted by Jefferies; he evokes the other side of the medieval world, the communal, egalitarian spirit of the peasants and guildsmen of the later Middle Ages. Finally, while Jefferies' world is largely devoid of man-made beauty, lacking books and even well-crafted artifacts, Morris fills Nowhere with beautiful objects, lovingly made by the inhabitants.

The vision of the future on which *News from Nowhere* seems most closely modeled is that presented in *A Crystal Age*, written by W. H. Hudson and anonymously published in London in 1887. Hudson's utopian fantasy, though considerably more sober in tone and mannered in style than Morris's, is clearly the source of incidents, themes, and characters which Morris assimilated and reutilized, some three years later, in his own romance. Interestingly, Hudson pays tribute to William Morris as a writer and as a designer in *A Crystal Age* (and even mentions *News from Nowhere* in the preface to the 1906 edition of his book).[7] The House of the Harvest Melody, the gens Roof where Smith, Hudson's visitor to the future, finds himself, appears to have been decorated by Morris and Company. Its communal dining hall, mosaic-floored and simply but exquisitely furnished, is illuminated by a stained glass window strikingly similar to those designed by Morris and Burne-Jones:

Below, with loosened dark golden-red hair and amber coloured garments fluttering in the wind, stood a graceful female figure on the summit of a grey rock. . . . Round the woman's head was a garland of ivy leaves, and she was gazing aloft with expectant face, stretching up her arms as if to implore or receive some precious gift from the sky. Above, against the slaty-grey cloud-rack, four exquisite slender girl-forms appeared, with loose hair, silver-grey drapery and gauzy wings as of ephermerae, flying in pursuit of the cloud. Each carried a quantity of flowers, shaped like lilies, in her dress, held up with the left hand; one carried red lilies, another yellow, the third violet, and the last blue. . . . Looking back in their flight, they were all with the disengaged hand throwing down lilies to the standing figure.[8]

Whether or not Morris was conscious of so doing, he reciprocated the tribute by incorporating elements of Hudson's romance into his own.

Like *News from Nowhere*, *A Crystal Age* is set in "an epoch of rest," an era of peace which has come about through cataclysmic change. Yet Hudson's world of the future, like Morris's, is based on the world of the distant past, made up of elements derived from the gens system and from the communal life of the Middle Ages. The men and women of *A Crystal Age* have abandoned the diseased life of the Victorian cities and gathered together under communal Roofs where they find joy in labor, happiness in aesthetic creation, and pleasure in observing and participating in the processes of the natural world. They have renounced large scale commerce and industry, rejecting both the Industrial Revolution and the principle of the division of labor. They no longer use money as a medium of exchange; when Smith, like Morris in *News from Nowhere*, tries to pay for services, he is laughed at. The people of the Crystal Age not only believe that work is necessary but that it is healthful and pleasurable. All are artist-craftsmen who sculpt, carve, decorate, embroider and blow glass; they create artistic works, including exquisite illuminated manuscripts and musical compositions, because they enjoy making beautiful things and because they wish to contribute to the pleasure of the group. They derive pleasure from beautiful clothing and all are attractively garbed in garments patterned on medieval costumes. Smith, yearning to shed his ugly Victorian clothes, requests and obtains a beautiful vestment, as Morris also does in *News from Nowhere*.

More important, the people of the Crystal Age are the regenerate products of a reborn world, an era which, like that described in *News from Nowhere*, has restored them to childhood, fellowship, and communion with external nature. They are more sensitive, fragile, and innocent than the Nowherians, but they are equally endowed with communal spirit and general benevolence. Furthermore, like the Nowherians, they are worshippers of earth who feel their lives akin to the cycle of the seasons. They are refreshed by the beauty of nature, joyfully celebrating such occasions as the blooming of the autumn rainbow lilies. Their great festival is a celebration of the harvest, a rite which culminates in the singing of a communal harvest melody. Revering the earth as the source, sustainer, and image of the beauty of life, they live according to their conceptions of the laws of nature and of human reason. To them, death is a return to mother earth, for they accept the limited life of every creature without needing a concept of personal immortality. Instead, they believe in survival through the continuity of the House and the race.

In general, the lives of the Crystal people are "healthy, and free from care and regret,"[9] a balance of pleasant work, joy in nature, and contentment derived from simple communal activities. Thus, the men and women of Hudson's utopia are attractive, healthy, and longlived. In the communal dining hall, Smith, talking to Edra, learns that though she looks twenty-eight, she is sixty-three, just as Morris (in a similar situation) learns that Annie, who appears to be twenty, is forty-two. All Crystal women, like Nowherian ones, are lovely, and Smith falls in love with Yoletta, the rarest and most beautiful of them, just as Morris does with Ellen, the paragon of her society. In both cases, though for different reasons, the loves cannot be happily fulfilled.

William Morris, as a character in *News from Nowhere*, is similar in behavior and in the experiences he undergoes to Hudson's Mr. Smith. Yet William Morris, as the author of *News from Nowhere*, pointedly rejects a number of ideas W. H. Hudson espouses in *A Crystal Age*. Because of his temperament and Marxist beliefs, Morris reinterprets Hudson's conceptions of childhood and nature and eliminates the hierarchical and ascetic elements of Hudson's utopian world. For an effete, delicate, and consciously aesthetic group of children, Morris substitutes the hearty, vigorous Nowherians, childlike mainly in their frankness and vitality. For Hudson's nature as the book-of-God, his pantheism and worship of the divine spirit manifested in the earth, Morris substitutes an essentially materialist and pagan veneration of the world of nature. He dismisses Hudson's concept of a return to a matriarchal stage of society in which the benevolent mother is worshipped and sexual relations exist only between her and the man selected as father of a House. Morris replaces these ideas with the concept of a society of equals united by the bonds of fellowship and free to experience all the pleasure and the pains of eros. For, while Hudson believes that sexual passion prevents peace and that abstinence is the way to control the threat of overpopulation,[10] Morris advocates a doctrine of healthy hedonism. He solves the population problem in Nowhere, at least, by having the inhabitants willingly emigrate to countries where they are both needed and wanted. In all, Morris uses material derived from Hudson in the same way he had been employing sources in his earlier literary works. Although he selectively borrows specific incidents, he either rejects or assimilates the general themes of the work he uses, transforming them to coalesce with his own original ideas and aims.

Morris's aim in *News from Nowhere* is complex: it is not only to write utopian romance, like Hudson, or to depict and thus relive or purge the important moments of his personal experience, but to integrate these elements with a Marxist vision of the future. Thus, *News from Nowhere* is unique; it is probably the only autobiographical Marxist utopian romance in literary history. The Marxism Morris's book depicts is not, however, in conflict either with its utopian scheme or romance form. Marx, in the *Manifesto*, had written of the ultimate synthesis, the time when the state has withered away and human beings "shall have an association, in which the free development of each is the condition for the free development of all,"[11] thus, almost calling out for fictional interpretations of his vision. Morris and Bax, echoing Marx in "Socialism Triumphant," the final section of their *Socialism: Its Growth & Outcome*, had commented that they could only guess at the life of the future and noted that their opinions would naturally be "coloured by . . .[their] own personal wishes and hopes."[12] And, to Morris, the genre of utopian romance was the appropriate form for such speculations. Not restricting him to the rationalistic and realistic conventions of the novel, the relative freedom of the romance form permitted the objectification of his private "wishes and hopes" for a future in which the communist ideal has triumphed.

There is nothing unorthodox, in Marxist terms, about the future which *News from Nowhere* presents. Patrick Brantlinger accurately observes that the major elements of Morris's utopia, "abolition of classes, of the state, of private property, and of money, the flexible and rational use of machinery, labor rendered 'attractive' . . . decentralization of cities and of working sites, freer relations among the sexes are one and all present in the writings of Marx and Engels."[13] Others have noticed that Morris's account of the revolution, in the chapter called "How the Change Came," follows the predictions made by Marx and Engels.[14] Moreover, Morris makes his romance an illustration of Marx's central belief that "man's ideas, views, and conceptions, in one word, man's consciousness, changes with every change in the conditions of his material existence, in his social relations and in his social life."[15] For Morris concentrates on depicting the world of regenerate men and women who will arise when the earth has been reborn through revolution. His interest is in the transformations of human nature that a Marxist Ragnarök will bring about, in how emancipated human beings will overcome their alienation from themselves, their fellows, and the world around them.

Morris cleverly fuses Marxism and the romance tradition when he presents himself as an enchanted figure wearing a "cap of darkness" and "seeing everything" (16:155) in a time and place different from Victorian England. As Morris, the romance character, quests for love and fellowship—and through them for a reborn self—he encounters romance archetypes in Marxist guises. Old Hammond is both the communist educator who teaches Morris the history and practice of the new world and the wise old man of romance. Dick and Clara are the good comrades and the married lovers who aid Morris in his wanderings. The journey on the Thames is both a voyage through society transformed by revolution and a quest for happiness. The quest's goal, met and found, though only transiently, is Ellen, the symbol of the reborn age and the bride the alien cannot win. Ellen herself is a multidimensional figure; a working-class woman emancipated under socialism, she is also a "good fairy" (16:155) and benign nature spirit as well as the soul in the form of a woman.

The earth itself has been improved as man has been perfected by socialism; it has become the ideal world of the romance tradition. The Nowherians have corrected man's mistake and capitalism's error; they do not look on external nature and human beings as separate from each other. Not only have they merged and revivified the town and country, but, like the "upper barbarians" who predated feudalism and capitalism, they are no longer alienated from nature. Even Dick, one of the less sensitive of the inhabitants of Nowhere, is profoundly moved by the changing drama of the year, announcing "I am part of it all" (16:207). Understanding their kinship with the processes of nature, responding to its many moods, the Nowherians find "delight in the life of the world, intense and overweening love of the very skin and surface of the earth on which man dwells, such as a lover has in the fair flesh of the woman he loves" (16:132). The freeing of their desire for the body of nature, a sexual yearning somewhat repressed within the Victorian world, is another important manifestation of the emancipation they have undergone. Now perceiving the universe as alive, Nowherians believe in the vitality of the earth and in their own continuity through their connection with it. Like the people of *A Crystal Age*, they are worshippers of earth. Like Morris, they are pagans in the original sense of the word.

Other than a love of the world around them, Nowherians accept no religion. They are regenerate enough to care for each other and join in fellowship without the command of a higher power, be it God or Mother. They neither fear fate nor need to confront it with heroism—though they stoically face their problems—for, as the economically and socially determined force that makes for the improvement of human life, fate is essentially benign. As in *A Crystal Age*, death is not important; Nowherians accept it as a return to earth, a necessary process like the turning of the summer into autumn. When Morris remarks to a ninety year old man that the people of Nowhere are longlived, the answer he receives—that what matters is that one "is healthy and happy while he *is* alive" (16:49)—indicates how little the inhabitants concern themselves with death.

Instead, Nowherians concentrate on life, particularly on childhood. While there are actual children in Nowhere, Morris's use of the concept to characterize his utopia is chiefly metaphorical in intention. He associates childhood with a stage of social and historical development, with imagination and creativity, and with energy and freedom. Nowhere is in its childhood, the stage of growth associated with virtue and noble barbarism in the historiography of Morgan and Engels. Old Hammond still remembers the problems of its infancy, the tempestuous times when peace and plenty were not constant; Ellen, young in the childhood of the new age, wonders about what changes the next epoch is to bring. Since lack of change implies death, Morris indicates that Nowhere will inevitably alter as it grows. Meanwhile, he shows Nowherians rejoicing because they "have got back . . . [their] childhood again" (16:102). When Morris, the alien, patronizingly comments that he feels himself in the "second childhood of the world," Old Hammond responds: "Yes, why not? And for my part I hope it may last long; and that the world's next period of wise and unhappy manhood, if that should happen, will speedily lead us to a third childhood—if indeed this age be not our third" (16:102). Thus, Morris as author creates the kind of world that Northrop Frye describes as "an analogy of innocence,"[16] stressing the joy, energy, and benevolence of those reborn as children. Moreover, he depicts youth as the blessed age in which human creative and imaginative powers are at their peak.

Creating an aesthetic appropriate to Nowhere, Morris states that "it is the child-like part of us that produces works of imagination" (16:102). Analogously, it is the past childhood of the world—prehistoric, heroic, and precapitalist culture—that has produced the literature that both Morris and the Nowherians venerate. Long before his conversion to Marxism, Morris had been a great admirer of the matter of the people, owning more than thirty-five books of and about folklore and knowing the epics and tales of places as diverse as India, Persia, Russian Georgia, Alaska, and Australia.[17] He considered such books as the

Grimms' *Märchen* or *Household Tales* among the great works of the world.[18] Therefore, he envisions the Nowherians as lovers of legend and folklore who choose to decorate their walls with characters and incidents from works like the Grimms'. The people of Nowhere admire the popular forms of visual and literary art which Morris believed existed before the destructive Renaissance division into high art and non-art or artisanship. Naturally, they reject much of Victorian literature, specifically disapproving of Victorian realistic novels.[19] Ellen, discussing them, suggests that "in spite of all their cleverness and vigour, and capacity for story-telling, there is something loathsome about them . . . we must be contented to see the hero and heroine living happily in an island of bliss on other people's troubles; and . . . after a long series of sham troubles (or mostly sham) of their own making, illustrated by dreary introspective nonsense about their feelings and aspirations" (16:151), watch the tales come to their end.

Not only does Morris believe that the novel as a literary genre "is based on bourgeois individualism with its cult of personality and its massive blindness to the larger workings of history and to the larger interests of society,"[20] but he also feels that the egoism and subjectivity of the form do not mesh with the life experiences of the people of the ideal Marxist future. Their art, objective in tone, imaginative in content, and at times communal in nature, reflects their society. Men like Boffin, the golden dustman, and Robert, the weaver, are writers, but they create "antiquarian novels" (16:22), historical fictions and romances. While Nowherians do not emphasize the study of history, Dick, one of the chief opponents of "reactionary" traditions, is well acquainted with medieval history and knowledgeable about Shakespeare's plays. Nowherians enjoy what Morris, in his lecture on "The Society of the Future," hoped the future generations would enjoy: the arts that "appeal to the senses [and to man's humanity] directly, just as the art of the past has done."[21] Thus, they value music and poetry, the most overtly sensual and emotional of the arts, and appreciate architecture, the most collective of forms, one which Morris believed would be the primary art of a society based on cooperation.[22] In another sense, as Patrick Brantlinger observes, Nowherian art is so meshed with Nowherian life "that genuine art is life, . . . and poetry and imagination have become one with it."[23]

The second childhood of the world has returned its inhabitants to an appreciation of the arts associated with the first childhood of the world and, by implication, freed creative energy in Nowhere. In a similar manner, the new young age has liberated the sexual energy of its people. The idea of women as property has died along with capitalism, and the tyranny of men over women has vanished. Thus, Nowherians can be sexually frank and open. Old Hammond comments that the idea of "the 'ruin' of women for following their natural desires in an illegal way" (16:81) (i.e., outside of marriage) is now dead and that Nowherians respect all varieties of heterosexual love. Relationships may be transient or permanent, and "contracts of sentiment or passion" (16:58) are not matters to be judged either by the law or Mrs. Grundy.[24]

Thus, Morris repudiates both the conventional mores of his time and the ascetic tendencies of some Victorian feminist beliefs, instead demanding "the utter extinction of all asceticism."[25] The men of Nowhere are quick to acknowledge the attractiveness of women, while the women, no longer "reared in an atmosphere of mingled prudery and prurience" (16:62), are equally quick to enjoy the attractiveness of men. It is not surprising that Dick should think of the beauty of Clara's tanned neck and hands and contemplate the covered parts of her body, "white as privet" (16:137), but in few places outside of Nowhere could Clara consciously muse on Dick's "man's beauty" as he shows "his splendid form at its best amidst the rhymed strokes of the scythes" (16:145). Ellen too, as George Levine comments, is "sexually alive and intellectually and physically the equal of any man in Nowhere."[26] In all, the men and the women of Morris's utopia are capable of enjoying healthy sensuality and of fully participating in the pleasures of erotic love.

Ironically, however, even in an ideal and liberated Marxist society, frustrated passion causes pain and crime. Morris indicates that, despite their union in fellowship, the people of Nowhere cannot always deal with eros. As Normal Kelvin notices, jealousy—though no longer socially caused or linked to legal infidelity—continues to trouble the inhabitants of the earthly paradise of the future.[27] Dick remarks that it is fortunate the Nowhere contains a plethora of beautiful women so that "every Jack may have his Jill," for he fears that otherwise "we should get fighting for them" (16:35). But the problem of choice and attraction is not so easily solved. Dick's wife, Clara, is envious when she believes that her husband and Ellen are attracted to each other. Her envy disappears only when she discovers that her fears are unfounded. Ellen sadly acknowledges that her beauty provokes jealousy in women and despair in men whose love she cannot reciprocate. She comments that she has "often troubled men's minds disastrously" (16:188), and her choice of a somewhat isolated habitation is an attempt to mitigate the situation. Morris, the guest, is told that two men and a woman have died because of a tragic love affair and listens to another account of a love triangle because of which one man is dead and the survivors are threatening suicide. Nowherians recognize that even in utopia "love is not a very reasonable thing, and perversity and self-will are commoner than some of our moralists think" (16:35). They admit that they can no more prevent the crimes and conflicts caused by eros than they can control "the earth-quake of the year before last" (16:166).

At least, Nowherian society does not additionally punish those already victimized by passion. No laws demand prosecution for the manslaughter of a rival or for attempted suicide. Public opinion does not condemn those whose love has led them to conflict or violence, nor does it "drive those who well know that they are incapable of it to profess an undying sentiment which they cannot really feel" (16:58). Should a marriage fail, separation and divorce are personal, nonlegal matters, for society recognizes that "if there must be a sundering betwixt those who meant never to sunder, so it must be: but there need be no pretext of unity when the reality of it is gone" (16:58). Because the world of the future has abandoned capitalism, Victorian marriage laws, and repressive attitudes toward sex, "there is not by a great way as much suffering involved in . . . [them] either to men or to women as there used to be" (16:59).

Instead, the reborn world accepts the pains caused by eros as usually concomitant with its pleasures. Nowherians "do not deceive . . . [themselves], indeed, or believe that . . . [they] can get rid of all the trouble that besets the dealings between the sexes"; they realistically accept love's mutability, knowing that sometimes they "must face the unhappiness that comes of man and woman confusing the relations between natural passion, and sentiment, and the friendship which, when things go well, softens the awakening from passing illusions." Enjoying the pleasures that attend love and desire, Nowherians "bear the sorrow which not unseldom goes with them also" (16:57). With the saga virtues of courage and stoicism fortifying their innate dislike of self-destructive sentimentality, they "shake off these griefs in a way which perhaps the sentimentalists of other time would think contemptible and unheroic," but which they consider "necessary and man-like" (16:58). Thus, they mitigate—although they cannot obliterate—the pain erotic love can cause.

Nevertheless, the problems of love that neither Nowherian

society nor improved human nature can solve remain to deeply trouble William Morris. In both his roles, as author of and as a character in *News from Nowhere*, Morris reveals that he cannot yet accept his personal frustration and that he has not yet successfully found the right road to love and self. The autobiographical element of the romance, usually pleasant and nostalgic, surfaces to reveal what is painful—in the accounts of love relationships scattered throughout the book. In depicting the separation and reunion of Dick and Clara, Morris describes his own marital problems and his dreams of reconciliation.[28] Through comments made by Old Hammond, one of Morris's alter-egos, he offers the reader a history and commentary of his erotic involvements;

> Calf love, mistaken for a heroism that shall be lifelong, yet early waning into disappointment; the inexplicable desire that comes on a man of riper years to be the all-in-all to some one woman, whose ordinary human kindness and human beauty he has idealised into superhuman perfection, and made the one object of his desire; or lastly, the reasonable longing of a strong and thoughtful man to become the most intimate friend of some beautiful and wise woman, the very type of the beauty and glory of the world which we love so well.
>
> (16:57)

While Morris can expose and purge his feelings of disillusionment about his wife and sense of separation from her, relegating them to a minor motif and creating a fictional resolution to his problems,[29] he cannot keep the "longing . . . to become the most intimate friend of some beautiful and wise woman"— perhaps one like Georgiana Burne-Jones—within the bounds of reason.

Thus, William Morris, the guest in utopia, is depicted as falling painfully in love with an ideal figure he cannot possess. Ellen, the beloved, is portrayed as richly human and yet as a creature of another order, an emblem of something beautiful but unobtainable. Her tanned face, which looks "as if the warmth of the sun were . . . in it," and her grey eyes, which shine like "light jewels" (16:155), suggest her closeness to the world of nature and her identity as a vegetative spirit or nonmortal. She is the epitome of joy, a personification of the exuberance of the reborn world, but she is also the voice and the spirit of both Morris the author and Morris the character. It is Ellen who responds to Morris's thoughts and verbalizes his deepest feelings. She loves what he loves, including the small river offshoot of the Thames and the old, beautiful home that is Kelmscott Manor.

When, experiencing the beauty of the house and the land around it, Ellen calls out: "O me! O me! How I love the earth, and the seasons, and weather, and all things that deal with it, and all that grows out of it,—as this has done! . . . The earth and the growth of it and the life of it! If I could say or show how I love it!" (16:202), the voice the reader hears in Morris's. For Ellen represents Morris's pure anima, the aspect of himself with which he should gain union. In his inability to do so lies the tragic element of *News from Nowhere*.

William Morris, the author, depicts William Morris, the character, as partially responsible for the failure to attain the ideal and thus to integrate his personality. As soon as Morris sees Ellen at Runnymede, he falls instantly in love with her. Intellectually unaware of his passion, he begins to experience jealousy and anxiety. For example, during the trip up the Thames, Ellen asks Dick to help her with her boat; Morris notices that "as the two beautiful young faces bent over the rudder, they seemed to me to be very close together." He ruefully confesses that "though it only lasted a minute, a sort of pang shot through me as I looked on" (16:181–82). When Ellen announces that she has come to join Morris, rather than Dick, his "uncomfortable feeling" (16:183) of jealousy vanishes, but he remains a prey to his anxieties. He fears that he will be forced to leave Nowhere. Like Smith, in *A Crystal Age*, he worries about the disparity in years between himself and the woman he loves. Bitter at being fifty-six, he thinks of himself as fit only to be Ellen's teacher. Afraid that his love will be unrequited, he broods on the end of the relationship and suffers from "anxiety as to the remedy of that age for the missing of something one might set one's heart on" (16:193).

Unlike the Nowherians, Morris, the alien, makes the pain of love worse than it need be. Ellen correctly accuses him "of wanting to nurse a sham sorrow, like the ridiculous characters in some of those queer old novels" (16:198), of behaving in the sentimental and melancholy manner of a Victorian rejected lover, and of asking for failure. Although she offers him fellowship, inviting him to live with her and her grandfather, he sees her gesture as insufficient. Finally, when he and Ellen together visit Kelmscott Manor, now blooming in perfection, "as if it had waited for these happy days" (16:201), he expects something—an avowal of love, an open discussion of feelings, a psychological or sexual consummation of his passion—to happen. But, as Ellen is about to speak, their moment of closeness is interrupted and neither he nor the reader learns what she would have said. Ironically, Morris is denied both the hope of fulfillment and the pain of rejection by the loss of the vision itself.

What is clear is that Morris fails to gain what he has set his heart on. Even were he to relinquish the dream of sexual communion and to accept friendly love with Ellen, he cannot wed himself to his soul or achieve the self-fulfillment of an integrated personality. Like Pharamond's in *Love is Enough*, Morris's quest in *News from Nowhere* is incomplete. Although he momentarily believes himself reborn, he is too much a product of his Victorian experience, too unregenerate, too ego-bound, too worldly wise to achieve his goal. Child of the old world, he must lose Ellen and the new golden age. As he is about to fade into the past, a look of recognition passes between him and Ellen, and she shakes her head mournfully. Interpreting her gesture as an expression of sorrow over the impossibility of their union, he imagines her saying: " 'No, it will not do; you cannot be of us; you belong so entirely to the unhappiness of the past that our happiness would weary you' " (16:210). Again shut out of paradise, Morris knows that ideal love has eluded him, but he does not succumb to despair.

Instead, he acknowledges Nowhere as a dream and knows that, though he and all men yearn to live reborn within its beautiful and harmonious order, they cannot yet do so. He sees that he cannot recapture the child lost with his childhood and is not ready for the new youth of a reborn self. The anima he seeks is separate from him; he cannot be the transformed personality correctly balanced between his unique consciousness and the collective psyche. Instead, he must return to the realities of the imperfect, once-born world from which he came. He is to go on "striving, with whatsoever pain and labour needs must be, to build up little by little the new day of fellowship, and rest, and happiness" (16:211). His duty is to speed the Ragnarök of Marxist revolution; remembering his dream and living by its light, he must strive to make it into a true vision.

News from Nowhere, therefore, becomes an important record of Morris's personal and political enlightenment. Although Morris cannot find the unified self he seeks, he can present his vision of the integrated world in which the search can best be made. For the romance successfully interweaves many of the most important strands of Morris's belief and feeling. Through the use of the genre of romance, *News from Nowhere* blends the traditional and the original and melds the utopian and Marxist components of Morris's thought. It depicts a future that retains the finest elements of the human past, yet is not frozen into time. It convincingly expresses Morris's belief that there can be a bridge between the world of nature and the works of man, that there can be a realm in which man lives in harmony with earth and in which man's art—connected to the earlier, more universal art-work of the people—can be almost as free and natural as life itself. In all, *Nowhere* is the portrait of an ideal world which is not static but alive and capable of growth, like those who will be fortunate enough to live in it.

In the romances that follow *News from Nowhere*, Morris begins to explore the process by which an unregenerate age may be redeemed. Realizing that personal rebirth must accompany the renewal of society—so that others will not lose utopia as he has done—he explores the essential qualities, developments, and quests of heroic men and women. As he traces their processes of growth and demonstrates their impact on their fellows and the world around them, he proceeds to show the human race how it can make a Nowhere into Somewhere.

SEVEN

THE WORLD BEYOND
THE WORLD

WILLIAM MORRIS's last romances, *The Story of the Glittering Plain, The Wood Beyond the World, Child Christopher and Goldilind the Fair*,[1] *The Well at the World's End, The Water of the Wondrous Isles,* and *The Sundering Flood* are journeys to worlds beyond the ordinary world in search of love and fellowship. Designed as much for the socialist utopia of the future as they are for Morris's own unregenerate age, they represent Nowherian ideals of art; they are tales to be depicted on the walls of the communal dining halls of Nowhere or to be told around the fireplace of a rejuvenated Kelmscott Manor. Their objectivity, fantasy, and vitality are qualities Nowherians would enjoy, and their sources, derived from the "Bibles . . . of the people" (22: xii) and the romance tradition of the Middle Ages, are those Nowherians would appreciate.

Even the themes of Morris's final romances are rooted in the ideology of Nowhere, for all the works trace the movement from individual alienation and social discord to union, harmony, and reconciliation. Yet, Morris emphasizes new aspects of this process. Employing the pattern of the quest, long a favorite vehicle for his ideas, but perhaps made more significant to him by his translation of Homer's *Odyssey* in 1887, Morris increasingly explores the problem of human maturation, the drama of spiritual death and rebirth, and the psychic miracle of the integration of the personality. Weaving together his literary, social, artistic, and psychological concerns, Morris makes of his last romances fascinating webs of much that he had felt and of much that he had read.

Morris was, first of all, an exceptionally knowledgeable reader of medieval romance, a literary genre he had loved since his Oxford days and had richly utilized in such poems as *The Earthly Paradise*. In addition to translating romances for his own use, he had written a redaction of *Havelock the Dane* and, in 1892 and

1893, translated and published a group of *Old French Romances*.[2] Along with perennial favorites like *Le Morte D'Arthur*, *Amadis of Gaul*, *Parzifal*, and *Sir Gawain and the Green Knight*, Morris knew and owned such medieval works as *Joseph of Arimathea*, *The History of the Holy Grail*, *Percival le Gaulois*, *Palmerin of England*, *Sir Eger and Grime*, *Lancelot du Lac*, *Le Chevalier de la Tour Landry*, *Le Chevalier Bayard*, *Ogier le Danois*, *Amadis et Ydoine*, *Houon de Bordeaux*, *Tristram de Lyones*, and *The Romance of Alexander*. He possessed important compilations of romance materials such as Lady Charlotte Guest's *Mabinogion*, Bishop Percy's *Folio Manuscript*, Ritson's *Ancient Engleish Metrical Romanceës*, Weber's *Metrical Romances*, Hunt's *Popular Romances of the West of England*, Ashton's *Romances of Chivalry*, and Joyce's *Old Celtic Romances*.[3]

His equally rich knowledge of the "Bibles . . . of the people" has already been examined in Chapter Five. These works, as previously mentioned, included ancient epics, myths, legends, and folk tales—many of which had become part of the romance tradition. Familiar, as well, with the important scholarly studies of mythology and folklore both previous to and current in his era, Morris considered Jacob and Wilhelm Grimms' *Teutonic Mythology* among his "Bibles," and greatly admired such works as John Brand's *Observations on Popular Antiquities*, Lady Wilde's *Ancient Legends, Mystic Charms, and Superstitions of Ireland*, and Eugene O'Curry's *On the Manners and Customs of the Ancient Irish* with its notes by W. K. Sullivan. He used other important scholarly works as "tools" (22:xii). Although he does not always mention their titles, he employs incidents and descriptions drawn from them. In addition, Morris's last romances show his awareness of still other major studies—a knowledge derived either through reviews and critical articles about them or through volumes he did own and read. In all, Morris was fully cognizant of the various theoretical methods and systems which attempted to demonstrate the interconnections among history, myth, folklore, literature, and life.

Morris was, however, especially interested in the emerging disciplines of comparative mythology and cultural anthropology which sought to explain the origin, transmission, and significance of myth, folklore, and romance.[4] His thorough grasp of Max Müller's philological and etymological method, and of Müller's thesis that all myth is solar has already been documented.[5] His agreement with the Grimms' treatment of folklore and fairytale as important survivals of a great Indo-European mythological system is manifested both in his admiration for

Teutonic Mythology and in his use, in the last romances, of materials drawn from it. A knowledge of the euhemeristic approach to mythology, utilized in his era by two of his heroes, Carlyle and Ruskin, may be assumed—since he had read virtually all their works—and his awareness of Ruskin's and Pater's aesthetic and humanistic approaches to the analysis of myth (demonstrated by such works as Ruskin's *Queen of the Air* [1869] and Pater's *Greek Studies* [1875–1889]) is equally apparent.

The final romances, however, reveal a fact which is less evident: Morris was cognizant of the new interpretations of myth and folklore which were flowering in the last quarter of the nineteenth century. Lewis H. Morgan's views of the life and beliefs of the ancient world, as described in *Ancient Society* (1877), had shaped Morris's ideas about the heroic peoples; E. B. Tylor's comparative method, demonstrated by his major work, *Primitive Culture* (1871), and Tylor's thesis that cultures pass through the same stages of development so that one may study modern primitive societies to understand ancient civilizations, had influenced both Andrew Lang, Morris's acquaintance and admirer, and Morris himself. Lang, in such books as *Custom and Myth* (1884), was interpreting ancient materials by comparing them to rituals employed in contemporary primitive societies. Challenging Müller's solar thesis, Lang was also seeking the roots of myth in vegetative and fertility cults, again influencing Morris. And, whether Morris knew James George Frazer's *Golden Bough* (1890) through Andrew Lang, through reviews of the work, or directly, he employs themes and descriptions clearly derived from Frazer in his own final works of art.

Even the language of Morris's last romances, though often attacked as quasi-archaic and unreadable "Wardour Street" English, is partially a result of his study of the past. It is his attempt to capture the qualities of the prose of epic and romance. Imitating more than the "whiloms" and "nonces" of medieval English, Morris tries to recreate what for him was the rich word-building and freshness of the language before it became merely "a dialect of French." Believing that if the English "could only have preserved our language as the Germans have theirs . . . we . . . would have made the world richer than it is now,"[6] he utilizes the complex syntax and archaic vocabulary he associates with Anglo-Saxon poetry, Icelandic saga, and the work of Chaucer and his predecessors. Although Morris's archaisms are sometimes pure inventions and the syntax of his sentences is sometimes obscure, his unique language serves an important aesthetic function in the final romances. Initially difficult to comprehend, it pulls the reader away from the words and objects of a modern, commercial society, gradually drawing him into the remote world of which it is a manifestation. Furthermore, words selected by Morris primarily for their connotative or root meanings become memorable. Because the reader is forced to analyze linguistic meaning, he must progress slowly; thus, he becomes aware of the romances' symbolic intentions and begins to participate in their events.

What is most significant about the ways in which Morris manipulates language and utilizes manifold and varied source materials is how they enhance his private vision. For, while Morris analyzes and interprets the sources he uses in varied ways, according to the theoretical structure he is following, he is always concerned with the same interlocking mythic patterns. Thus, he depicts the "green world" of medieval romance, but places within it groups living in various stages of social evolution or moving from savagery to barbarism or civilization, as described by anthropologists like Morgan or Tylor. For the structure of his plots, he utilizes the pattern of the quest, derived from epic and romance and from his contemporaries' analyses of them; for his major characters, he draws upon the conventions of romance and upon the speculations of his era as to their nature. Assimilating a remarkable range of source materials, utilizing them without pedantry or self-consciousness, Morris creates a new personal and social mythology for himself and for his audience.

The framework of Morris's final romances is the world depicted according to ancient and medieval romance conventions, a realm in which the ordinary laws of nature are slightly rather than radically suspended. Morris's basic terrain is the woodland and forest, well supplied with castles and hermitages, and broken, occasionally, by small medieval towns or larger (and almost always evil) cities. Morris's world includes false paradises, places of illusion and artifice where the hero may be trapped, natural valleys and gardens of love and education, and realms of negation symbolized by wastelands. Blue Calhoun, analyzing the landscape of the romances, describes how Morris evaluates different views of nature and natural life by moving from the simple pastoral setting, through the supernatural complexity of the wilderness and the sophisticated complexity of the city, back to the idyllic pastoral.[7] Morris's convictions as a socialist and as a romancer coalesce in his preference for places where nature requires that man must work. His beliefs again merge in his depiction of cities which manifest the evils of capitalism and of small Nowherian communities which are filled with the spirit of the golden age.

Yet the world of the last romances is animistic, full of elemental spirits, not all of whom are benevolent. The evil witches, wise

old men and crones, saintly hermits and fairy folk common to the
genre of romance are present. In addition, savages, barbarians,
and civilized men fill the landscape. Abandoning the essentially
historical treatment of "upper barbarism" he had employed in
The House of the Wolfings and *The Roots of the Mountains*,
Morris turns to depicting anthropologically identifiable groups
at various levels of social development coexisting within the same
imaginary time and place. Using anthropological sources mythically and psychologically, he demonstrates how cultures in various stages of growth may aid or injure each other.

The heroes of the final romances also demonstrate the fusion
of many strands of Morris's thought, for they are drawn from the
romance tradition, the nineteenth-century idea of the cultural
hero, and the Morgan-Engels description of the ideal upper barbarian. Essentially, they are modeled upon the simplified, idealized figures of medieval romance, men superior to others not in
kind but in degree, yet they are not of aristocratic birth or lineage.
Clearly manifesting his socialist sensibilities, Morris makes
Walter, in *The Wood Beyond the World*, merely the son of a merchant and Osberne, in *The Sundering Flood*, the child of a free-
holder. Ralph, in *The Well at the World's End*, is the figure highest in rank, but he is only the youngest of the four sons of a minor
ruler. All the heroes are strong and courageous warriors who
joust, battle, and rescue damsels in the best medieval manner. Yet,
they fight only when they deem it necessary to preserve their lives
or those of others. Their courage is coupled with humility and
wisdom, and they have often been educated in these values by
supernatural figures. They themselves are not divine or even
demi-gods; instead, they are culture heroes, figures who represent
the highest ideals of their given social groups. Like the culture
heroes described by John Rhys in his *Lectures on the Origin and
Growth of Religion as Illustrated by Celtic Heathendom* (1888),
Morris's heroes add to their anonymous or obscure parentage
courage in war, wisdom, and "creative power."[8] The mothering
or fathering force of imagination is theirs.

In this way, they show their cultural inheritance of the best
qualities of "upper barbarism," even when, like Ralph, they are
nominally Christian. They retain the simplicity, vitality, and
sense of duty to home and kindred of the barbaric peoples; they
have the barbarians' sense of their correct role in a rightfully con-
stituted group, and they possess, as well, that barbaric inheritance
which Morris believed would again blossom in the future: "that
higher form of conscience that would impel . . . [men] to action
on behalf of the future of the race."[9]

But the heroes must leave their groups; as culture heroes, all are wanderers journeying on quests for life-giving goals.[10] Their quests are richly symbolic, and Morris derives the structure, imagery, and symbolism of the journey from many sources: the bridequests seem drawn from folklore, the *Mabinogion*, and ancient epic and saga; the grailquests from the Sangraal romances he knew and admired. Devising a series of journeys whose goals are the bride, the grail, or both, Morris dismisses the alternative aims of questers—treasure and empire—as unworthy of socialists. Instead the goals of his journeys are happiness through wisdom and love, and the quests are metaphors for the process of regeneration. Whether they are land journeys or *imrama*—the sea-voyages of Celtic legend—their stages follow the same basic pattern and the experiences within them constitute what Joseph Campbell calls "the monomyth of the hero."[11] F. A. C. Wilson, in analyzing the structure of the quest in *The Well at the World's End*, virtually describes the basic design of all the last romances.[12] All Morris's heroes are called to adventure, sometimes by a vision, as in *The Wood Beyond the World*, or by a rumor, as in *The Well at the World's End*, or by a direct challenge to them or their loved ones. Leaving the world of common day, they enter a supernatural realm; here, they undergo their "Katabasis" or initiation by ordeal. Separated from others, they undergo the experience of evil and the confrontation with death. Hallblithe, in *The Story of the Glittering Plain*, must voyage to the Isle of Ransom; Birdalone, the female hero of *The Water of the Wondrous Isles*, must encounter the ordeals imposed on her at several of the islands; Golden Walter must traverse the varied dangers of *The Wood Beyond the World*.

All the male heroes survive their initiation by ordeal to encounter the Virgin—often a figure for both the Great Mother and the anima in Morris's romances—and to free the pure anima and emanation who is the female part of their soul. The women (or, in the case of Birdalone, the men) with whom they unite are the images of their marriage with self and of their union with the life-force. The bride *is* the grail, even in *The Well at the World's End*, where the objects of the quest are ostensibly twofold; the quests always culminate in success. When the hero and his anima unite, what Charlotte Oberg calls "the pattern of separation and isolation ended by union and generation"[13] is not yet complete. The lovers do not live in isolation but return, instead, to the world to exercise the wisdom and grace they have gained. They may discover and rule a new society as in *The Wood Beyond the World*, create their own utopian community as in *The Water of the Wondrous Isles*, or simply return to their pastoral homes. Wherever they end their journey, they bring to their final residence both personal and societal regeneration.

While all of Morris's last romances follow the pattern outlined above, they are richly various in incident and setting. They do not replicate each other in the emphases they place on stages in the pattern of the quest or on specific major themes. Instead, each romance may be thought of as representing Morris's last words on an issue that has preoccupied him throughout his literary career. Thus, *The Story of the Glittering Plain* contains Morris's final repudiation of escape, while the literary works which follow it illustrate Morris's metamorphoses of the figure of the dark anima, his increased understanding of the nature of erotic passion, and the many facets of his vision of the world rejuvenated through the individual, male and female, reborn to new heroic stature.

I

The Story of the Glittering Plain, or the Land of Living Men is Morris's final study of the human desire to avoid the limitations imposed by age and death by finding an earthly paradise in which the golden age survives intact. In the romance, Morris returns to the motifs he had first explored in "The Hollow Land" and *The Defence* volume and had fully developed in *Jason* and in the "Prologue" and a number of the tales of *The Earthly Paradise*. Yet, in *The Glittering Plain*, the drive for such escape is unambivalently condemned and the alternative to it—life working for and in the purely human world—is roundly praised.

Published in 1891, *The Glittering Plain* is closest in theme, detail, and heroic tone to the historical romances of the 1880s. However, the world of the romance is no longer that of an identifiable place or time. The people Morris describes resemble the Norse and some dwell in lands reminiscent of Iceland, but the work is as much influenced by Celtic folklore as by Norse saga. Morris derives elements of his story from the tales of "Connla of the Golden Hair" and "Oisin in Tirnanoge," as retold in P. W. Joyce's *Old Celtic Romances* (1879) and from O'Curry's account of the Druid Dallan's rescue of Queen Edain from the earthly paradise of the fairies.[14] Perhaps speculating on the historical connections between the Norse and the Irish, Morris makes his hero, Hallblithe, a member of a northern gens, the House of the Raven, and Hallblithe's betrothed, the Hostage, a member of another gens "wherein it was right and due that the men of the Raven should wed" (14:211), but sets some of the book's action in a realm drawn from Irish legend. When the Hostage is kidnapped by Vikings, Hallblithe embarks on a quest to find and free her. Seeking her first on the Isle of Ransom, a land described as an underworld and modeled on Iceland, he next journeys to a terrestrial Eden, patterned after Tir-na-mbeo, "The Land of the Living" visited by Oisin and Connla.[15]

The quest in *The Story of the Glittering Plain* leads from an ideal pastoral home through a realm of death, to a paradise exposed as false and, finally, back to home. Hallblithe—the hearty spirit of his House—must triumph over the forces that oppose life and natural fertility, but are disguised as their counterparts. Again utilizing the bridequest, Morris further develops the motif he had employed in "Rapunzel," "The Land East of the Sun," and *Love is Enough*, concentrating even more explicitly on how the hero finds himself through the search for a fulfilling woman. The romance is essentially a *Bildungsroman*, an account of how Hallblithe, in maturing, learns to separate appearances from realities.

In search of his beloved, Hallblithe must leave Cleveland by the Sea, a natural land where things are as they seem, and journey to the Isle of Ransom, a "land of lies" (14:267). Hallblithe's first initiation by ordeal occurs in Ransom, after an almost classic descent to the underworld. The island, a realm of black-robed figures, strange rituals, and false values, can be approached only through a dangerous underground cave. Modeled on those aspects of Iceland which, during his journey of 1871, became for Morris the symbols of the bare and terrible in life, Ransom contains high mountains, glacial rocks, and a wasteland of black volcanic sand marked only by a few dwarfed, wind-bitten trees. Like the Iceland of Morris's day, it lies beyond the edge of the ordinary world and suggests experience beyond the norm. Like the Iceland of Morris's mind—before the restorative journey of 1873—it is a place of despair and death which must be confronted and finally conquered.

Puny-Fox, Hallblithe's guide, honored among the Ransomers as "chief liar" (14:229), subjects Hallblithe to a series of trials, deserting him in the wilderness and subjecting him to tests of silence and self-control. Only when Hallblithe has proved himself, may he resume his journey. But he is sent on a false quest, that of accompanying Sea-Eagle, a dying chieftain, to the land of the Glittering Plain. The Plain or "the Land of Living Men" is the other half of Morris's psychological underworld and the second site of Hallblithe's initiation. Ruled by an immortal king, called the "Glittering Plain" because its unchanging sun shines even in the depths of winter, this "Acre of the Undying" (14:253) is a terrestrial Eden in all externals:

> A land of youth, a land of rest,
> A land from sorrow free;
> It lies far off in the golden west,
> On the verge of the azure sea.[16]

But Hallblithe learns to see and, thus, to reject the land for its internal flaws: exclusivity, sloth, and false eroticism.

Those who enter the land regain their youth and are granted personal immortality. But only the few (the oldest chiefs of the Ransomers) may go and, of these, some refuse. Not seeking to separate their fates from those of their people, the best of the chieftains prefer death and a return to the earth to the death in life the Glittering Plain actually offers.[17] For, once on its shores, men lose their memories of the past, forgetting kinsmen, deeds, and communal responsibilities. The Plain, however benevolent it appears, is in reality a tyranny, in which the old structures and customs of the gentes have been abrogated; it offers its inhabitants an existence devoid of adventure and even of change. Lacking both the natural processes of growth and decay and the external goads to action, it lures men to sloth, a vice, which to Morris the socialist is as insidious as exclusivity. Hallblithe learns that the "plenty and peace and good will and pleasure without cease" (14:272) within the borders of this Lotos Land are goods whose price is the relinquishment of manhood and duty.

But the lack that Hallblithe finds most troubling is the absence of the correct variety of love. The Glittering Plain is filled with beautiful and eager women; it permits spontaneous relationships and promises the fulfillment of desire. The ladies of the land are revealed as sirens, made for pleasure only, and its princess, condemned to unrequited love, is shown as born to grieve. Hallblithe rejects them all. Not only are they not of the Houses into which he may wed, but they seem to him alien to "the old laws of marriage" (14:256) in which he believes. With them, he cannot find the friendly love which must be the basis of a true union of body and soul. He is never even really tempted to forget the woman he considers his appropriate and rightful bride.

After Hallblithe has confronted death, rejected immortality in a realm devoid of fellowship, and repudiated inappropriate erotic passion, he is free to seek and find the Hostage. Returning to the Isle of Ransom, he rescues her through his truthfulness and the constancy of his love. When he publicly admits that his victory over the Ransomers' champion has been based on fraud, he moves his hosts to help him. When he rejects the beautiful maidens offered to him, he convinces the Ransomers to restore his bride.[18] Demonstrating the strength of his values to his hosts, he begins to reform them. Once he has infused his civilizing power into their culture, he may return, with his bride and his blood brother, Puny-Fox, to the ordinary land of normal life, Cleveland by the Sea. There, where "men die when their hour comes . . . and they [the hours] are long enough for the doing of deeds that shall not die" (14:212), he may wed the Hostage amid promises of good and fertile life to come.

Thus, Morris, through his account of Hallblithe's experiences, offers a final statement on the matter of the earthly paradise. Showing that "the quest for immortality ends in living death and that true life is experienced only through acquiescence to natural process,"[19] he drives home the point he had announced in his earlier works. Though, as in *Jason* and *The Earthly Paradise*, he reveals his understanding of the human urge to avoid the limitations of mortality, he no longer sees escape as even mildly tempting or attractive. Like Hallblithe, Morris seeks "no dream but rather, the end of dreams" (14:273), finding man's true life in participation in the joys, sorrows, and struggles of the mortal world. For Morris, man's role lies in improving himself, others, and the world in which he lives, in accepting his death as life's just end, and in finding his immortality in "the continuous life of the world of men" (16:132) and of the world of nature.

While *The Story of the Glittering Plain* emphasizes the problems one faces in choosing the correct mode of human life, *The Wood Beyond the World*, begun in 1891 and published in 1894, concentrates on the issue of differentiating between appearance and reality in selecting the correct partner in romantic love. Having effectively dealt with man's need to accept the processes of change and death, Morris moves to what to him seemed the more complex question of the constructive and destructive aspects of erotic passion. Like *The Glittering Plain*, *The Wood Beyond the World* is structured as a bridequest. Again, Morris depicts a hero undergoing trial and temptation and eventually moving from falsehood to truth and from death to life as he obtains union with the virgin who is his soul. Following the strategy of *The Glittering Plain*, Morris keeps his canvas small, emphasizing the fortunes of a few individuals whom he names symbolically and characterizes archetypally. Morris's recognition that he is using archetypal figures and his clear depiction of them is already evident in such characters as the Friend and the Bride in

The Roots of the Mountains and in the Hostage of *The Glittering Plain*. But the depiction of all the major characters as archetypes differentiates *The Wood Beyond the World* from its predecessors among the romances. The intensification of archetypal figures and patterns in this romance may have been due to Morris's increased contact with the contents of his subconscious mind—the last romances were written during his bouts of insomnia—to the aging artist's impulse to universalize his fictions, or to his readings in comparative mythology which emphasized the pervasiveness and underlying similarity of seemingly disparate deities and culture heroes. Whatever the causes, types, especially female archetypes, dominate the romance.

The hero and heroine of *The Wood Beyond the World*, Golden Walter and the Maid, though not dissimilar to Hallblithe and the Hostage in appearance and actions, are even more reduced to their central and essential characteristics. Golden Walter, so named to associate him with the brightness of the sun (perhaps as a vestigial tribute to Max Müller's solar theory), is the only figure in the book who bears a Christian name. The others are designated by their characteristics and functions. The Maid's name connotes her magical virginity and her condition of servitude, the Lady's name indicates her roles as goddess, witch, and ruler of the wood beyond the world. The King's Son is the Lady's royal, if temporary, consort and a child both in terms of his maturity and of her power. The Dwarf, a Browningesque Caliban, is a representative of the primitive, demonic forces in the world.

The most striking figures in the romance are the two women with whom Golden Walter becomes erotically involved. Each is an aspect of his inner self; the Lady is his dark anima, the Maid, his pure anima or emanation. Each is envisioned in terms of fertility and vegetative power, for, deriving the connections from the Grimms, Lang, and Frazer, Morris links human sexuality and the processes of nature. Indeed, beyond its general similarity to folklore, *The Wood Beyond the World* specifically resembles *The Golden Bough*. Like Frazer's book, Morris's romance is a quest in search of the explanations of a mystery. Like *The Golden Bough*, it begins with a re-enactment of a ritual of love, pain, and death, while each of the two women between whom the hero is caught is eventually revealed as an aspect of one goddess, the Great Mother. At the beginning of Morris's romance, Golden Walter finds himself involved in a mysterious rite of fertility and death, for his first meeting in the woods is with an old man who functions as a Frazerian priest of Nemi. The old man describes his former participation in a bloody ritual, telling Walter that he has slain his predecessor and supplanted him in order to possess the Lady. His warnings: that evil has come of his act, and that he too would have been killed (were it not for the Maid) are meant to discourage Walter from entering the forbidden precincts of the valley. But Walter, called to adventure by a vision of the Lady, feels compelled to explore the mystery. He too is almost lured to his death, for the Lady wishes him to kill and replace the King's Son as her consort. She will, in turn, eventually tire of Walter and persuade her next male victim to destroy him.

Walter's first series of ordeals ensue partially from his initial failure to clearly ascertain the meaning and goal of his quest. He is in search of the wrong woman. The Lady he believes he is seeking is only a more potent version of the cruel and unchaste wife from whom he is in flight. Not a man whom all women love, Walter has already married and been betrayed:

when they had been wedded some six months he found by manifest tokens, that his fairness was not so much to her, but that she must seek to the foulness of one worser in all ways; wherefore his rest departed from him, whereas he hated her for her untruth and her hatred of him, yet would the sound of her voice . . . make his heart beat; and the sight of her stirred desire within him, so that he longed for her to be sweet and kind with him, and deemed that, might it be so, he should forget all the evil gone by.

(17:1)

Walter is as attracted to the Lady as he had been to his wife and equally unable to see her true nature. The Lady, however, is more powerful and seductive than an ordinary mortal woman. She is an Acrasia, modeled on Spenser's character, luring men to her artificial Bowre of Bliss and leaving them dishonored and destroyed.[20] More significantly, she is a passionate and cruel fertility figure whose love demands the shedding of blood, a Diana of Nemi who represents the fearsome aspects of the Great Mother. She is described both as Diana, appearing garbed like "the hunting-goddess of the Gentiles" (17:50) in a tunic and sandals, with a bow and arrows slung across her back, and as the carnal Venus, arising from the bed of love, clothed only in her flowing golden hair.[21] Hunting or loving, men are her prey. Her wantonness, "a disordered abundance like that of weedy places,"[22] is a form of natural fertility run wild.

At first, unable to break the masochistic pattern of his past, Walter succumbs to the Lady. When he is overpowered by his mixed passion and fear, he yields to her advances. But he is not destroyed, for, aided by the Maid, he begins to purge the elements within him which have prevented him from loving appropriately and from integrating his psyche. The Maid, his pure anima, represents the creative life-giving aspects of the Great Mother. Her potency, like the Lady's, is that of a nature goddess, but she is associated with the Maiden Korê[23] and her magic powers depend on her remaining chaste. Employing both her supernatural and her human powers, she destroys the Lady and the King's Son and leads Walter out of "the wilderness fruitful of evil" (17:33).

In the realm through which she takes him, she must employ her power as a fertility figure, for the two—friends but not lovers—must pass through the valley of the People of the Bear. The Bear tribesmen are enormous figures, larger and stronger than civilized men, ignorant of iron weapons and even of the bow, and dressed only in the skins of beasts. They have evolved to what Morgan and Engels catagorize as "middle savagery,"[24] worshipping an Ancient Mother of Tribes to whom they offer human sacrifices. Using only their primitive bone and flint tools, they have built a doom-ring and an altar to their goddess. Since they have worshipped the Lady as her incarnation, they must be persuaded by the Maid that she, not the Lady, is "the new body" of their "God" (17:106). Thus, she appears to them as Korê or Demeter, clothed in a flower bedecked gown. When they demand proof of her powers, she makes the faded blossoms that adorn her bloom again. Like Frazer's May Spirit or May Queen,[25] she manifests herself as the "Mother of Summer" (17:97), a vegetative force who can send rain from the mountains to make the earth bear fruit and whose very footsteps on the meadows will make them thrive. Though virgin, she is the bringer of fecundity, "the very heart of the year's increase" (17:108). Serving as an Isis figure or civilizer, she issues new edicts which will raise the Bears from savagery to ideal barbarism. No longer are they to practice the customs of slaying all aliens or offering them as sacrifices to the Great Mother. Instead, they are to adopt into their tribe the strong and worthy and to enthrall only the weak or degenerate among their captives. The Maid's final gift to the People of the Bear assures their gradual evolution to "upper barbarism"; she sends them iron tools, seed corn, and the men to educate them in the art of tillage.

Only after this second set of trials do the Maid and Golden Walter find the realm in which they are to live. Still led by the Maid, Walter sees from afar the land of Stark Wall. By arriving from the hills where local legend indicates the people's tribal heritage began, by being unflawed in body, and by selecting the correct role in life—symbolized by his choice of the worn battle garb of deeds as opposed by the opulent robes of peace[26]—Walter becomes the ruler of the land. The Maid's work done, she may renounce her chastity and magic and become, as Walter's bride, a fully mortal woman. When Walter consummates his friendly love with the Maid, he achieves union with his anima. Thus, he becomes a whole man, ready to transmit his wisdom to a new society. The type of the good king, he creates within Stark Wall a realm of justice and mercy based on the finest aspects of barbarism. The ultimate fruit of the personal love of Walter and the Maid is a kingdom rooted in fellowship and growing toward utopia.

To explore the problem of escape in *The Story of the Glittering Plain* and to examine the nature of love in *The Wood Beyond the World*, Morris synthesizes elements derived from his own psyche, the romance tradition, myth and its study, and socialist doctrine. Morris creates an especially powerful amalgam of these in *The Wood Beyond the World*. From his subconscious mind comes the projection of submerged parts of himself as benign and malign female figures. Reinforced by the experiences of his life, these figures emerge as images of the sexually unfaithful wife-mistress and the loving friend who becomes the ideal beloved. Following the tradition of medieval romance, in which life may be viewed as a quest for love, the same female figures are metamorphosed into those of the enchantress, who must be defeated and the maiden, who must be rescued and wed. Through the mythological and folkloric motives embedded in romance, the hero becomes the representative of the force, be it solar or cultural, which undergoes the processes of birth and death through an encounter with a dual-natured goddess who is the symbol of the earth. A successful encounter leads, in Morris's socialist view, to the hero's return to and rejuvenation of the ordinary world. Ideal erotic love helps forge an ideal world, for the integrated man can transform his private passion into acts of general benevolence.

Morris enriches these patterns, through variation and expansion, in the next of the romances, *The Well at the World's End*. No longer seeing the feminine components of the self in the form of two opposing figures, he creates a female character whose dichotomous nature incorporates the qualities of each. Developing his social theme, he broadens his focus to describe the rise, fall, and rebirth of a series of communities. Depicting an entire imaginary world, he demonstrates how the power of human love transforms both those who share it and the realms through which they pass.

II

Written between 1892 and 1894 and published in 1895, *The Well at the World's End,* Morris's most elaborate and detailed romance, is again structured as a bridequest. Beginning with the *enfance* of the hero and depicting his education through preliminary adventures and ordeals, the romance carefully develops the twofold pattern of a search: first, for an appropriate woman and the love she represents; second, for the secular grail of the well at the end of the world. The romance centers on the triumph of the hero once he has passed through temptation, a confrontation with death, and the experience of rebirth. Significantly, however, *The Well at the World's End* concentrates as much on the societal aspects of life as it does on the destinies of individuals, showing the hero's impact on his world after the integration of his personality. Filling a huge canvas, Morris shapes a myth about the connections between romantic love and communal fellowship and demonstrates how both are forces which can conquer evil and, thus, redeem the earth.

The characters and incidents in the romance are derived from such disparate sources as the Grimms and Frazer, the medieval romances of Alexander and of the holy grail, Celtic folklore, and contemporary adventure tales like Rider Haggard's *She.* While *The Well at the World's End* is not allegorical, it is a "romance of types,"[27] in which sections of pure narrative are interspersed with symbolic incidents and descriptions. A "stream of conscious symbolic intention" runs through the work,[28] as images of the inner life are projected by means of the exterior world. One of the main sources of the romance is autobiography; much of the inner life depicted in it is Morris's own—distilled into fiction. Like *News from Nowhere, The Well at the World's End* obliquely depicts Morris's feelings and experiences, here, his childhood joy, his somewhat aimless and frustrated youth, his rejection of the ministry, his call to social activism, and the problems of his twofold love: initially, for a fatal woman who brings both joy and sorrow; later, for a friend who becomes his love and finer spirit. Though Ralph, the hero of the romance, is a man all women love and, thus, something of a compensatory figure for Morris,[29] he displays a number of his creator's essential traits—bluntness, rapid shifts of mood, a passionate love of the world of nature, and a concern with political and economic justice.

Morris's own preoccupations with social evolution and revolution are embodied in Ralph's travels to various lands, many of them countries of the mind. Ralph moves from the pastoral world of Upmeads, modeled on Kelmscott Manor and its

Edward Burne-Jones, J. H. Dearle, and William Morris: *The Arming and Departure of the Knights of the Round Table on the Quest of the Holy Grail.* Tapestry of 1895–96. Second panel of the *San Graal* series designed by Burne-Jones for Morris & Company.

neighboring villages, through cities, the places of corruption which reflect Morris's hatred of Victorian London, through the realms of romance, the forest and the wasteland—the latter derived from the Iceland Morris perceived on his 1871 sojourn—and then to the place of reward, an Iceland transformed by the journey of 1873. Not content with depicting the attainment of the goal, Morris shows how Ralph, on his return trip to his home, witnesses or aids in the rejuvenation of the societies through which he passes.

Upmeads, Ralph's first and final home in this circular romance, is one of the most tenderly depicted of Morris's peaceable kingdoms. A medievalized Nowhere by which all other communities are measured, it is a land of simple living, firmly independent people, whose rulers have "but scant dominion save over their horses and dogs" (18:1). Although Ralph, leaving Upmeads in search of adventure, is attracted to Higham-on-the-Way because of its wealth, culture, and well developed guild system, he is repelled by its theocratic rule and by the priestly vocation itself. In terms reminiscent of Morris, Ralph observes that those who choose the church do so not because they find the world lacking, but because it finds them so. His rejection of Higham and priesthood lead him to the Wood Perilous, the green world threatened, and to the Burg of the Four Friths. A capitalistic tyranny built on slavery, the Burg exploits its female captives, the Wheat-wearers. These beautiful women lack all legal and personal rights and are forced to serve as laborers or are purchased as concubines. Yet, even the Burg's free citizens are not truly so; they cannot openly criticize their government or buy and bear weapons. Corrupted by the system under which they live, they resent Ralph's "manly bearing," "free tongue," and hatred of "cruel deeds and injustice" (18:90) and force him to flee the city.

Ralph next enters the magic realm of the Land of Abundance, a beautiful place of fertility and propagation, though one not devoid of their darker aspects. Abundance must be left behind, however, and, grieving at the loss of love, Ralph must confront the land of Whitewall. Imaginatively depicting England gone wrong, Morris shows how the countryside of Whitewall has been deformed. Ralph cannot even locate a yeoman's cottage or farmer's house; all dwellings are either the manorial estates of the rich or the foul slave barracks and "long rows of ugly hovels" of the impoverished laborers (18:253).[30] Goldburg, whose name connotes its dedication to Mammon as well as its role as the chief mercantile and commercial city of Whitewall, is still more diseased. In a city that is "half marble and half slums,"[31] the sumptuous houses of the rich are juxtaposed with the miserable hovels of the poor, while the "two nations" live in mutual enmity. The poor lack even the care that Carlyle's Garth the thrall received from Cedric the Saxon:

> they belonged not to a master, who must at worst feed them, and to no manor, whose acres they might till for their livelihood, and on whose pastures they might feed their cattle; nor had they any to help or sustain them against the oppressor and the violent man; so that they toiled and swinked and died with none heeding them, save that they had the work of their hands good cheap; and they forsooth heeded them less than their draught beasts whom they must needs buy with money, and whose bellies they must needs fill; whereas these poor wretches were slaves without a price, and if one died another took his place on the chance that thereby he might escape present death by hunger, for there was a great many of them.
>
> (18:261–62)

Ruled by an ineffectual queen, perhaps a Morrisian caricature of Victoria in medieval dress, Goldburg encourages commercial anarchy, the exploitation of labor, and the inhumane treatment of the poor. While Whitewall embodies the worst corruptions of the civilized world, it also marks its terminus, and Ralph leaves Christian and feudal realms to journey back into history.

One of his first encounters in the uncharted lands beyond Whitewall is with a group of living barbarians, the vigorous Kindred of the Bull. The members of this gens are pagans who dwell in the hidden places of the fell, worshipping their ancestral totem and the forefathers of their clan. In the tradition of "upper barbarism," they follow a blood code and adopt worthy aliens into their tribe. But they are slavers, and Ralph must later wean them from this vice. In selling Ralph as a slave in Utterbol, they bring him into a city resembling the early despotisms Morris and Bax had described in *Socialism*.[32] Ralph escapes from Utterbol and, after adventures in a supernatural wilderness, is finally succoured by the Innocent Folk. They are the people of the age of gold. Dressed in wool and feathers, ignorant of iron, they are noble savages who live in peace and harmony and neither need nor desire the water of the Well at the World's End. As they tell Ralph:

> ye of the World beyond the Mountains are stronger and more godlike than we, as all tales tell; and ye wear away your lives desiring that which ye may scarce get; and ye set your hearts on high things, desiring to be

masters of the very Gods. Therefore ye know sickness and sorrow, and oft ye die before your time, so that ye must depart and leave undone things which ye deem ye were born to do; which to all men is grievous. And because of all this ye desire healing and thriving. . . . Therefore ye do but right to seek to the Well at the World's End.

(19:66)

The Innocent Folk are the last human beings Ralph encounters; the earliest children of the earth, they partake of the spirit of the golden age and of the nature of the prelapsarian realm of the Well, at which Ralph finally arrives.

The lands through which Ralph travels function both as cultural and historical symbols and as images of Ralph's psychological transformation. They and the people who live within them indicate stages in Ralph's life journey. When, for example, Ralph leaves home and childhood behind, he enters the Wood Perilous, the world of uncertain but exciting growth. There he first meets Ursula,[33] the anima he is not mature enough to recognize, and the Lady of Abundance, an incarnation of the mother of the earth.

The Lady, connected by her title and attributes to Frazer's corn goddess and the Grimms' *domina Abundia*,[34] rules both the region of the Dry Tree and the fecund Land of Abundance. The Lady's paradoxical nature is manifested by more than the differing characteristics of her two provinces. Though the folk of the Land of Abundance believe that "when she came . . . increase became more plenteous" (19:152), other peoples see her as "devil" and "mahmet" (18:69), "the evilest woman who ever spat upon the blessed Host of the Altar" (18:81). The Lady is an embodiment of the Great Mother, a personification of the earth in all its aspects. "From her hands goeth all healing" (18:137), but also the inadvertent destruction of men and their kingdoms. The Lady is seen as creator and destroyer, enemy and kindly guide, mother and harlot. Although she is wed to the Knight of the Sun, she freely gives herself to Ralph; her actions, like the processes of fertility, are unconditioned by the usual morality.

Morris's Lady of Abundance is somewhat reminiscent of Rider Haggard's She, in the popular romance of the same name. Like She-who-must-be-obeyed, the Lady is feared and hated by most women but fatally charming to all men. Protected from change and age by the magic of the Well, she has lived long past the ordinary span of life. "Lovely as no woman was lovely or ever had been,"[35] she is loved by the Black Knight, the Chief of the Dry Tree, and the Knight of the Sun, yet causes the demise of each. But she does no injury to Ralph, who, like Leo Vincy in Haggard's tale, is the handsome man all women love. Like Leo, Ralph, despite his passion, has an unsettling sense of his beloved's power and mystery. When he asks her if she is good or evil, she replies: "whatsoever I have been, I am good to thee" (18:145), thus evading, while answering, his question. Ralph's illicit sexual union with the Lady is described by Morris, in startlingly Laurentian terms,[36] as utterly fulfilling:

He drew her down to him as he knelt there, and took his arms about her, and though she yet shrunk from him a little and the eager flame of his love, he might not be gainsayed, and she gave herself to him and let her body glide into his arms, and loved him no less than he loved her.

(18:145)

Initiating the hero into love and manhood, the Lady tells him of her past, in which she has been victim and victimizer both, and indicates the nature of the future life he is to lead. Through an act provoked by her fatal beauty, the Lady is slain, but, like the corn goddess and the fertile grain, she dies to be reborn in a new form. Although Ralph grieves for her, he senses that she is not the mate intended for him and learns that he must move beyond the memory of her.

Only after he has left the Land of Abundance is Ralph prepared to begin his quest. *Enfance* and first love are behind him, and he is now ready to recognize the woman who is his soul. She is Ursula, named after the saint who is "the Friend of Maidens" (19:14), and a fully mortal "sending" of the Lady of Abundance. Frank, courageous, and natural, a child of the woodlands which bore her, Ursula incarnates only the benevolent aspects of the Great Mother. Like Ellen in *News from Nowhere*, whom she resembles in body and spirit, she is the Jungian anima in all her positive attributes. Kidnapped and enslaved in Utterbol—a hell on earth that is a metaphor for the life of lust and violence on the outmost promontory of existence—she is capable of evading the desire of its rapacious lord and of engineering her own escape. When she joins Ralph, himself endangered by the lord of Utterbol's determination to castrate him, she becomes the hero's sworn companion on the quest. As Ralph's friend—for their love begins as friendship—she aids in his plans and deeds. As his anima, she senses and responds to the inner workings of his mind. As his guide, she leads him through all barriers to the well of life, herself unprotected by the talisman she wears.

In the finest section of the romance, "The Road to the Well at the World's End," Morris's use of symbolic landscape illuminates

Ralph's gradual transformation: the death of his old egocentric self, the birth of an altruistic identity, and the integration of the personality. Ralph and Ursula are initially educated and purified in preparation for their perilous journey by the Sage of Swedenham, the wise old man of romance. Accompanied by the Sage, who takes them as far as he may go, the couple undergo a test of courage and endurance as they traverse the barren Sea of Molten Rock, modeled on an Icelandic lava sea, and pause beside the statue of "The Fighting Man," a figure carved from living rock and an emblem of dedication to a life of deeds, which guards the passage to an unknown world. Then, bidding farewell to their teacher, they enter the pass, the long and narrow way to a new world and life. Spending fall and winter within its confines, they emerge from the pass in the spring to find themselves, appropriately, within the land of the Innocent Folk. There, they become one flesh. Sexually united, they are ready to undertake their last symbolic trial—the journey through the Thirsty Desert to the Dry Tree.

Ralph has read of the Dry Tree, for he is cognizant of the deeds of Alexander the Great, who, according to medieval romance, had been to see it.[37] But neither he nor Ursula is prepared for its horrors or for those of the barren wasteland they must cross to reach the Tree. Entering the desert of negation whose sands are strewn with desiccated corpses, they look upon the remains of those who have sought and failed, of those dead of their frustration and despair:

> So came they to the brow and looked over it into a valley, about which on all sides went the ridge, save where it was broken down into a narrow pass on the further side, so that the said valley was like to one of those theatres of the ancient Roman Folk, whereof are some to be seen in certain lands. Neither did those desert benches lack their sitters; for all down the sides of the valley sat or lay children of men; some women, but most men-folk, of whom the most part were weaponed, and some with their drawn swords in their hands. Whatever semblance of moving was in them was when the eddying wind of the valley stirred the rags of their raiment, or the long hair of the women.
>
> (19:73)

Finally, Ralph and Ursula confront the Dry Tree—an image of death itself:

> But a very midmost of this dreary theatre rose up a huge and monstrous tree, whose topmost branches were even the horns which they had seen from below the hill's brow. Leafless was that tree and lacking of twigs,

and its bole upheld but some fifty of great limbs, and as they looked on it, they doubted whether it were not made by men's hands rather than grown up out of the earth. All round about the roots of it was a pool of clear water, that cast back the image of the valley-side and the bright sky of the desert, as though it had been a mirror of burnished steel.

(19:73)

Death's other kingdom is before them: the dead who, like the mummified corpses in *The Earthly Paradise*, ironically appear alive in death, the water which, though clear, is poisonous, and the Tree itself, a perversion of the force of life from which it sprang. Leafless, twigless, barren, death's trophies hung upon its rigid boughs, it is the Tree of Life transformed into the Tree of Death. With burning cheeks and sparkling eyes, the lovers go to investigate its mysteries. Although they see that "each of the dead leathery faces [of its victims] was drawn up in a grin, as though they had died in pain and yet beguiled" (19:74), they are unaware of their own enthrallment. Ursula first prevents Ralph's destruction by noticing that although the wind blows, the water surrounding the Tree remains unrippled and, thus, according to medieval lore, is poisoned. Subduing her own attraction to death, she next saves Ralph from his desire to die by pretending that a more heroic doom awaits him in the form of horsemen waiting to attack. Functioning as his anima, Ursula rescues Ralph from his temptation by death, and, having successfully confronted the specter, the two lovers may traverse the remainder of the Thirsty Desert. When they cross the Wall of the World, a range of mountains based on those Morris saw in Iceland, they find themselves in a small valley filled with living trees and intersected by a flowing river—a memory of the peaceful spots that Morris found on his return to the Icelandic world. At the edge of the sea, they find the Well. At last, they are fully ready to drink of the water of life.

The Well at which they do so is pagan. Their quest for it has been condemned by a priest as "a memory of the customs of the ancient gentiles and heathens" (18:214), and the talisman that each wears, though derived from Sarras, the city of the Christian Grail, may not be blessed or exchanged for a rosary. The rituals necessary to prepare them for their quest include pagan rites of purification, the wearing of toga-like garments, and the study of ancient books which must be pursued in the groves where the old gods of earth were worshipped. Even the sign of the quest which is carved on rocks and trees, found in the wasteland, and marked on the sacred Well, is the ancient pagan emblem of a sword crossed by a three-leaved bough. A symbol known only to initiates, it is the Golden Bough of the *Aeneid* and, possibly, of Frazer's book.

The Well itself has the properties of the many Irish wells that confer the blessings of wisdom or eternal youth; its description is derived from O'Curry's account of Connla's Well, O'Grady's passage on the fountain of youth located at Slieve Gullian, and Lady Wilde's depiction of St. Seenon's Well, whose curative waters run close to the sea but remain untouched by salt.[38] In Morris's romance, however, the Well is clearly a new and secular grail to be enjoyed by humanists. It does not grant men physical immortality—an ignoble goal to Morris—but it offers long and happy life devoid of sorrow, weariness, and sickness. It is a fountain of love; to Ursula, its water tastes as if Ralph's "love were blended with it" (19:83). A spring of wisdom, it enables those who drink to see into the life of things, offering them "the Clearing of the Eyes that they might behold" (18:168). Its symbol, the interwoven sword and bough, is the sign of its ability to integrate the human personality, but for an end beyond the merely personal.

When Ralph and Ursula drink the water of the Well they experience a brief epiphany and fall into a profound sleep. Their physical regeneration manifests itself when, after their immersion in the sea, they discover that their scars and blemishes have vanished; the merging and regeneration of their spirits is demonstrated by their sense of oneness, their ability to love each other totally. Because "they are one which were twain,"

> The Tree bloometh again,
> And the Well-spring hath come
> From the waste to the home.
>
> (19:196)

The Well's gifts of wisdom, love, and wholeness will help them redeem the societies through which they pass. As the Tree of Death becomes the Tree of Life, the water of goodness and fellowship, which is no longer inaccessible to men, begins to irrigate the entire created world.

Thus, Morris indicates how the integration of the personality leads naturally to the betterment of society. When Ralph drinks the Well's waters, he does not toast either himself or his beloved, but "the Earth and the World of Manfolk" (19:83). In drinking of the Well, Ralph knowingly assumes a responsibility to society, for its waters are only for those who love the earth and its inhabitants. The Well carries with its gifts the obligations to "be the friends of men," to "succour the oppressed," and to create a better world, thus bringing "Heaven to the Earth for a little while" (19:36). Ralph willingly accepts his duty to "serve . . . [his] fellows and deliver them from the thralldom of those that be strong and unwise and unkind" (19:66). Now leading Ursula, he and his beloved both directly and obliquely aid in reforming the corrupt and blighted regions through which they had previously passed. They arrive at Utterbol to find that Bull Shockhead, the barbarian they have reformed, has conquered it and eliminated its cruel and decadent practices. They discover that Goldburg and the land of Whitewall have improved, for, driven by her unrequited love for Ralph, the Queen of Whitewall has either fled or killed herself. A successful revolution, helped by Ralph, makes the Burg of the Four Friths a free land. The Wheat-wearers and the Men of the Dry Tree have captured the city and banished its old masters. The two groups, united in marriage, will generate a new and uncorrupted people. The Kindred of the Bull, the Men of the Dry Tree, and the Shepherds—a semi-barbaric people who remember their ancient customs and their descent from a clan of the Bear (perhaps from the old savage tribe depicted in *The Wood Beyond the World*) join with Ralph to help him free his threatened homeland.[39]

Thus, the end of the romance demonstrates that the product of an integrated personality is the liberation of others and the development of fellowship with them. Ralph and Ursula return to a life of dedication within Ralph's small realm filled with the power, wisdom, and love to revitalize and live purposively within their world. "They have learned to love the world almost as abundantly as they love each other, almost as naturally as they love themselves."[40]

In all, *The Well at the World's End* represents both the fruition of Morris's consciously held views of what constitutes the correct life in this world—ideas that he had suggested in his two previous romances and in *News from Nowhere*—and the flowering of Morris's less conscious examination of his past inner history. In symbolically recounting the experiences of his life, Morris depicts his gradual acceptance of the flaws in his love relationships and of the fate that seemingly ordains that one must suffer on the road to wisdom. Accepting his fears of physical extinction and psychic paralysis, he vividly describes—through a quest in which he imaginatively relives his two Icelandic journeys—both the dark night of the soul and the dawn which he now knows will follow it. Moreover, accepting the destructive power of passion, he explores his infatuation with the dark anima, both as a projection of the self and a figure for the faithless but alluring mistress-wife. Significantly, when the Lady of Abundance dies, the writer who created her is born again. The figure of the *femme fatale* is put to rest and although there are enchantresses in the remaining works, they are grotesque or sexually unappealing characters whose power is never really felt as menacing. Even the Lady, though seen as dichotomous in nature, is not perceived as intentionally malevolent. Rather, she is a necessary tutor, an essential predecessor of the woman who will be the soul and rightful partner of the integrated man. In the same vein, Morris no longer sees romantic love and social fellowship as separate or opposing forces. Instead, he carefully delineates the process by which passion generates the fellowship of all and shows how the two forces can work together to create more truly human lives within a fully humane world. Thus, Morris's examination of the truths of existence becomes, for him, purgation leading to a sense of renewed life. The joyous ending of *The Well at the World's End* marks the imaginative flowering of Morris as a writer of romances; his two final works of fiction continue the celebration of good and joyous life, paradoxically carrying Morris both further from the ordinary world and nearer to its essence.

III

Morris's death in 1896 cut short his experimentation in the genre of romance, yet his last two works, *The Water of the Wondrous Isles* and *The Sundering Flood*, suggest new insights in his exploration of his inner being. Both romances, issued posthumously in 1897, are works of acceptance, in which Morris either treats ideas he had not earlier developed or comes to terms with problems he had not resolved in a hitherto satisfactory manner. The last romance, *The Sundering Flood*, closely analyzes the *enfance* of the hero, a period of human development Morris had only previously sketched even in the vast *Well at the World's End*. *The Water of the Wondrous Isles*, Morris's sole prose romance treating the adventures of a female hero, is a symbolic and psychological study of the development and maturation of the anima. In delineating the figure of Birdalone—derived from Psyche in *The Earthly Paradise* and the most convincing portrait of a woman since Guenevere—Morris concentrates on the feminine aspects of the self, thus exploring and liberating his unconscious feelings. In the process, he resolves the problem of the triangle of love.

The controlling idea of *The Water of the Wondrous Isles*, that of a young woman embarking on a quest for selfhood, love, and wisdom, was clearly important to Morris. He had written and discarded three earlier partial drafts of the romance,[41] but despite a tendency to abandon works which caused him undue difficulty, he continually returned to the concept and the problems it presented. In 1895, the year before his death, he found an appropriate vehicle for his theme and apparently became emotionally free enough to utilize it. The romance, unpolished in language but complete in plan and structure, is his most symbolic work. Unique among the prose romances, yet arising naturally from the reconciliation with the female aspects of the self indicated in *The Well at the World's End*, *The Water of the Wondrous Isles* begins where Morris's other romances end.

Birdalone, whose name denotes both her isolated condition and her nature as the soul, embarks on a search for freedom and identity. The quest again involves the call to adventure, the perilous journey, the period of trial and purgation, the eventual union with the beloved—this time in the guise of a fulfilling husband—and the return to fellowship with others. Birdalone's initial adventures, identical with the experiences described by the Lady of Abundance, include enslavement and torture by a witch who has kidnapped her in hopes of raising her to lure and destroy men.[42] Like the Lady of Abundance, Birdalone is educated and helped to free herself by a wise and kindly surrogate mother, here a supernatural being called Habundia. Habundia, whose name means "lady of abundance," is the wise woman of the romance tradition. She is also a goddess of plenty who bestows prosperity and blessings upon the mortals who obey her. Her name may be derived from that of Dame Habond in *The Romance of the Rose*, but her essential characteristics are those of the *domina Abundia* as delineated by the brothers Grimm in their *Teutonic Mythology*. Believing that all female deities were one and their names merely different titles for various aspects of a primal earth and mother goddess, the brothers Grimm identify the *domina Abundia* as another form of Diana, Venus, and the German goddess, Folla. Like the Grimms, Morris characterizes Habundia as an essentially benevolent deity who is, however, limited in power and in domain. She is a wood-mother or wood-wife who rules lesser deities within a forest and who may enter man-made dwellings only at her own peril.[43] Linking her to both external nature and the human spirit, Morris makes her the guide and tutor of the female hero. Her physical appearance is that of Birdalone's identical twin, a mirror of the self; her spiritual powers are those of guiding and informing the hero's conscience and intelligence. As a nature spirit, Habundia teaches Birdalone the lore of earth; as an alter-ego, she teaches Birdalone about herself. Herself unchanging, she can, nevertheless, educate Birdalone about change. But, because she cannot feel or understand erotic passion, she cannot totally prepare the female hero for the journey to maturity.

The quest upon which Birdalone embarks derives its imagery from Spenser's *Faerie Queene*, from Celtic *imrama* or voyage myths—such as those of Maildun or Mannanan's Canoe—from Richard Jefferies' *After London*, and from Morris's Icelandic journey of 1873. More important, the quest symbolically depicts the major phases of the journey that is life. Naked, in token of the infancy of her experience, Birdalone enters a magic Sending Boat, which, like Phaedria's bark in *The Faerie Queene*, glides without any visible means of propulsion through a vast lake—a transmutation of Grimmtaþir, the Icelandic tarn which Morris had described in his 1873 journal—and stops at sundry islands. Birdalone disembarks first at the Isle of Increase Unsought, a land like Phaedria's, where, controlled by a sorceress, the earth thrives without man's "toilsome paines."[44] A false earthly paradise, the island is ruled by a witch who is a sister both to Birdalone's wicked mistress and to such grotesque folklore figures as the witch, Rapunzel, in Morris's early poem. The Isle of Increase Unsought is a travesty of natural growth both in terms of external environment and of human development[45]; a place in which increase is unearned by labor, and disorder and exploitation appear initially attractive, it is simultaneously the fantasy world of the child, filled with imaginary terrors and products. The nature of the three "real" maidens, Aurea, Viridis, and Atra, who are prisoners on the island remains unclear, though each is associated with the symbolism of the color after which she is named.[46] However, the maidens' function in the romance is obvious; unable to free themselves, they enable Birdalone to free them and, thus, define her quest.

Before Birdalone can achieve her goal, she must encounter the perils of the remaining Wondrous Isles, lands whose mystery links them to the islands visited by Maildun or the Sons of Corra.[47] All are realms where natural growth is lacking or perverted; all seem to symbolize arrested phases of human development. The Isle of the Young and Old is an isle of no increase, devoid of all forms of maturity. Its sole inhabitants are two children, trapped in an eternal childhood, and an ancient, senile man. The mirror isles of Kings and Queens are realms of sterility, in which love and violence have been enshrined by death. In imagery reminiscent of that of *The Earthly Paradise*, the dead knights of the Isle of Queens are ringed, as if alive, around their royal mistress; the maidens of the Isle of Kings surround the monarch who has slain her, and both Queen and King are sleeping beauties who will not awaken. After leaving their realms of destructive passion, Birdalone next confronts death itself, symbolized by the Isle of Nothing. A wasteland, veiled in fogs like the pestilent London in Richard Jefferies' *After London*,[48] the island brings destruction to all who land upon its shores. Lost in its perilous mists and theatened by despair, Birdalone must call upon Habundia's supernatural aid. Once she has received it, she may reach the mainland and the Castle of the Quest.

Although Birdalone's childhood and initiation are completed, she has not yet reached maturity. Mortal and fallible, she has still to learn of human love. Her trials, as indicated in the fourth section of the romance, "Of the Days of Abiding," include the difficult feats of learning to accept, abide, and suffer. When Birdalone and Arthur, the Black Squire betrothed to Atra, fall in love, they must deal with a painful triangle of passion. Atra knows that Arthur loves another, but she cannot gracefully relinquish him. Birdalone, in turn, suffers the guilt of knowing that she must hurt her female friend and of realizing that she causes Arthur to experience a conflict between passion and a sense of obligation. The situation is not resolved by the death of the less sympathetic female rival, as it is in *The Wood Beyond the World* and *The Well at the World's End*, nor by the pairing off of the rejected woman with a new lover, as in *The Roots of the Mountains*. Instead, Atra's initial bitterness fades with time and she comes to terms with her rejection.

In the interim, however, Birdalone's desire to do but not to suffer—her lack of patience and endurance—lead to pain for all. Too eager to act, Birdalone is responsible for the murder of a knight who meets and kidnaps her and for the death of Aurea's beloved, the Gold Knight. Banishing herself to the City of the Five Crafts, she begins the process of regeneration through self-sacrifice and patient labor. Significantly, her death to egoism and rebirth to altruism is neither magical nor external in causation. Instead, in becoming a master embroideress, Birdalone finds consolation in creation, making works that are both beautiful and useful, and in sharing the rewards of her labor with those she employs. She gains an additional sense of identity and worth by finding her biological mother and devoting herself to caring for her needs. After five years have passed, Birdalone is ready to

resume her voyage. Called by a vision of Arthur and in need of the
aid which Habundia can offer, she embarks upon a second
journey which completes her maturation.

Birdalone again passes through the Wondrous Isles and finds
them, like her inner being, changed and ripened. The Isle of
Nothing, no longer a place of death, has become a young and
fertile land filled with the spirit of the golden age. Its inhabitants
are innocent folk who worship Birdalone as their founding deity
and civilizing power, an Isis who has come to bless them and then
mysteriously departed. The isles of Kings and Queens, though
still imperfect, are now filled with life and house the reborn
knights and maidens who attended the dead rulers. The young
men and women, directed by their impulses of desire, are destined
to locate each other and to generate a fresh, new race. The Isle of
Young and Old has also undergone a transformation; its aged
man has died, its children have matured, and its population has
magically increased. In all, the power that thwarted normal
growth has been vanquished. Only the Isle of Increase Unsought,
the realm of the sorceress, has declined. Its false fertility destroyed,
it has become a wasteland which Birdalone must cross. Naked
and hungry, she swims from its shore back to the home from
which she came. Her swim, a rite of purification and a final
indication of her rebirth, marks the last step in her maturation.
Fully loving and humanly perfect, she is ready to first heal and
then unite with Arthur.[49]

When Birdalone and Arthur consummate their love, creating a
new integrated self, they bring their fruitful union back into the
world. Gathering their friends together, they build in Utterhay—
a place near the wood where Birdalone was born—an ideal community of fellowship. Atra is among its members and she neither
dies nor comes to love and wed a man other than Arthur. Instead,
she becomes a friend to the married lovers and a participant in the
communal joys of a utopia, deriving her solace and pleasure from
labor, nature, and the friendship of Habundia: aspects of life
different from but equally as important as erotic passion.

In *The Water of the Wondrous Isles*, Morris reviews and completes a number of recurrent thematic patterns. Again exploring
the triangle of love, he accepts but ceases to concentrate upon its
painfulness, and stresses, instead, the ways in which the human
beings involved may deal with it. He postulates a Nowhere in
which frustrated love is sublimated into useful personal and
social action. No longer separating the figure of the fertile
woman who represents the creative and destructive aspects of the
earth into two opposing images, he does not see the force as

supernatural in essence. Instead, he envisions Birdalone as entirely mortal, incorporating within herself all aspects of the world of nature; she is the last, most fully realized of all the "sendings" of the Lady of Abundance. Moreover, Morris no longer divides the female aspects of the self into distinct projections of the dark and fatal or the white and pure animas. In Birdalone, capable of both good and evil, courageous but fallible in thought and deed, Morris creates a believably human female and hero. Equally important, he depicts the death of the egocentric self and the birth of the altruistic spirit not as sudden or miraculous events but as results of self-examination, patient labor, and a life of service to others. *The Water of the Wondrous Isles*, the most fantastic and privately symbolic of the last romances becomes, paradoxically, the site of Morris's most profound examination of the ways in which the individual can change, develop, and mature.

As the depiction of the development and integration of Birdalone is the focal point of *The Water of the Wondrous Isles*, so the growth of Osberne is the main theme of *The Sundering Flood*. Morris's final romance is incomplete and unrevised, yet its very bareness and lack of polish reveal the new directions in which Morris's mind was turning. *The Sundering Flood* is Scandinavian in inspiration, folkloric rather than mythic in tone, and realistic rather than symbolic or "typical" in atmosphere and incident. Morris derived the romance's controlling motif, that of two lovers divided by a great river, from an Icelandic novel and its beginning, an account of the childhood love of Osberne and Elfhild, from Bjørnstjerne Bjørnson's *Synnøve Solbakken*. Again returning to the Norse materials he knew so well, Morris drew from them much of the tone and spirit of his romance.[50]

Thus, reutilizing the same mythic construct he had employed in *The Water of the Wondrous Isles*, Morris created a considerably different effect. Again, the romance is patterned on the quest whose object is the bride and the maturity and wholeness which are represented by a union with her. Again, the hero is aided in preparing for his journey by a kindly supernatural guardian. This time the figure is called Steelhead; not subject to change or death, he is a tribal barbarian ancestor garbed in human form who is a wise, benevolent foster father to the orphaned Osberne.[51] Like Habundia, he is the giver of magic gifts as well as the hero's teacher and the voice of his conscience.

After receiving the education that Steelhead provides, Osberne undergoes initiation, chiefly through a perilous journey. Once again, his reward is the winning of the rightful bride, the integration of the self, and the return to a life of fellowship in a simple, pastoral home. Yet, the adventures of Osberne lack both overt allegory and symbolic complexity. Instead, Morris's emphasis is on a closely observed analysis of human growth, the tracing of Osberne's emotional and sexual maturation from childhood to adulthood.

The most richly developed section of *The Sundering Flood* is the account of the youth of the hero. Perhaps Morris intended to elaborate more fully upon the adventures of Osberne's adulthood, but, cut off by death, could not complete his plan. However, he carefully depicted the childhood of the hero and his beloved through a series of incidents derived from *Synnøve Solbakken*.[52] While Elfhild is Morris's now familiar joyous child of nature and Osberne's anima, Osberne is the child as hero, slaying savage wolves like the young Sigmund and defeating Hardcastle, the adult champion and bully. The romance describes the growth of Osberne's fortitude and courage, and, equally important, the development of his adolescent sexuality and tenderness: how he first looks upon Elfhild as a childhood playmate, how he comes to be attracted to her, and how, awakened by an older, more accessible woman, he begins to suffer the pangs of desire. Osberne's shooting of gifts to Elfhild across the river that divides them is not, as Northrop Frye believes, an act filled with unconscious sexual symbolism, but one of which the implications are clear to both Osberne and Morris. Osberne's gifts are the first fruits of his yearning to embrace his sweetheart; he acknowledges them as a sublimation of his wish.[53] As he matures, his longing for Elfhild strengthens, and it is when he has decided to try to cross the river that she is kidnapped. Once again, the hero must go in search of the enslaved anima; again, he must be initiated into adult life before he may find and free her. In *The Sundering Flood*, however, the hero does not go to worlds beyond his world, but to the more usual realms of men.

Assuming the benevolence of fate and thus placing himself "in the hands of Weird, to wend as she will have me" (21:142), Osberne visits human societies and participates in their struggles. Although his experiences are sketched rather than developed or explained, many deal with his education in fellowship; his tests involve the learning of the correct political and social attitudes toward other human beings. Coming to understand the spirit of social equality, he refuses to accept a knighthood. Teaching others the spirit of political and economic justice, he aids the Lesser Craft Guilds in their formation of a socialist society in the City of the Sundering Flood.[54] He becomes a champion of the weak and oppressed, a man who has, in effect, drunk of the Well at the World's End and is, therefore, without the need for personal aggrandizement or power. Once he has shown his merit and demonstrated his desire to serve society, he is permitted to unite with his beloved. Suddenly, if inexplicably, the dividing river, symbolizing the psychological and sexual barriers which prevent the lovers' union, may be crossed. Osberne and Elfhild return together to their simple Northern home to live a life of love and fellowship with those around them.

Through his two final romances, Morris unconsciously indicates the reintegration of his own personality. *The Water of the Wondrous Isles*, Morris's myth of the anima, is his remotest and deepest fantasy, focusing on what he had hitherto only implied, beginning where he had previously ended. When Morris depicts the female spirit—free, kind, and loving—returning from her journey to a world beyond the world and uniting with a man who has failed and suffered but has been restored to wisdom and humaneness, he has completed his own long quest. Thus, circling home—in the pattern he had established for the heroes of all the last romances—he returns to a more ordinary world. *The Sundering Flood*, his final romance, becomes a somewhat "unromantic" work, one which derives its adventures from experience within the norm, its atmosphere from the depiction of reality, and its strength from the analysis of growth and change in character.

In yet another sense, the romances of the 1890s, *The Glittering Plain*, *The Wood Beyond the World*, *The Well at the World's End*, *The Water of the Wondrous Isles*, and *The Sundering Flood*, mark Morris's last journey and return, for they recapitulate and distill the forms and themes of his first published works, the prose tales of the 1850s. Linked by the employment of the *topoi* and generic structure of romance and by a set of common themes, the two groups of works use similar materials for different ends. The early prose romances pose the problems—those of frustrated love, the triangle of passion, the proper roles of the heroic man and of the woman who is his soul, the consummation or destruction wrought by death—but they resolve these tragically, finding solutions solely in an afterlife or in another world. The late romances postulate a realm in which these problems may be faced, accepted, and comedically resolved. Constituting a holistic vision of life within a full and variegated world, they interweave—at last—the many strands of Morris's protean thought and work. Not only do they demonstrate his movement from a fragmented view of self and an uneasy mental dialectic to a new synthesis of integrated thought and psychic wholeness, but they also incorporate, without pyrotechnics or overt polemics, the many aspects of Morris's being. In the romances of the 1890s, Morris manifests his care for the art and all the useful crafts of man, his interest in the mythic and folkloric pasts that still inform the human spirit, and his deep love of earth. He fuses with these his abiding certainty that men can join in fellowship and that, reborn through socialism, the spirit of the golden age shall thrive.

As a whole, the last romances show how Morris gradually evolved the vision that led William Butler Yeats to describe him as "the happiest of poets." Coming to an inner comprehension of the "perfect fullness of natural life,"[55] Morris sees human love as only one of its components. No longer troubled by the imperfections and the pains of eros, he neither degrades nor excessively idealizes romantic passion. His imagination liberated, Morris vividly depicts both lust and the ambiguous and fatal power of the dark anima, but he has overcome his obsession with them, laying them to rest in *The Well at the World's End*. He ceases to reiterate the theme of two men trapped by love for the same woman and credibly resolves its obverse in *The Water of the Wondrous Isles*. In all, Morris comes to see erotic passion not as man's major goal but as simply one part of his natural fulfillment. He implies that each soul's quest is not for what is unattainable in either a love-object or the world but for those elements within the self which make one lovable and loving. He indicates, as well, that personal romantic love is not opposed to but a necessary step in human progress toward a love for all one's fellows.

Morris ceases to envision fate as an indifferent or malevolent force. In terms of groups and societies, destiny becomes Marx's historical process, optimistically perceived and mythically rendered. Corrupt societies are fated to fall, new groups to rise and prosper; men of good will are destined to unite in justice and equality. Some individuals are, indeed, more fortunate than others, but human beings, basically good if not corrupted by their social systems, can and do make their own fates. They may choose or refuse to strive, and they are free to act in either righteous or wrongful ways. For all, change is the sign and law of life. To accept it as one does the cycle of the world of nature is to live the way man should.

Death, examined and acceded to in the romances of the 1880s, is not a major issue in the works of Morris's last years. When it is timely and peaceful, death is assented to as an essential, positive return to earth, a final step in merging with the world. When it is cruel or unexpected, it is accepted as a natural phenomenon which must be borne. The point of man's existence is to live "without shame" and die "without fear" (20:387). No longer seeking immortality through earthly paradises, both Morris and the heroes of the last romances strive to make a paradise of earth.

Thus, in the romances of the 1890s, Morris offers his readers convincing embodiments of the vision he had hoped to see during the period of his personal anguish. Affirming the belief that he had stated in a letter written in the 1870s, "that life is not empty nor made for nothing, and that the parts of it fit one into another in some way; and that the world goes on, beautiful and strange and dreadful and worshipful,"[56] he creates a series of last literary works that richly celebrate the life and world of man.

APPENDIX

"Lonely Love and Loveless Death," *A Book of Verse*,
pp. 44–46.

O HAVE I been hearkening
To some dread new-comer?
What chain is it bindeth
What curse is anigh,
That the World is a-darkening
Amidmost the summer,
That the soft sunset blindeth
And Death standeth by?

Doth it wane, is it going,
Is it gone by forever,
The life that seemed round me
The longing I sought?
Has it turned to undoing
That constant endeavour
To bind love that bound me
To hold all it brought?

I beheld till beholding
Grew pain thrice told over;
I hearkened till hearing
Grew woe beyond speech;
I dreamed of enfolding
Arms blessing the lover
Till the dream past all bearing
The dark void did reach.

Beaten back, ever smitten
By pains that none knoweth
Did love ever languish
Did hope ever die?
I know not, but litten
By the light that love showeth
I beheld her through anguish
Never lost, never nigh.

191

I know not: but never
The day was without her,
I know not; but morning
Still woke me to her;
The miles that might sever
All faces about her
Weary days, and self-scorning
Ah easy to bear!

Look back, while grown colder
The sunless day lingers,
And the tree-tops are stirring
With the last wind of day—
If thou didst behold her
If thine hand touched her fingers
If her breath thou wert hearing
What words wouldst thou say?

Words meet for the hearkening
Of Death, the new-comer,
For the new bond that bindeth,
The new pain anigh:
For the World is a-darkening
Amidmost the summer,
Death sickeneth and blindeth
No love standeth by.

NOTES

INTRODUCTION

1. Peter Floud, "Dating Morris Patterns," *The Architectural Review* 126 (1959) :14–20.
2. E. P. Thompson, *William Morris: Romantic to Revolutionary*, rev. ed. (London: Merlin Press, 1979), p. 273, pp. 784–87.
3. Northrop Frye, *Anatomy of Criticism: Four Essays* (Princeton: Princeton University Press, 1957), p. 305.
4. Ibid., p. 187.

1 THE HOLLOW LAND

1. William Morris, *The Collected Works of William Morris*, ed. May Morris, 24 vols. (London: Longmans, Green, 1910–15), 1:60. All further references to the *Collected Works* appear in the text and are cited by volume and page numbers.
2. James D. Merrit, ed., *The Pre-Raphaelite Poem* (New York: Dutton, 1966), p. 11.
3. John Dixon Hunt, "A Moment's Monument: Reflections on Pre-Raphaelite Vision in Poetry and Painting," in *Pre-Raphaelitism: A Collection of Critical Essays*, ed. James Sambrook (Chicago: University of Chicago Press, 1974), p. 252.
4. J[ohn] W. Mackail, *The Life of William Morris*, 2 vols. (London: Longmans, Green, 1899), 1:63 (hereafter cited as *Life*). Mackail quotes a letter written in 1853 by Edward Burne-Jones.
5. See Mackail, *Life*, 1:92, for a list of Morris's contributions to the magazine.
6. Benjamin Thorpe, *Northern Mythology*, 3 vols. (London: E. Lumley, 1851–52), 2:14–15.
7. R. C. Ellison, "'The Undying Glory of Dreams': William Morris and the 'Northland of Old,'" in *Victorian Poetry*, Stratford-upon-Avon Studies, no. 15 (London: Edward Arnold, 1972), p. 143.
8. Cf. the ending of "The Fall of the House of Usher": ". . . there was a long tumultuous shouting sound like the voice of a thousand waters—and the deep and dank tarn at my feet closed sullenly and silently over the fragments of the *House of Usher*" (*The Complete Poems*

and Tales of Edgar Allan Poe, [New York: Modern Library, Random House, 1938], p. 245).

9. See John Hollow, "William Morris and the Judgment of God," *PMLA* 86 (1971) :446-47; and Kenneth Deal, "Acts of Completion: The Search for Vocation in Morris' Early Prose Romances," in *The Golden Chain: Essays on William Morris and Pre-Raphaelitism,* ed. Carole G. Silver (New York: William Morris Society, 1982), p. 73, for two valuable views of the tale's color symbolism.

10. Childe Roland, whom Morris envisioned (rather like his own characters Hugh and Leuchnar) as "so very, very lonely" (1:339) on his courageous but fatal quest, is the inspiration for the figures of Lawrence in "A Dream," and Lionel in "Golden Wings." Morris indicates that he loves Browning's poem "the best of all" (1:340) the poet's works.

11. Mackail, *Life,* 1:119.

12. Hugh and Leuchnar not only resemble each other but, like Palomydes, function as Morris's doppelgängers. Both, like Morris, are accused of lacking a firm sense of vocation and direction. The charge made against Hugh, for example: "People think me now a weak man, with no end to make for in the purposeless wanderings of my life" (1:309) is similar to the accusation that Morris replies to in a letter to his mother: "Perhaps you think that people will laugh at me, and call me purposeless and changeable; I have no doubt they will" (Philip Henderson, ed., *The Letters of William Morris to His Family and Friends* [London: Longmans, Green, 1950], p. 16; hereafter cited as *Letters*). Despite their surface appearances, all three figures share the "wonderful power of concentrating every thought, every least spark of passion, on some one thing" (1:185)—when they care about it. Hugh and Leuchnar's self-vindication, that beneath their exterior lethargy lies a strong undercurrent of single-minded dedication to work and duty—once they have found the appropriate duty—is Morris's own.

13. See "Concerning Geffray Teste Noire" (1:75-81) for a darker and more ironic version of this motif.

14. See Swinburne's letter of 1858 to Edwin Hatch. Despite the playful tone of the note and its discussion of "kisses in Paradise" and "the celestial development of that necessity of life," it is apparent that the idea of a fleshly reunion of lovers was taken seriously (Cecil Y. Lang, ed., *The Swinburne Letters,* 6 vols. [New Haven: Yale University Press, 1959-62], 1:17-18).

15. John Dixon Hunt, *The Pre-Raphaelite Imagination, 1848-1900* (London: Routledge and Kegan Paul, 1968), p. 80.

16. Morris's use of the word "Hollow" in the title of the tale refers both to the land's terrain—it is into a hollow that Florian falls in finding the mysterious realm—and to the quality of the country—it is a hallow or holy place. Lionel Stevenson notes the similarity of the tale to Rossetti's "Hand and Soul" as "a projection of the author's personal objectives" (*The Pre-Raphaelite Poets* [Chapel Hill: University of North Carolina Press, 1972], p. 133).

2 IN DEFENSE OF GUENEVERE

1. William Morris, *The Defence of Guenevere and Other Poems,* ed. Robert Steele (London: A. Moring, 1904), p. 251. Steele is quoting Morris.

2. The speaker may also be indicating that his lady is crimson-stained, i.e., that she has been slain. I am grateful to Professor Robert Keane for this suggestion.

3. The painting of 1849, also known as *Lorenzo and Isabella,* is presently in the Walker Art Gallery, Liverpool. In the foreground, Lorenzo and Isabella are shown wistfully sharing the halves of a blood orange in token of their love. Isabella's brothers, one of whom is kicking her dog, are eyeing Lorenzo and clearly contemplating his murder.

4. Walter Pater, "Aesthetic Poetry," in *Appreciations: With an Essay on Style* (London: Macmillan, 1889), p. 218.

5. Morris's poems are often set in the grayness before dawn as in "King Arthur's Tomb," "Summer Dawn," "The Wind," and "Shameful Death," or in the gray of twilight as in "The Blue Closet," "Sir Galahad," and the first episode of "Rapunzel." Morris seems to employ visual imagery as much for creating tension as for sensuous effects. His auditory images, often battle cries or sounds like that of the splashing of rain in "The Haystack in the Floods" and that of the shifting of the speaker's chair in "The Wind," add to the intensity of the poems.

6. See Elizabeth Barrett Browning's medievalized poems: "The Romaunt of Margret," "The Romaunt of the Page," "The Lay of the Brown Rosary," and the "Rhyme of the Duchess May." See also Scott's poetic works, especially: "The Eve of Saint John," "The Fire-King," "Frederick and Alice," "The Monks of Bangor's March," and *The Lay of the Last Minstrel, Marmion,* and *The Bridal of Triermain.*

7. Algernon Charles Swinburne, *Essays and Studies,* 4th ed. (London: Chatto and Windus, 1897), p. 133; Dixon Scott, *Men of Letters* (London: Hodder and Stoughton, 1923), p. 259; and Pater, *Appreciations,* p. 218. See Scott, *Men of Letters,* pp. 258–73, for a good early study of the impact of the volume.

8. A major source of my approach is Cecil Y. Lang's statement that "Morris demonstrated how verse could be both poetic and brutal" (*The Pre-Raphaelites and Their Circle* [Boston: Houghton Mifflin, 1968], p. 510).

9. The terms are those used by Ralph Berry, "A Defense of Guenevere," *Victorian Poetry* 9 (1971) :278; and Patrick Brantlinger, "A Reading of Morris' *The Defence of Guenevere and Other Poems,*" *Victorian Newsletter,* no. 44 (1973): 18. Both Berry and Brantlinger, who derives his term from Pater, provide valuable studies of *The Defence* volume.

10. Two other poems may be included in the Malory group, though they are less central to it. "Near Avalon" utilizes Malory in its title and employs Guenevere as a symbol of love's fatality, and "A Good Knight in Prison" employs Launcelot as the figure who rescues the captive knight.

See 1:xix for "The Maying of Queen Guenevere"; see 24:68–69 for "St. Agnes [sic] Convent," a fragment of the dramatic monologue of Iseult of Brittany, consisting of her reflections on her wretched present and the happier past she experienced in loving Tristram; and see 24:70–71 for "Palomydes' Quest," a fragment, dealing with Palomydes' dreams of capturing the Questing Beast and winning fame and the love of Iseult of Cornwall.

11. Morris's volume appeared a year before the first series of Tennyson's *Idylls of the King* (1859). He knew the early Tennyson poems: "Morte D'Arthur," "Sir Galahad" (which he disliked), and the fragment, "Sir Launcelot and Queen Guinevere." Only the last—with its images of spring and description of the passionate kiss of the lovers—seems to have influenced him, and the appearance of the *Idylls* may well have made him abandon his own plan for an Arthurian cycle.

12. See Chapter 1 and note 10 above. Morris's identification with Palomydes clearly intensified. The rejected knight was the subject of Morris's contribution to the Oxford Union frescoes: *How Sir Palomydes loved La Belle Iseult with exceeding great love out of measure, and how she loved not him but rather Sir Tristram*, and was mentioned in the canceled opening of "The Defence" (1:xx). Morris's painting of Jane Burden was seemingly first named *La Belle Iseult* (before its title was changed to *Guenevere*) and perhaps he again visualized himself as Palomydes. Indeed, his one physical description of the knight is of a man with "red heavy swinging hair" (1:21) like his own.

13. Meredith Raymond, "The Arthurian Group in *The Defence of Guenevere and Other Poems*," *Victorian Poetry* 4 (1966): 213.

14. The following discussion of "The Defence" appeared, in slightly different form, in my article "'The Defence of Guenevere': A Further Interpretation," *Studies in English Literature: 1500–1900* 9 (1969): 695–702.

15. Laurence Perrine, "Morris's Guenevere: An Interpretation," *Philological Quarterly* 39 (1960) :241. See also Mother Angela Carson, "Morris' Guenevere: A Further Note," *Philological Quarterly* 42 (1963): 131–34. For recent articles which concentrate on the poem see Raymond, "The Arthurian Group"; Robert L. Stallman, "The Lovers' Progress: An Investigation of William Morris' 'The Defence of Guenevere' and 'King Arthur's Tomb,'" *Studies in English Literature: 1500–1900* 15 (1975) :657–70; and Dennis R. Balch, "Guenevere's Fidelity to Arthur in 'The Defence of Guenevere' and 'King Arthur's Tomb,'" *Victorian Poetry* 13, nos. 3–4 (1975) :61–70.

16. Perrine, "Morris's Guenevere," p. 237. See also Carson, "A Further Note," pp. 132–34 for an explanation of Guenevere's probable innocence on the occasion of Launcelot's visit.

17. Sir Thomas Malory, *Le Morte D'Arthur*, intro. Sir John Rhys, 2 vols. (London: J. M. Dent, 1906), 2:324.

18. Ibid.

19. Ibid., 2:314–15.

20. Ibid., 2:326.

21. Perrine, "Morris's Guenevere," p. 239. In indicating that the queen's body cannot be defiled, Guenevere suggests her awareness of the doctrine of the king's two bodies. As queen royal, she is above judgment and incapable of evil; as queen natural, she is graceful and beautiful in proof of innocence.

22. Guenevere, like the other fatal women of the volume, is not intentionally evil. She is to be compared to Yoland in "The Tune of Seven Towers," and the nameless lady in "Concerning Geffray Teste Noire." Her role as an embodiment of love's fatality is made evident in the lyric "Near Avalon" (1:40).

23. It is clear that the color blue is also associated with King Arthur. See Balch, "Guenevere's Fidelity," pp. 61–70, for a reading of the symbolism of the cloths which differs from mine.

24. The role of Gauwaine as the accuser in the poem is not, as Perrine thinks in "Morris's Guenevere," p. 235, a mistake. Morris casts Gauwaine in this role to create an important antagonist to Guenevere and to make the accuser someone who understands the ramifications of adultery and its punishment. Moreover, Morris compresses the events that follow the incident, for it is as a result of Launcelot's killing of Gauwaine's relatives during the rescue of Guenevere that Gauwaine becomes the enemy of the lovers.

25. Morris's description of Guenevere resembles Rossetti's studies and paintings of Lizzie Siddal, which were executed during the early 1850s—especially the study for *Regina Cordium*, which shows Lizzie before her illnesses, and before Rossetti had fully spiritualized and desexualized his portraits of her. The implications of Morris's selection of her as a prototype for Guenevere are interesting: they suggest the strength of Morris's worship of Rossetti and the adoption of Rossetti's ideal standard of beauty and/or they suggest Morris's sexual attraction to Lizzie. Since she seems to have disliked Morris, his choice of her as an ideal may have reinforced his identification with Palomydes.

26. David Staines, "Morris' Treatment of His Medieval Sources in *The Defence of Guenevere and Other Poems*," *Studies in Philology* 70 (1973) :444. Morris changes the scene of the parting from Almsbury to Glastonbury, since the latter place is the site of Arthur's tomb—a monument which provides much of the poem's drama. He again compresses events described by Malory in order to make the death of Guenevere simultaneous with the severing of the lovers.

27. *Arthur's Tomb*, dated 1854 but actually completed in 1855, was initially purchased by John Ruskin. The faces of the lovers are those of Rossetti and Lizzie, and the painting depicts Launcelot leaning over the Queen, who appears to be resisting him. The symbolic use of the images of apple trees and of a snake suggests that Rossetti is treating the incident as an analogy to the Fall.

28. Malory, *Morte D'Arthur*, 2:395.

29. Despite his appreciation of the poem, Swinburne failed to recognize the relationship between the poem's intense passion and broken utterance, and found it in need of "combing and trimming." He

felt that the work, though powerful, "had not been constructed at all; the parts hardly hold together; it has need of joists and screws, props and rafters" (*Essays*, pp. 112–13).

30. See, for example: "This he knew also; that some fingers twine, / Not only in a man's hair, even his heart, / (Making him good or bad I mean,) but in his life" (1:11), and Guenevere's cry of anguish, "not / Ever again shall we twine arms and lips" (1:17).

31. Guenevere describes Launcelot's serpentine "long lips" (1:18) cleaving to her hand and imagines his body "curl'd, . . . in agony" (1:22). All her images of him are phallic, and he is equated with a viper and a sword.

32. Cf. Malory's account of Guenevere's final speech to Launcelot: "Through this man and me hath all this war been wrought, and the death of the most noblest knights of the world; for through our love that we have loved together is my most noble lord slain. . . . Therefore, Sir Launcelot, I require thee and beseech thee heartily, for all the love that ever was betwixt us, that thou never see me more in the visage" (*Morte D'Arthur*, 2:394).

33. Raymond, "Arthurian Group," pp. 214–15.

34. Berry, "Defense of Guenevere," p. 279.

35. One possible explanation for Ozana's plight is that he is being punished for his failure to aid Guenevere. Malory mentions him as one of the ten knights who failed to save her from Meliagraunce's attack and could not, because of his wounds, defend her at her trial.

36. The group also contains "The Eve of Crecy," "The Judgment of God," and "Sir Giles' War-Song." "The Judgment of God" and "Sir Giles' War-Song" are both linked to Froissart, the former by the statement that Roger's foe is the "flower of all the Hainault knights" (1:96) and the latter by the mention of Clisson.

37. Dougald B. MacEachen, "Trial by Water in William Morris' 'The Haystack in the Floods,'" *Victorian Poetry* 6 (1968) :74–76, suggests that Jehane would have had a good chance of surviving the *judicium aquae frigidae*, but Morris seems to have misunderstood the nature of the trial and assumes that Jehane's death will result from it.

38. Jean Froissart, *The Chronicle of Froissart*, trans. Sir John Bourchier, Lord Berners, intro. William Paton Ker, 6 vols. (1901–3; reprint ed., New York: AMS Press, 1967), 1:291–92. The battle occurred in 1346.

39. Margaret Gent, in an otherwise excellent article ("'To Flinch from Modern Varnish': The Appeal of the Past to the Victorian Imagination," in *Victorian Poetry*, Stratford-upon-Avon Studies, no. 15 [London: Edward Arnold, 1972], p. 35), seems wrong in suggesting that the reader's judgment of Jehane and her conduct must be unfavorable.

40. Dianne F. Sadoff, "Erotic Murders: Structural and Rhetorical Irony in William Morris' Froissart Poems," *Victorian Poetry* 13, nos. 3–4 (1975) :18.

41. Frank J. J. Davies, "William Morris's 'Sir Peter Harpdon's End,'" *Philological Quarterly* 11 (1932) :314–15, identifies Peter with

Sir John Harpendan (or Harpedon) who was Seneschal of Rochelle in 1372 and Marshal of Bordeaux in 1385. It is more probable that Morris envisions Peter as Sir John's nephew, since the poem alludes to a powerful old uncle who will be angered at Peter's execution.

42. Froissart, *Chronicle*, 2:484–85.

43. Sadoff, "Erotic Murders," p. 14.

44. Ibid., p. 16. There is no evidence to support Sadoff's contention that Peter castrates Lambert; indeed, he has been merciful in slicing off Lambert's ears, since Lambert has treacherously used a truce to try to murder him.

45. For Geffray's life and career see Froissart, *Chronicle*, 5:80–112, 254–57, and 330–41. "Concerning Geffray Teste Noire" is, perhaps, Morris's closest imitation of a Browning dramatic monologue. For verification, compare Morris's closing lines: "This Jaques Picard, known through many lands, / Wrought cunningly" (1:81) with the last line of Browning's "My Last Duchess": "Which Claus of Insbruch cast in bronze for me."

46. Froissart, *Chronicle*, 2:446, mentions a man of this name.

47. Gent, "'To Flinch from Modern Varnish,'" pp. 23, 28.

48. Mario Praz, *The Romantic Agony*, trans. Angus Davidson, 2nd ed. (New York: Oxford University Press, 1951), p. 31.

49. Brantlinger, "A Reading of Morris' *Defence*," p. 20.

50. See Geoffrey Grigson, *The Contrary View: Glimpses of Fudge and Gold* (London: Macmillan, 1974), pp. 81–83, for a brief appreciation of the poem. "Shameful Death" may be considered a Froissart poem on the basis of its subject and grim tone.

51. Note the folkloric motifs of the animal enemy—here a kingfisher—and of the necessity of avoiding a body of water.

52. Cf. "Welland River" to tales such as "Roland," and "The True Bride" in Jacob and Wilhelm Grimm, *German Popular Tales and Household Stories, Collected by the Brothers Grimm* (Philadelphia: Porter and Coates, 1869), pp. 282–86, 324–27. Also compare the poem to "Goldmaria and Goldfeather," in *Yule-Tide Stories*, ed. Benjamin Thorpe (London: H. G. Bohn, 1853), p. 450. Thorpe's collection of folk tales is an important source of several of Morris's poems. Several lines of "The Eve of Crecy," for example, are derived from Thorpe's tale of "The Ness King." Cf. Morris's "'Sir Lambert du Bois, with all his men good, / Has neither food nor fire-wood'" (1:94) with Thorpe's "Ebbe from Nebbe, with all his men good, / Has neither food nor fire-wood" (Thorpe, *Yule-Tide Stories*, p. 398).

53. Cf. "Rapunzel," in Grimm, *German Popular Tales*, pp. 98–102.

54. For detailed examinations of Morris's "Rapunzel," see Robert L. Stallman, "'Rapunzel' Unravelled," *Victorian Poetry* 7 (1969) :221–32; and Dianne F. Sadoff, "Imaginative Transformation in William Morris' 'Rapunzel,'" *Victorian Poetry* 12 (1974) :153–64.

55. See Chapter 3, especially pp. 66–69 and the discussion of *Love is Enough* in Chapter 4, pp. 87–89.

56. Stallman, "'Rapunzel' Unravelled," pp. 221–32, passim.

57. Morris purchased both watercolors from Rossetti in 1857. In both

cases his poems record—but go beyond—the visual details of the paintings. In "The Tune of Seven Towers," Morris is clearly creating the song the lady plays on her musical instrument. In "The Blue Closet," Morris follows Rossetti's color scheme and symbolism; the walls and floor of the mysterious chamber are tiled in blue, and damozels behind the queens are wearing "purple and green," etc.

58. Barbara Charlesworth Gelpi, "The Image of the Anima in the Work of Dante Gabriel Rossetti," *Victorian Newsletter*, no. 45 (1974) :1.

59. Scott, *Men of Letters*, p. 297.

60. Pater, *Appreciations*, p. 222.

3 THE LOSS OF EDEN

1. See Peter Faulkner, ed., *William Morris: The Critical Heritage* (London: Routledge and Kegan Paul, 1973), pp. 31–49, for the unfavorable reviews of *The Defence* volume written by Morris's contemporaries.

2. Of the twelve poems that were to comprise Morris's Trojan cycle only eight (nine, if one counts the two versions of "Helen's Chamber") were written. Morris planned but did not execute scenes on "The Wedding of Polyxena," "The Last Fight Before Troy," "The Wooden Horse," and "Aeneas on Shipboard."

3. See "Song" in "Ogier the Dane" (4:247–48). Morris also calligraphed and illuminated the poem for *A Book of Verse*, Victoria and Albert Museum, R. C. AA. 17.

4. *Jason*, written in 1866, was published in January 1867. It is predated by a number of *Earthly Paradise* tales which Morris seems to have begun in the early 1860s.

5. The passage (2:140–41) is significant as the first evidence of Morris's interest in the life and customs of the prehistoric European peoples.

6. The poem was included in *A Book of Verse* and republished in *Poems By the Way* (9:149).

7. Maude Bodkin, *Archetypal Patterns in Poetry* (London: Oxford University Press, 1934), pp. 116, 118. With the exception of Bodkin's brilliant reading of the "Song," to which I am indebted, and Charlotte Oberg's recent *Pagan Prophet: William Morris* (Charlottesville: University Press of Virginia, 1978), *Jason* has been largely ignored by critics.

8. For a discussion of the poem's reception see Oscar Maurer, Jr., "William Morris and the Poetry of Escape," in *Nineteenth Century Studies*, ed. Herbert Davies et al. (Ithaca: Cornell University Press, 1940), pp. 247–73. For the reviews by Morris's contemporaries see Faulkner, *Critical Heritage*, pp. 79–151.

9. Alfred Noyes, *William Morris* (London: Macmillan, 1908), p. 144. A slightly briefer version of my discussion of *The Earthly Paradise* has appeared as "*The Earthly Paradise*: Lost," *Victorian Poetry* 13, nos. 3–4 (1975) :27–42.

10. Paul Thompson, *The Work of William Morris* (New York: Viking Press, 1967), p. 171.

11. See, for example, E. P. Thompson, *William Morris: Romantic to*

Revolutionary (London: Lawrence and Wishart, 1955), pp. 144–62 and rev. ed. (London: Merlin Press, 1977), pp. 143–50; Philip Henderson, *William Morris: His Life, Work and Friends* (New York: McGraw-Hill, 1967), pp. 87–92; and Jack Lindsay, *William Morris, Writer* (London: William Morris Society, 1961), pp. 12–15.

12. Maurer, "Poetry of Escape," p. 249.

13. Paul Henri Mallet, *Northern Antiquities*, trans. Bishop [Thomas] Percy (London: H. G. Bohn, 1847), p. 267.

14. Through this incident Morris dates the Wanderers' expedition as beginning no earlier than 1349 when the Black Plague reached Scandinavia and when Edward III and the English fleet met the Spaniards in battle off the coast of Calais. The King, accompanied by the Black Prince and Sir John Chandos, whom the Wanderers see, was again invading France. The meeting could also have occurred in 1359 when Edward returned to France to attempt to enforce the Treaty of Bretigny.

15. For details about South American geography, culture, and customs, Morris seems to have used such works as Alexander Von Humboldt's *Personal Narrative of Travels to the Equinoctial Regions of America*, ed. and trans. Thomasina Ross, 3 vols. (London: H. G. Bohn, 1852–53); and William H. Prescott's *History of the Conquest of Peru*, 2 vols. (New York: Harper, 1847–48). Von Humboldt provides the description of the mummies of rulers dried in sacred caves, 1:121–23; and Prescott is the source of the account of murdered royal servants embalmed to look alive, 1:61.

16. Joseph Dunlap persuasively argues that the Greek Elders are descendants of the Greeks who fled from the Persian destruction of Miletus and the surrounding islands in 494 B.C., in "'Your Peaceful and Delicious Land': Or the Last Home of the Wanderers," a paper read at the Modern Language Association Convention, Session 635: William Morris' *Earthly Paradise*, 30 December 1978, New York Hilton Hotel.

17. See Mackail, *Life*, 1:204–6 for an account of the sources of the individual tales. As Douglas Bush notes, the Greek Elders tell their tales as if they were medieval romances (*Mythology and the Romantic Tradition in English Poetry* [Cambridge: Harvard University Press, 1937], p. 320). Although Morris does not directly explain the anachronism, his reasons for it lie in his bardic pose. As he had done in "Lindenborg Pool" and would do again in *A Dream of John Ball*, Morris sees himself both as a Victorian narrator and as a medieval chronicler, free to adapt and reshape his source materials.

18. Graham Hough, *The Last Romantics* (London: Duckworth, 1949), p. 123.

19. Although the four remaining tales do not deal with erotic love, they do illuminate other major themes in the work. "The Golden Apples" is an account of the successful quest of Hercules for the terrestrial paradise of the Hesperides and, thus, an ironic contrast to the Wanderers' failure. "The Writing on the Image," "The Proud King," and "The Son of Croesus" are centered on man's inability to control or overcome his fate; the two latter tales also describe varieties of non-erotic love, caritas and friendship.

20. See, for example, the two tales for March—"Atalanta's Race" and "The Man Born to Be King"—in which love is miraculously born in time to save men doomed to death; the tales for September—"The Death of Paris" and "The Land East of the Sun and West of the Moon"—which illustrate the ambivalence of passion; and the stark love tragedies of November, January, and February—"The Lovers of Gudrun," "The Ring Given to Venus," and "The Hill of Venus."

21. Mackail, *Life*, 1:210. The lyrics replaced earlier poems on the months, some of which were printed by May Morris in the *Works* (6:xxvii–xxx and 24:345–46). All the earlier lyrics are polished works and several deal with fulfilled, happy love. Their replacement may have been due more to Morris's need to express his pain than to a low estimation of their worth.

22. I am indebted to E. P. Thompson's autobiographical reading of a number of the poems to the months in *Romantic to Revolutionary*, rev. ed., pp. 153–55.

23. See *Letters*, pp. 43, 45; and Rosalie Glynn Grylls, *Portrait of Rossetti* (London: Macdonald, 1964), p. 141.

24. Morris often also uses kinetic imagery, alternating scenes of stillness and scenes of motion as correlatives to emotion. Pygmalion's restlessness is reflected in the landscape through which he wanders (4:192), and John's serenity (in "The Land East of the Sun") is reflected in the quiet land to which he returns (5:58).

25. Jessie Kocmonová believes that "Orpheus" was excluded not, as Morris said, because it was too long, but because of its revelation of his personal unhappiness and failing marriage (*The Poetic Maturing of William Morris* [1964; reprint ed., Folcroft Library, 1970], p. 37).

26. *Letters*, p. 50.

27. Morris's dedication of *The Earthly Paradise* to his wife is somewhat ironic. In a work written by a man "late made wise in love" (6:332) as an attempt to exorcise the ghosts which surround his empty life, many of the female figures, particularly the remote, cool, and passively rejecting women who are images of the dark anima, are reminiscent of Jane Morris.

28. Lindsay, *William Morris, Writer*, p. 16.

29. The similarities between the two figures are clearly indicated by their final statements; cf. Sthenoboea's "I have loved one man alone, / And unto him the worst deed have I done / Of all the ill deeds I have done on earth" (6:130) and Gudrun's "I did the worst to him I loved the most" (5:395).

30. May Morris, ed., *William Morris: Artist, Writer, Socialist*, 2 vols. (1936; reprint ed., New York: Russell and Russell, 1966), 1:433.

4 "THE STORMY YEARS": AN INTERLUDE

1. Quoted in Henderson, *Life, Work and Friends* p. 93.

2. See Henderson, *Life, Work and Friends*, pp. 79–116; and Jack Lindsay, *William Morris: His Life and Work* (London: Constable, 1975), pp. 146–89.

3. For a list of unpublished poems and fragments see K[enneth] L. Goodwin, "Unpublished Lyrics of William Morris," in *The Yearbook of English Studies*, no. 5, ed. T. J. B. Spencer (London: Modern Humanities Research Association, 1975), pp. 194–95.

4. See R. C. Ellison, "An Unpublished Poem by William Morris," *English* 5 (1964) :100–102; and Goodwin, "Unpublished Lyrics," pp. 190–206.

5. A number of the personal poems are not intelligible unless read biographically. For my biographical reading see "No Idle Singer: A Study of the Poems and Romances of William Morris," Ph.D. dissertation, Columbia University, 1967, pp. 99–154.

6. Goodwin, "Unpublished Lyrics," p. 193.

7. *A Book of Verse*, Victoria and Albert Museum, R. C. AA. 17, is a beautiful, calligraphic illuminated manuscript of some fifty pages made by Morris as a present for Georgiana Burne-Jones in 1870. Its title has been identified by Joseph Dunlap as a quotation from the first version of Edward FitzGerald's *Rubáiyát of Omar Khayyám*; the relevant lines read: "Here with a Loaf of Bread beneath the Bough, / a Flask of Wine, a Book of Verse—and Thou / Beside me singing in the Wilderness— / And Wilderness is Paradise enow." The manuscript consists of twenty-five poems, some of which were lyrics from *The Earthly Paradise*, some of which were later published in *Poems by the Way* (1891) and by May Morris in volume 24 of the *Works*, and several of which were not published until Goodwin's "Unpublished Lyrics."

8. See Chapter 3, p. 63.

9. May Morris, *Artist, Writer, Socialist*, 1:538–39.

10. Morris, *A Book of Verse*, pp. 44–46.

11. See Henderson, *Life, Work and Friends*, pp. 93–94; and Lindsay, *Life and Work*, pp. 182–84.

12. Goodwin, "Unpublished Lyrics," pp. 198-99. The poem continues:

> Ah do you lift your eye-brows in disdain
> Because I dare to pity or come nigh
> To your great sorrow, helpless weak and vain
> E'en as I know myself?—ah rather I
> On you my helper in the darkness cry
> For you alone unchanged now seem to be
> A real thing left of the days sweet to me.
>
> Dreamy the rest has grown now that my lips
> Must leave the words unsaid my heart will say
> While I grow hot, and o'er the edge there slips
> A word that makes me tremble and I stay
> With fluttering heart the thoughts that will away.
> We meet, we laugh and talk but still is set
> A seal o'er things I never can forget
>
> But must not speak of, still I count the hours
> That bring my friend to me, with hungry eyes

I watch him as his feet the staircase mount
Then face to face we sit, a wall of lies
Made hard by fear and faint anxieties
Is drawn between us, and he goes away
And leaves me wishing it were yesterday.

Then when they both are gone, I sit alone
And turning foolish triumph's pages o'er
Now think how it would be if they were gone
Not to return, or worse if the time bore
Some seed of hatred in its fiery core
And nought of praise were left to me to gain
But the poor [deed?] we talked of as so vain.

The poem's margin bears a note, obviously intended for Georgie, which reads: "Was dull but all right now [—] poets unrealities [—] x tears can come with verse [—] we are in the same box and need conceal nothing—dont [sic] cast me away—scold me but pardon me[.] What is all this to me (say you) [—] shame in confessing ones [sic] real feelings—"

13. See Chapter 3, pp. 65–66.

14. May Morris sees the poem—perhaps because of the "Music"—as the greatest revelation of Morris's deepest feelings. She indicates that "no glimpse of the inner life of Morris was ever vouchsafed to his closest friends—*secretum meum mihi*. It was a subject on which he never spoke except in Love is Enough" (*Artist, Writer, Socialist*, 1:144).

15. Lady Charlotte Guest, *Mabinogion: Mediaeval Welsh Romances* (London: David Nutt, 1902), p. 85.

16. Ibid.

17. Frederick Kirchhoff, "*Love is Enough*: A Crisis in William Morris's Poetic Development," *Victorian Poetry* 15 (1977) :304. I am indebted, in general, to Kirchhoff's valuable reading of the poem.

18. Cf. "Hope dieth: Love liveth" in *A Book of Verse*, pp. 23–25; and in *Works*, 9:106–7.

19. William Morris, British Museum Additional Manuscript, 45, 328, ff. 1–53 (hereafter cited as Br. Mus. Add. MS).

20. Jessie Kocmanová, "'Landscape and Sentiment': Morris' First Attempt in Longer Prose Fiction," *Victorian Poetry* 13, nos. 3–4 (1975) :115. I am indebted to Kocmonová's summary of the novel's plot, pp. 105–15.

21. Morris, Br. Mus. Add. MS, 45, 328: f. 16r, 32v.

22. John, like Morris, is described as light-haired, full-mouthed, large-chinned and jawed, and somewhat short and husky—as opposed to Arthur, who is slighter in build, but taller, darker, and more sensitive in appearance.

23. Morris, Br. Mus. Add. MS, 45, 328: f. 51r–v. The letter advises the lover to "heed nothing heed nobody live your life through with her, crushing everything that comes in your way" (f. 50v). It orders him to "stoop to any humiliation, tell any lie, commit any treachery—but do not die as—as some people must, with your love barren and unsatisfied when you can make it otherwise" (f. 51r).

24. See Chapter 1. The epigraph to "Gertha's Lovers," taken from the opening stanza of Samuel Taylor Coleridge's poem, "Love," seems to inspire this letter: "All thoughts, all passions, all delights, / Whatever stirs this mortal frame, / All are but ministers of love, / And feed his sacred flame" (1:76).

25. Morris, Br. Mus. Add. MS, 45, 328: f. 38r.

26. Cf. Arthur's dream with Pharamond's dream vision of Azalais singing amid the apple orchard (9:27). Both women are clearly depicted in these visions as animas and inspiring muses.

27. Morris, Br. Mus. Add. MS, 45, 328: f.38r–v.

28. See *Letters*, pp. 46–47 on his "abortive novel," of which he says: "I sent it to Georgie to see if she could give me any hope: she gave me none, and I have never looked at it since"; and note Morris's belief that "one ought to be able to write a novel in six weeks, and . . . then it ought to be so good or so bad that no subsequent revision could alter it materially" (Mackenzie Bell, "William Morris: A Eulogy," *Fortnightly Review* 66 [1896] :695). Kocmonová's argument in "'Landscape and Sentiment,'" pp. 116–19, that Morris's lack of sympathy with the realism, formalism, and moral constraints of Victorian novels hindered him is also to the point.

29. May Morris, *Artist, Writer, Socialist*, 1:540.

30. The poem was printed as "O Far Away to Seek" by May Morris in *Works*, 24:364.

31. The published lines read: "Where we may sit apart / Hapless, undying still" (24:364).

32. Goodwin, "Unpublished Lyrics," p. 201.

33. Ibid., p. 202.

34. Ibid., my italics.

35. A slightly different version of the poem was printed by David J. DeLaura, "An Unpublished Poem of William Morris'," *Modern Philology* 62 (1965) :340–41. For the version in *A Book of Verse*, see Appendix.

36. Goodwin, "Unpublished Lyrics," p. 197.

37. May Morris, *Artist, Writer, Socialist*, 1:538–39.

38. E. P. Thompson, *Romantic to Revolutionary*, rev. ed., p. 153.

39. Kirchhoff, *"Love is Enough,"* p. 299.

40. Bodkin, *Archetypal Patterns in Poetry*, p. 118.

41. Kirchhoff, *"Love is Enough,"* p. 298. See also Kirchhoff's excellent reading of the *Journal* of 1871, to which I am indebted for the concept of the work's importance and tone ("Travel as Anti-Auto-biography: William Morris' Icelandic Journals," in *Approaches to Victorian Autobiography*, ed. George Landow [Athens, Ohio: Ohio University Press, 1979], pp. 292–309).

42. Cf. Kirchhoff, "Travel as Anti-Autobiography," p. 296, for a different view.

43. Ellison, "An Unpublished Poem," p. 100.

44. Ibid., p. 101.

45. *Letters*, p. 59.

46. Cf. p. 101.

47. *Letters*, p. 59.

48. May Morris, *Artist, Writer, Socialist*, 1:232, reprints Morris's review of "The Exhibition of the Royal Academy," in which Morris suggests that John Brett, one of the few exhibitors whose work he liked, might have his landscape painting further enriched by utilizing Icelandic scenery. He comments: "I could tell him of places there as wild and strange as the background of a fairy tale, every rood of which has a dramatic tale hanging by it."

49. Quoted in Henderson, *Life, Work and Friends*, p. 116. The poem was in the possession of Georgiana Burne-Jones.

50. Ibid.

51. Mackail, *Life*, 1:310.

5   PARABLES FOR THE TIMES

1. See "The Early Literature of the North—Iceland," in *The Unpublished Lectures of William Morris*, ed. and comp. Eugene D. Lemire (Detroit: Wayne State University Press, 1969), pp. 181–85.

2. See Chapter 1.

3. Ellison, " 'The Undying Glory of Dreams,' " p. 152, makes the important point that the early translations which were available to Morris softened the tone of the originals and elaborated upon the details within them—a practice Morris himself followed until his study of the Icelandic language.

4. For a discussion of the materials that were available to Morris, see Karl Litzenberg, "The Victorians and the Vikings: A Bibliographical Essay on Anglo-Norse Literary Relations," *University of Michigan Contributions in Modern Philology*, no. 3 (Ann Arbor: University of Michigan Press, 1947), pp. 1–27.

5. This "Translators' Preface," retained from the 1870 edition of the work, is by Morris.

6. During the same period, Morris began, but did not complete, a verse translation of the *Nibelungenlied*.

7. See *Works*, 7. Significantly, all three of the short sagas that comprise the bulk of the translation deal with triangles of love. The tale of Gunnlaug ends in tragedy, while the stories of Frithiof and Viglund end in the happy union of the lovers for whom the reader feels sympathy.

8. Among them are "To the Muse of the North," "Iceland First Seen," "Gunnar's Howe above the House at Lithend," a second sonnet to "Gunnar Asmundson," and "Anthony."

9. *Letters*, p. 106.

10. Anthony Ugolnik, "The Victorian Skald: Old Icelandic and the Evolution of William Morris' *Sigurd the Volsung*," in *The After-Summer Seed: Reconsiderations of William Morris's "The Story of Sigurd the Volsung,"* (hereafter cited as *After-Summer Seed*), ed. John Hollow (New York: William Morris Society, 1978), p. 43.

11. *Letters*, p. 32.

12. Morris did not change the spelling of the word, subtilty—obsolete in his day—in any of the editions of the saga.

13. Bernard Shaw, "William Morris as I Knew Him," in May Morris, *Artist, Writer, Socialist,* 2:48.

14. Ibid., 1:474.

15. He had, however, dealt with the fate of Gudrun's children in "The Wooing of Swanhild" which was written for, but not included in, *The Earthly Paradise.*

16. Conrad H. Nordby, *The Influence of Old Norse Literature upon English Literature* (New York: Columbia University Press, 1901), p. 59.

17. Ibid., p. 60.

18. J. W. Blench, "William Morris's *Sigurd the Volsung*: A Re-Appraisal," *Durham University Journal,* o.s. 41 (1968), n.s. 30 (1968) :3.

19. Dennis Balch, "'The Lovers of Gudrun,' *Sigurd the Volsung,* and *The House of the Wolfings*: Three Chapters in a Tale of the Individual and the Tribe," in *After-Summer Seed,* p. 92.

20. Kocmonová, *Poetic Maturing of William Morris,* p. 141.

21. In the case of the Volsungs, however, the poem traces how the qualities of the hall—courage and community—are initially transformed rather than destroyed. Descriptions of halls and of Icelandic landscape account, in part, for the fact that the poem is four times the length of the saga.

22. See Hartley S. Spatt, "Morrissaga: *Sigurd the Volsung,*" pp. 140–41; and Balch, "Individual and the Tribe," pp. 109–13, in *After-Summer Seed* for two analyses of the images of the tree and the fire—to which I am indebted.

23. Max Müller, *Chips from a German Workshop* (1871–72), 5 vols. (New York: Scribner, 1890–93), 2:106–9. Müller's lectures and books were extremely popular in England in the 1870s.

24. That Morris knew Müller's works is certain. Although the lists of Morris's library holdings (which are not complete and do not always list individual books) do not show his ownership of *Chips,* they do indicate his possession of two books that discuss and utilize Müller's thesis: Julia Goddard's *Wonderful Stories from Northern Lands* (London: Longmans, Green, 1871) and, more important, Rasmus B. Anderson's *Norse Mythology* (Chicago: Scott, Foresman, 1875).

25. See *Volsunga Saga,* "A Prologue in Verse" (7:290).

26. To achieve this effect, Morris, who had written several versions of an emotional last meeting between Brynhild and Sigurd, eliminated them in favor of a bare understated version. He also modeled his Gudrun more on the stoical figure depicted in the *Nibelungenlied* than on the more emotional but passive woman of the *Volsunga.*

27. *Letters,* p. 84.

28. Dorothy M. Hoare, *The Works of Morris and Yeats in Relation to Early Saga Literature* (Cambridge: At the University Press, 1937), p. 14.

29. Ibid., p. 141.

30. The entire group of poems was privately reprinted from *Commonweal* in 1886, and three episodes, "The Message of the March Wind," "Mother and Son," and "The Half of Life Gone," appeared in *Poems by the Way* (1891). Morris seems to have felt that the other sections of the poem should not be officially published without extensive revision.

31. See Chapter 4. See also Kocmonová, *Poetic Maturing of William Morris*, pp. 190–91, for the new use of seasonal imagery.

32. Thompson, *Romantic to Revolutionary*, rev. ed., p. 670. See Thompson's reading of the work, pp. 669–72.

33. William Morris and E[rnest] Belfort Bax, *Socialism: Its Growth & Outcome* (London: Swan Sonnenschein, 1893), p. 201. This volume is a reprint of Morris and Bax, "Socialism from the Root Up," printed in installments in *Commonweal* in 1886.

34. Oswald Doughty, *A Victorian Romantic: Dante Gabriel Rossetti*, 2nd ed. (London: Oxford University Press, 1960), pp. 458–68.

35. For discussions of Morris's use of medieval and contemporary sources in *John Ball* see John Goode, "William Morris and the Dream of Revolution," in *Literature and Politics in the Nineteenth Century*, ed. John Lucas (London: Methuen, 1971), pp. 247–49; and Alice Chandler, *A Dream of Order: The Medieval Ideal in Nineteenth-Century English Literature* (Lincoln, Neb.: University of Nebraska Press, 1970), pp. 221–26.

36. See Chapter 1. See also Goode, "Dream of Revolution," p. 251 on the use of dream in the work.

37. *Letters*, p. 302.

38. John Hollow's suggestion that the tribe consists of "those 'Sons of the Wolf' with whom Beowulf's father had a feud" is equally possible, especially in view of Morris's translation of *Beowulf* some years later ("Deliberate Happiness: The Late Prose Romances of William Morris," in *Studies in the Late Prose Romances of William Morris* [hereafter cited as *Studies*], intro. Frederick Kirchhoff, ed. Carole Silver and Joseph Dunlap [New York: William Morris Society, 1976], p. 84).

39. May Morris, *Artist, Writer, Socialist*, 2:67.

40. Goode, "Dream of Revolution," p. 261.

41. Morris and Bax, *Socialism*, pp. 16, 25. Morris's statement in a letter is equally clear: "I have [no] more faith than a grain of mustard seed in the future history of 'civilization,' which I *know* now is doomed to destruction, and probably before very long: what a joy it is to think of: and how often it consoles me to think of barbarism once more flooding the world, and real feelings and passions, however rudimentary, taking the place of our wretched hypocrisies" (*Letters*, p. 236).

42. William Morris, "How I Became a Socialist," in *William Morris*, ed. G. D. H. Cole (London: Nonesuch Press, 1948), p. 658; and *Letters*, p. 236. Parts of the following discussion of "upper barbarism" and its impact on the romances have appeared in my article, "Myth and Ritual in the Last Romances of William Morris," in *Studies*, pp. 121–24.

43. Frederick Engels, *The Origin of the Family, Private Property and*

the State, intro. Eleanor Burke Leacock (London: Lawrence and Wishart, 1972), p. 237. Engels quotes and adds italics to L. H. Morgan's statement in *Ancient Society* (ed. Eleanor Burke Leacock [Cleveland: World Press, 1963], p. 562). Although Morris sorrowfully announced that he could only read "even *old* German with great difficulty and labour" (22:xiv), Bax, with whom he worked on socialist documents, was proficient in the language and served as translator. Moreover, an Italian edition of the *Origin of the Family* had become available in 1886.

44.   Engels, *Origin of the Family*, pp. 215, 216. Like Engels, Morris praises the Teutonic tribes for adding morality and a high valuation of women to the virtues of the gens system.

45.   See "Art and Socialism," *Works*, 23:204–5 and passim.

46.   Ibid. See also Margaret Grennan, *William Morris: Medievalist and Revolutionary* (New York: King's Crown Press, 1945), p. 111.

47.   Barbara J. Bono, "The Prose Fictions of William Morris: A Study in the Literary Aesthetic of a Victorian Social Reformer," *Victorian Poetry* 13, nos. 3–4 (1975) :47.

48.   Ibid., p. 48.

49.   It is significant that Thiodolf, who saves the Wolfings, is of alien blood. Morris thus hints at the extension of ideal fellowship beyond the ties of blood and gens. The hope is again expressed in "The Society of the Future," when Morris predicts that, in the higher barbarism to come, "the family of blood-relationship would melt into that of the community and of humanity" (May Morris, *Artist, Writer, Socialist*, 2:466).

50.   Grennan, *Medievalist and Revolutionary*, p. 120.

51.   Morris changed his original plan to have the Bride die in battle and spared her to promote a marriage which he believed would "be a good alliance for the Burgdalers and the Silverdalers both" (15:x1). Again, both rivals for the hero's love in the romance seem to derive from the figure of Clara in the novel and to influence the figure of Ellen in *News from Nowhere*. They are active, tall, well-knit, sun tanned, and well adapted to labor and to war.

52.   Blue Calhoun, "'The Little Land of Abundance': Pastoral Perspective in the Late Romances of William Morris," in *Studies*, p. 67.

53.   E. P. Thompson, *Romantic to Revolutionary*, rev. ed., pp. 678–79.

6 *NEWS FROM NOWHERE*: A SECOND INTERLUDE

1.   May Morris, *Artist, Writer, Socialist*, 2:502. May Morris reprints Morris's review of Bellamy's *Looking Backward* (2:501–7), originally written for *Commonweal*, 22 June 1889.

2.   See *Works*, 22:xvi–xxii. Among Morris's contemporary favorites were the gypsy romances of George Borrow, *Lavengro* and *Romany Rye*; comic novels such as Robert Surtee's *Handley Cross*, Mark Twain's *Huckleberry Finn*, and Chandler Harris's *Uncle Remus*; historical novels such as Charles Reade's *Cloister and the Hearth*; and all the

novels of Charles Dickens. He seems to have respected rather than enjoyed the great realistic fiction of Meredith, Eliot, and Tolstoy.

3.   May Morris, *Artist, Writer, Socialist*, 2:502.

4.   See Samuel Butler, *Erewhon, or Over the Range* (1872). Morris may also have been influenced by Butler's view of art as a living organism which must be born and die and by his idea of death as simply a quiet slumber. He clearly agrees with Butler's dislike of hypothetical education, preferring practical and vocational learning, and with Butler's belief in leisure, exercise, and freedom for children. Morris does not, however, ban technology or machinery from Nowhere; instead he utilizes it to do that work which men would find truly irksome.

5.   Jessie Kocmonová, *The Poetic Maturing of William Morris*, pp. 124–25.

6.   J. R. Ebbatson, "Visions of Wild England: William Morris and Richard Jefferies," *Journal of the William Morris Society* 3, no. 3 (1977): 16.

7.   W[illiam] H[enry] Hudson, *A Crystal Age*, 2nd ed. (London: Unwin, 1906), pp. v–vi. Few critics have considered the possibility of Hudson's work serving as an influence on Morris, since *A Crystal Age* is usually thought of as first appearing in 1906. Morris's attention might have been drawn to the book by one of the many acquaintances the two men shared in common—H. H. Champion, Cunningham Graham, Wilfrid Scawen Blunt, and William Rossetti, among them—or by Hudson himself, since the Hudsons were living in Westbourne Park, London, from 1886 on.

8.   Hudson, *A Crystal Age*, pp. 45–46.

9.   Ibid., p. 159.

10.   John T. Frederick, *William Henry Hudson* (New York: Twayne, 1972), p. 44.

11.   Karl Marx and Friedrich Engels, *The Communist Manifesto*, intro. A. J. P. Taylor (London: Penguin Books, 1967), p. 105. The first English translation of the work had been published in 1850; a new English translation, with a preface by Engels, had appeared in 1888.

12.   Morris and Bax, *Socialism*, p. 288.

13.   Patrick Brantlinger, "*News from Nowhere*: Morris's Socialist Anti-Novel," *Victorian Studies* 19 (1974) :39.

14.   See, for example, E. P. Thompson, *Romantic to Revolutionary*, rev. ed., p. 694.

15.   Marx and Engels, *Manifesto*, p. 102.

16.   Northrop Frye, *Anatomy of Criticism* (Princeton: Princeton University Press, 1957), p. 151.

17.   For an idea of the large scope of Morris's library and of the works of and about folklore he owned, see: "A List of Books and Manuscripts bought by William Morris . . . " (begun in 1876), British Museum Manuscript 86; "A Catalogue of the Library at Kelmscott House" (begun in 1890), Library of J. R. Abbey; and *A Priced Catalogue of a Portion of the Valuable Collection of Manuscripts, Early Printed Books and Etc. of the late William Morris, of Kelmscott House Hammersmith* (London: Sotheby, 1898).

18.   See Morris's list of his choice of the greatest books ever written—including a number of folkloric works—reprinted from the *Pall Mall Gazette* in *Works* (22:xii–xvi).

19.   Brantlinger, "Morris's Socialist Anti-Novel," pp. 39–41.

20.   Ibid., p. 41. Brantlinger quotes and analyzes Morris's view of Victorian realistic novels.

21.   See May Morris, *Artist, Writer, Socialist*, 2:465.

22.   Ibid.

23.   Brantlinger, "Morris's Socialist Anti-Novel," p. 49.

24.   Women continue to bear children and to keep house, even serving the food in the communal dining halls. They do these things, however, because they enjoy them; their functions are now respected. They are also depicted as performing vigorous outdoor labor, being as adept as men in such sports as rowing and sailing, and functioning as equal and active members of the Nowherian community.

25.   May Morris, *Artist, Writer, Socialist*, 2:457.

26.   George Levine, "From 'Know-not-Where' to 'Nowhere': The City in Carlyle, Ruskin, and Morris," in *The Victorian City: Images and Realities*, ed. H. J. Dyos and Michael Wolff, 2 vols. (London: Routledge and Kegan Paul, 1973), 2:515.

27.   Norman Kelvin, "The Erotic in *News from Nowhere* and *The Well at the World's End*," in *Studies*, pp. 100–102. I am indebted to Kelvin's argument on jealousy in Nowhere.

28.   Not only are the circumstances of the separation similar to Morris's own—Clara falls in love with a man other than her husband, leaves her husband for him, and lets the two children of the marriage be reared partially by relatives—but the characters resemble the originals. Clara is initially depicted as being somewhat discontented and wishing that she was "interesting enough to be written or painted about" (16:103), while Dick is portrayed as bluff, emphatic, and stubborn.

29.   In reality, Jane Morris cohabited with Rossetti only briefly, the Morris children spent much time at their grandmother's house, and the Morrises continued to maintain appearances—while going their separate ways. Jane Morris was further alienated from her husband by her dislike of Morris's socialist friends and of his politics and consequent public activities. She almost miraculously regained her health after his death in 1896 and lived until 1916. There is no indication that the emotional reunion depicted in the book ever occurred. Morris seems to indicate, however, that in a world unlike Victorian England in which a couple would not be forced to "profess an undying sentiment" (16:50), maintain a marriage of pretense, or experience public disapproval for infidelity, such a true reconciliation would have been possible.

7 THE WORLD BEYOND THE WORLD

1.   I have not included a discussion of *Child Christopher* (1895), since it is as much a translation of *Havelok the Dane* as an original romance. It is worth noting, however, that the adventures of Christopher follow the

pattern of those of the other heroes who become forces for social redemption and that Goldilind, imprisoned by a wicked surrogate mother, is another captive benign anima who is freed and won by the hero.

2. See *Works*, 17. The Old French romances translated are "The Tale of King Florus and the Fair Jehane," "The Friendship of Amis and Amile," "The Tale of King Coustans the Emperor," and "The History of Over-Sea." Morris had planned but not written a verse rendition of "Amis and Amile" for *The Earthly Paradise* but had included in it versions of two other Old French romances, "Ogier the Dane" and "The Man Born to Be King" (modeled on *Havelok*).

3. See Chapter 6, note 17 for an account of the library lists which contain the names of many of the romances Morris owned.

4. E[rnest] Belfort Bax, Morris's friend and co-author in the 1880s and 1890s, points to Morris's unacknowledged excellence as an historian, especially to his "marvelous" knowledge of "the by-ways of history." Bax continues: "To this, he added, especially latterly, the study of comparative mythology and what may be termed the newer anthropology" (*Reminiscences and Reflections of a Mid and Late Victorian* [London: Allen and Unwin, 1918], p. 120).

5. See Chapter 5, pp. 115–16, 139 and notes 23–24 of Chapter 5.

6. Lemire, *Unpublished Lectures*, p. 177. For a discussion of Morris's invention of words, see Paul Thompson, *Work of William Morris*, p. 160.

7. Calhoun, "'Little Land of Abundance,'" in *Studies*, p. 56.

8. John Rhys, *Lectures on the Origin and Growth of Religion as Illustrated by Celtic Heathendom* (London: Williams and Norgate, 1888), pp. 284–87, 305.

9. Morris and Bax, *Socialism*, p. 299.

10. Rhys, *Lectures*, pp. 345–47.

11. Joseph Campbell, *The Hero with a Thousand Faces*, Bollingen Series 17 (Princeton: Princeton University Press, 1968), p. 30.

12. F. A. C. Wilson, *Yeats's Iconography* (New York: Macmillan, 1960), pp. 53–56.

13. Charlotte Oberg, "Motif and Theme in the Late Prose Romances of William Morris," in *Studies*, p. 46.

14. See P. W. Joyce, *Old Celtic Romances*, 3rd ed. (London: Longmans, Green, 1914), pp. 106–9 and 386–90; and Eugene O'Curry, *On the Manners and Customs of the Ancient Irish: A Series of Lectures*, ed. W. K. Sullivan, 3 vols. (London: Williams and Norgate, 1873), 2:193–94.

15. Joyce, *Old Celtic Romances*, p. 74.

16. Ibid., p. 76.

17. Hallblithe asks Sea-Eagle, the chief who has chosen to go to the false earthly paradise, how the leader can bear a life devoid of action. He warns him that he may someday weary of the land and yearn for the peace of death. Sea-Eagle, on the other hand, believes that his only choices are existence on the Glittering Plain or existence elsewhere as a "gibbering ghost" (15:257) and imminent death. Morris indicates that Sea-Eagle has

mistakenly chosen death in life instead of the peace of a natural demise.

18. The incident is derived from O'Curry's account of Druid Dallan and Queen Edain in *Ancient Irish*, 2:194.

19. Calhoun, "'Little Land of Abundance,'" p. 63.

20. See Edmund Spenser, *The Faerie Queene*, intro. J. W. Hales, 2 vols. (London: J. M. Dent, 1910), 1:331-32.

21. For a further discussion of Morris's witch and anima archetypes, see Norman Talbot's excellent article, "Women and Goddesses in the Romances of William Morris," *Southern Review* (Australia) 3 (1969): 342-55. See also Oberg, *Pagan Prophet*, pp. 61-64 for a view of Diana and Venus as conflicting symbols. Both Oberg and Talbot seem unaware that Morris, supporting the theories of Jacob and Wilhelm Grimm, depicts all female deities as varied, but essentially interchangeable, aspects of one primal earth goddess.

22. W[illiam] B[utler] Yeats, "The Happiest of the Poets," in *Ideas of Good and Evil* (London: A. H. Bullen, 1903), p. 80.

23. Jane Morris had been painted as Proserpine or Korê by Dante Gabriel Rossetti. Morris was aware of her significance as a daughter and aspect of Demeter and as a symbol of the fertile but ambiguous earth goddess, not only through Frazer but also through J. J. Bachofen's *Mutterrecht*. See *Myth, Religion, and Mother Right*, trans. Ralph Manheim, Bollingen Series 84 (Princeton: Princeton University Press, 1967), pp. 26-195, passim.

24. See Engels, *Origin of the Family*, p. 88.

25. James George Frazer, *The Golden Bough*, 2 vols. (London: Macmillan, 1890), 1:87. Frazer (2:344) also identifies the Maid[en] as a name for the young corn and the spirit which inhabits it.

26. Oberg, *Pagan Prophet*, p. 118.

27. Graham Hough, *A Preface to the Faerie Queene* (New York: W. W. Norton, 1962), p. 14.

28. Wilson, *Yeats's Iconography*, p. 53. See Wilson's Jungian analysis of the romance, pp. 52-56.

29. Harold Bloom, *Yeats* (New York: Oxford University Press, 1970), p. 296.

30. Morris's description appears to be modeled on William Cobbett's *Rural Rides*, ed. G. D. H. Cole and Margaret Cole, 3 vols. (London: J. M. Dent, 1930), 3:726-63, a work Morris knew well and valued highly. See Cobbett's account of the farms of Scotland and descriptions of the barracks and boothies in which poor hired laborers were lodged.

31. Grennan, *Medievalist and Revolutionary*, p. 126.

32. Morris and Bax, *Socialism*, pp. 31-47.

33. The damsel of Bourton Abbas is first named "Dorothy" by Ralph. She is perhaps called so after the virgin martyr about whom Morris had written "The Story of Dorothea," planned for but not included in *The Earthly Paradise*.

34. See Frazer, *Golden Bough*, 1:310; and Jacob Grimm and Wilhelm Grimm, *Teutonic Mythology*, trans. James Steven Stallybrass, 4 vols.

(London: G. Bell, 1882), 1:97–98, 1:286–87. Dame Habond and Habundia are identified as various names for a Lady of Abundance or goddess of plenty.

35. H[enry] Rider Haggard, *She* (1887), in *Five Adventure Novels of H. Rider Haggard* (New York: Dover, 1951), p. 69. Morris knew and corresponded with Haggard.

36. Norman Kelvin, "The Erotic in *News from Nowhere* and *The Well at the World's End*," in *Studies*, p. 110.

37. For a discussion of the use of Alexander in the romance, see Oberg, *Pagan Prophet*, p. 121.

38. See Standish O'Grady, *History of Ireland: Critical and Philosophical* (London: Sampson, Low, 1881), p. 136; O'Curry, *Ancient Irish*, 2:143; and Lady Jane Wilde, *Ancient Legends, Mystic Charms, and Superstitions of Ireland* (Boston: Ticknor, 1888), p. 241.

39. Richard Jefferies, *After London, or Wild England* (London: Duckworth, 1885), pp. 292–304, may well be the source of this incident. Felix Aquila, the hero, is aided by the Shepherds, a noble and simple people, who wish him to become their king. Instead, he becomes their war-leader and helps them gain a righteous victory.

40. Talbot, "Women and Goddesses," p. 334.

41. Three fragments of other versions exist: one in verse, one in mixed prose and verse, and a long prose fragment called "The Widow's House by the Great Water" (British Museum Additional Manuscript 45324 613B). The extant portion of the "Widow's House" differs from the published version in both tone and incident. It is folkloric and full of allusions to folk tales; the heroine, Katherine, is depicted as being raised by a loving mother and beset by suitors within a "normal," rather than enchanted, world.

42. Both Birdalone and the Lady of Abundance are stolen children who witness the evil sorcery of their mistresses and are threatened with death and punished for their actions by being temporarily transformed into animals. Both are aided in escaping their thralldom by supernatural female guardians. The Lady's mysterious Teacher of Lore seems a proto-type of the more fully characterized Habundia.

43. See Grimm and Grimm, *Teutonic Mythology*, 1:97, 1:286–87, 3:xxi. The Grimms see all goddesses as "divine mothers . . . from whom the human race learns the occupations and arts of housekeeping and husbandry" (1:250). Morris's Habundia, directly derived from *Teutonic Mythology*, is a wood-mother, purely local in power, who shrinks in size when she enters a manmade house.

44. Spenser, *The Faerie Queene*, 1:230–32.

45. Talbot, "Women and Goddesses," p. 353.

46. The three maidens, clad in the colors after which they are named, resemble the three maidens of Morris's early poem, "The Sailing of the Sword." As in the poem (in *The Defence* volume), each is connected to her lover by a token, and Atra, like the "white maid" of the poem, is deserted for another woman by the man she loves. Perhaps the maidens in the romance are meant to represent the attributes Morris associates

with the colors gold (richness and ripeness), green (happiness), and black (absence and sorrow), or perhaps they are seasonal symbols.

47. See Joyce, *Old Celtic Romances*, pp. 60–64, 124–53, 390–96.

48. Ebbatson, "Visions of Wild England," p. 25.

49. Arthur, however, is not prepared for the fertile marriage with his anima. Reducing the main plot of previous romances to a subplot in this volume, Morris shows how the necessity of rejecting Atra and the loss of Birdalone have driven Arthur to despair and isolation. Living as a hermit—a state Morris finds unnatural—Arthur has been smitten by madness and has become the semi-human wildman of the medieval romance convention. Habundia aids him, but only integration with Birdalone can fully heal him.

50. Note, for example, Osberne's skill as a scald and the fact that his songs imitate Icelandic verse, his mastery of the smith's art, his sword, "Broadcleaver," and its relationship to the swords of such figures as Sigurd and Thiodolf.

51. Cf. the relationship between Pharamond and Oliver in *Love is Enough*.

52. Bjørnstjerne Bjørnson, *Synnøve Solbakken*, trans. Rasmus B. Anderson (London: n. p., 1884). Morris utilizes the novel's structural pattern—the neighboring but separated steads, the love that begins as childhood play, and the placing of obstacles between the lovers. He even borrows such specific motifs as "the Luck of the Stead"; both Thorbjorn and Osberne are born into families in which good fortune skips a generation and passes from grandfather to grandson. Both are fated to good fortune.

53. Frye, *Anatomy of Criticism*, p. 200. See also *Works*, 21:41–44 and 74–75.

54. The small craft guilds, in which Morris had found the seeds of true democratic and communal practices in medieval Europe, are victorious. Representing the larger part of organized labor, they win just representation from the richer middle-class merchant guilds, and drive out the king. The entire account, especially the rising of the masses and the battle in the square, is reminiscent of "How the Change Came" in *News from Nowhere*. It is also modeled on an historical event in which Morris was interested—the uprising in Ghent in the fourteenth century.

55. Yeats, "Happiest of the Poets," pp. 71–72.

56. *Letters*, p. 78.

BIBLIOGRAPHY

Anderson, Rasmus B. *Norse Mythology; or, The Religion of Our Fore-fathers, Containing All the Myths of the Edda, Systematized and Interpreted*. Chicago: Scott, Foresman, 1875.

Apollonius of Rhodes. *The Voyage of Argo: The Argonautica*. Translated by E. V. Rieu. Harmondsworth: Penguin Books, 1959.

Apuleius Madaurensis. *The Golden Ass; being the Metamorphoses of Lucius Apuleius*. Translated by W. Adlington (1566). London: W. Heinemann, 1919.

Ashton, John. *Romances of Chivalry Told and Illustrated in Facsimile*. London: Unwin, 1887.

Bachofen, J. J. *Myth, Religion, and Mother Right*. Translated by Ralph Manheim. Bolingen Series 84. Princeton: Princeton University Press, 1967.

Balch, Dennis R. "Guenevere's Fidelity to Arthur in 'The Defence of Guenevere' and 'King Arthur's Tomb.'" *Victorian Poetry: An Issue Dedicated to the Work of William Morris* 13, nos. 3–4 (Fall-Winter 1975): 61–70.

———. "'The Lovers of Gudrun,' *Sigurd the Volsung*, and *The House of the Wolfings*: Three Chapters in a Tale of the Individual and the Tribe." In *The After-Summer Seed: Reconsiderations of William Morris's "The Story of Sigurd the Volsung."* Edited by John Hollow. New York: William Morris Society, 1978.

Bax, E[rnest] Belfort. *Reminiscences and Reflections of a Mid and Late Victorian*. London: Allen and Unwin, 1918.

Bell, Mackenzie. "William Morris: A Eulogy." *Fortnightly Review* 66 (Nov. 1896): 693–702.

Bellamy, Edward. *Looking Backward: 2000 - 1887*. New York: New American Library, Signet Classic, 1960.

Berry, Ralph. "A Defense of Guenevere." *Victorian Poetry* 9 (1971): 277–86.

Bjørnson, Bjørnstjerne. *Synnøve Solbakken*. Translated by Rasmus B. Anderson. London: n.p. 1884.

Blench, J. W. "William Morris's *Sigurd the Volsung*: A Re-appraisal." *Durham University Journal*, o.s. 41 (1968), n.s. 30 (1968): 1–17.

Bloom, Harold. *Yeats*. New York: Oxford University Press, 1970.

Bodkin, Maude. *Archetypal Patterns in Poetry: Psychological Studies of Imagination*. London: Oxford University Press, 1934.

Bono, Barbara J. "The Prose Fictions of William Morris: A Study in the Literary Aesthetic of a Victorian Social Reformer." **Victorian Poetry: An Issue Dedicated to the Work of William Morris** 13, nos. 3–4 (Fall-Winter 1975): 43–59.

Borrow, George. *Lavengro: The Scholar—the Gypsy—the Priest*. London: J. Murray, 1851.

_____*The Romany Rye: A Sequel to "Lavengro."* London: J. Murray, 1857.

Brand, John. *Observations on Popular Antiquities Chiefly Illustrating the Origin of Our Vulgar Customs, Ceremonies, and Superstitions*. New rev. ed. London: Chatto and Windus, 1877.

Brantlinger, Patrick. "*News from Nowhere*: Morris's Socialist Anti-Novel." *Victorian Studies* 19 (1974): 35–49.

_____"A Reading of Morris' *The Defence of Guenevere and Other Poems*." *Victorian Newsletter*, no. 44 (1973): 18–24.

Browning, Elizabeth Barrett. *The Complete Works of Mrs. E. B. Browning*. 6 vols. New York: Sproul, 1901.

Browning, Robert. *The Poetical Works of Robert Browning: Complete from 1833 to 1868 and the Shorter Poems Thereafter*. London: Oxford University Press, 1940.

B[urne]-J[ones], G[eorgiana]. *Memorials of Edward Burne-Jones*. 2 vols. London: Macmillan, 1904.

Bush, Douglas. *Mythology and the Romantic Tradition in English Poetry*. Cambridge: Harvard University Press, 1937.

Butler, Samuel. *Erewhon, or Over the Range*. New York: Dutton, 1920.

Calhoun, Blue. "'The Little Land of Abundance': Pastoral Perspective in the Late Romances of William Morris." In *Studies in the Late Romances of William Morris*. Introduction by Frederick Kirchhoff. Edited by Carole Silver and Joseph Dunlap. New York: William Morris Society, 1976.

_____*The Pastoral Vision of William Morris: The Earthly Paradise*. Athens, Ga.: University of Georgia Press, 1975.

Callisthenes, Pseudo-. *The Romance of Alexander the Great*. Translated by Albert Mugrdich Wolohojian. New York: Columbia University Press, 1969.

Campbell, Joseph. *The Hero with a Thousand Faces*. Bollingen Series 17. Princeton: Princeton University Press, 1968.

Carlyle, Thomas. *Past and Present*. Introduction by Douglas Jerrold. London: J. M. Dent, 1960.

_____*Sartor Resartus—On Heroes and Hero Worship*. Introduction by W. H. Hudson. London: J. M. Dent, 1908.

Carson, Mother Angela. "Morris' Guenevere: A Further Note." *Philological Quarterly* 42 (1963): 131–34.

Chandler, Alice. *A Dream of Order: The Medieval Ideal in Nineteenth-Century English Literature*. Lincoln, Neb.: University of Nebraska Press, 1970.

Chaucer, Geoffrey. *The Works of Geoffrey Chaucer*. Edited by F. N. Robinson. 2nd ed. Boston: Houghton Mifflin, 1957.

Clemens, Samuel Langhorne, [Mark Twain]. *The Adventures of Huckleberry Finn (Tom Sawyer's Comrade)*. Introduction by Brander Matthews and Dixon Wecter. New York: Harper, 1948.

Cobbett, William. *Rural Rides*. Edited by G. D. H. Cole and Margaret Cole. 3 vols. London: J. M. Dent, 1930.

Cole, G. D. H., ed. *William Morris: Studies in Prose, Stories in Verse, Shorter Poems, Lectures and Essays*. London: Nonesuch Press, 1948.

Coleridge, Samuel Taylor. *The Poems of Samuel Taylor Coleridge*. Introduction by Sir A. T. Quiller-Couch. London: Oxford University Press, 1930.

Commonweal (London). Vols. 1–7, Feb. 1885 - Sept. 1892. (Edited by William Morris from 1885 to June 1890.)

Dasent, George Webbe, trans. *East of the Sun and West of the Moon: Old Tales from the North*. London: Hodder and Stoughton, n.d.

_____*Tales from the Fjeld. A Second Series of Popular Tales from the Norse of P[eter] Chr[isten] Asbornsen*. London: Chapman and Hall, 1874.

Davies, Frank J. J. "William Morris's 'Sir Peter Harpdon's End.'" *Philological Quarterly* 11 (1932): 314–17.

Deal, Kenneth. "Acts of Completion: The Search for Vocation in Morris' Early Prose Romances." In *The Golden Chain: Essays on William Morris and Pre-Raphaelitism*. Introduction by Carole Silver. Edited by Carole G. Silver. New York: William Morris Society, 1982.

DeLaura, David J. "An Unpublished Poem of William Morris'." *Modern Philology* 62 (1965): 340–41.

Doughty, Oswald. *A Victorian Romantic: Dante Gabriel Rossetti*. 2nd ed. London: Oxford University Press, 1960.

Dunlap, Joseph R. *The Book That Never Was*. New York: Oriole Editions, 1971.

Ebbatson, J. R. "Visions of Wild England: William Morris and Richard Jefferies." *Journal of the William Morris Society* 3, no. 3 (1977): 12–29.

Ellison, R. C. "'The Undying Glory of Dreams': William Morris and the 'Northland of Old.'" In *Victorian Poetry*. Edited by Malcolm Bradbury and David Palmer. Stratford-upon-Avon Studies, no. 15. London: Edward Arnold, 1972, pp. 139–75.

_____"An Unpublished Poem by William Morris." *English* 5 (1964): 100–102.

Engels, Frederick. *The Origin of the Family, Private Property and the State*. Introduction by Eleanor Burke Leacock. London: Lawrence and Wishart, 1972.

Faulkner, Peter, ed. *William Morris: The Critical Heritage*. London: Routledge and Kegan Paul, 1973.

Fredeman, William E. *Pre-Raphaelitism: A Bibliocritical Study*. Cambridge: Harvard University Press, 1965.

FitzGerald, Edward. *The Rubáiyát of Omar Khayyám* [first version]. Vol. 1 of *The Variorum and Definitive Edition of the Poetical and*

Prose Writings of Edward FitzGerald. Edited by George Bentham. Introduction by Edmund Gosse. New York: Doubleday, Page, 1902.

Frazer, James George. *The Golden Bough: A Study in Comparative Religion*. 2 vols. London: Macmillan, 1890.

Frederick, John T. *William Henry Hudson*. New York: Twayne, 1972.

Freud, Sigmund. *The Interpretation of Dreams*. Translated by James Strachey. New York: Avon, 1965.

Froissart, Jean. *The Chronicle of Froissart: Translated out of French by Sir John Bourchier, Lord Berners*. Introduction by William Paton Ker. 6 vols. 1901–3. Reprint. New York: AMS Press, 1967.

Frye, Northrop. *Anatomy of Criticism: Four Essays*. Princeton: Princeton University Press, 1957.

Gelpi, Barbara Charlesworth. "The Image of the Anima in the Work of Dante Gabriel Rossetti." *Victorian Newsletter*, no. 45 (1974): 1–7.

Gent, Margaret. "'To Flinch from Modern Varnish': The Appeal of the Past to the Victorian Imagination." In *Victorian Poetry*. Edited by Malcolm Bradbury and David Palmer. Stratford-upon-Avon Studies, no. 15. London: Edward Arnold, 1972, pp. 11–36.

The Germ: Thoughts toward Nature in Poetry, Literature, and Art. Nos. 1–4, Jan.-May 1850.

Gesta Romanorum: or, Entertaining Moral Stories; . . . Translated by Rev. Charles Swan. 1876. Reprint. New York: Dover, 1959.

Goddard, Julia. *Wonderful Stories from Northern Lands*. London: Longmans, Green, 1871.

Goode, John. "William Morris and the Dream of Revolution." In *Literature and Politics in the Nineteenth Century: Essays*. Edited by John Lucas. London: Methuen, 1971, pp. 221–80.

Goodwin, K[enneth] L. "Unpublished Lyrics of William Morris." In *The Yearbook of English Studies*, no. 5. Edited by T. J. B. Spencer. London: Modern Humanities Research Association, 1975, pp. 190–206.

Grennan, Margaret. *William Morris: Medievalist and Revolutionary*. New York: King's Crown Press, 1945.

Grigson, Geoffrey. *The Contrary View: Glimpses of Fudge and Gold*. London: Macmillan, 1974.

Grimm, Jacob and Wilhelm [Grimm]. *German Popular Tales and Household Stories, Collected by the Brothers Grimm*. Philadelphia: Porter and Coates, 1869.

_____*Teutonic Mythology*. Translated by James Steven Stallybrass. 4 vols. London: G. Bell, 1880–88.

Grylls, Rosalie Glynn. *Portrait of Rossetti*. London: Macdonald, 1964.

Guest, Lady Charlotte. *Mabinogion: Medieval Welsh Romances*. London: David Nutt, 1902.

Haggard, H[enry] Rider. *She*. (1887) In *Five Adventure Novels of H. Rider Haggard*. New York: Dover, 1951.

Harris, Joel Chandler. *Uncle Remus and His Friends*. Introduction by Myrta Lockett Avary. Boston: Houghton Mifflin, 1914.

Henderson, Philip, ed. *The Letters of William Morris to His Family and Friends*. London: Longmans, Green, 1950.

_____*William Morris: His Life, Work and Friends*. New York: McGraw-Hill, 1967.

Hoare, Dorothy M. *The Works of Morris and Yeats in Relation to Early Saga Literature*. Cambridge: At the University Press, 1937.

Hollow, John. "Deliberate Happiness: The Late Prose Romances of William Morris." In *Studies in the Late Prose Romances of William Morris*. Introduction by Frederick Kirchhoff. Edited by Carole Silver and Joseph Dunlap. New York: William Morris Society, 1975, pp. 79–94.

_____"William Morris and the Judgment of God." *PMLA* 86 (1971): 446–51.

Hough, Graham. *The Last Romantics*. London: Duckworth, 1949.

_____*A Preface to the Faerie Queene*. New York: W. W. Norton, 1962.

Hudson, W[illiam] H[enry]. *A Crystal Age*. (1887) 2nd ed. London: Unwin, 1906.

Hunt, John Dixon. "A Moment's Monument: Reflections on Pre-Raphaelite Vision in Poetry and Painting." In *Pre-Raphaelitism: A Collection of Critical Essays*. Edited by James Sambrook. Chicago: University of Chicago Press, 1974, pp. 243–64.

_____*The Pre-Raphaelite Imagination: 1848-1900*. London: Routledge and Kegan Paul, 1968.

Hunt, Robert. *Popular Romances of the West of England; or, The Drolls, Traditions, and Superstitions of Old Cornwall*. 3rd ed., 1881. Reprint. New York: Benjamin Blom, 1968.

Jefferies, Richard. *After London, or Wild England*. London: Duckworth, 1885.

Joyce, P. W. *Old Celtic Romances: Tales from Irish Mythology*. 3rd ed. London: Longmans, Green, 1914.

Jung, Carl Gustave. *The Archetypes and the Collective Unconscious*. Translated by R. F. C. Hull. New York: Pantheon, 1959.

_____*Symbols of Transformation: An Analysis of the Prelude to a Case of Schizophrenia*. Translated by R. F. C. Hull. New York: Pantheon, 1956.

Keats, John. *The Complete Poetical Works of Keats*. Boston: Houghton Mifflin, 1953.

Kelvin, Norman. "The Erotic in *News from Nowhere* and *The Well at the World's End*. In *Studies in the Late Romances of William Morris*. Introduction by Frederick Kirchhoff. Edited by Carole Silver and Joseph Dunlap. New York: William Morris Society, 1976, pp. 97–114.

Kirchhoff, Frederick. "*Love is Enough*: A Crisis in William Morris' Poetic Development." *Victorian Poetry* 15 (1977): 297–306.

_____"Travel as Anti-Autobiography: William Morris' Icelandic Journals." In *Approaches to Victorian Autobiography*. Edited by George Landow. Athens, Ohio: Ohio University Press, 1979, pp. 292–310.

_____*William Morris*. Boston: Twayne, 1979.

Kocmonová, Jessie. "'Landscape and Sentiment': Morris' First Attempt in Longer Prose Fiction." *Victorian Poetry: An Issue Dedicated to the Work of William Morris* 13, nos. 3–4 (Fall-Winter 1975): 103–17.

————*The Poetic Maturing of William Morris: From "The Earthly Paradise" to "The Pilgrims of Hope."* 1964. Reprint. New York: Folcroft Library, 1970.

Lang, Andrew. *Custom and Myth.* London: Longmans, Green, 1884.

Lang, Cecil Y., ed. *The Pre-Raphaelites and Their Circle.* Boston: Houghton Mifflin, 1968.

————*The Swinburne Letters.* 6 vols. New Haven: Yale University Press, 1959–62.

Lemire, Eugene D., ed. *The Unpublished Lectures of William Morris.* Detroit: Wayne State University Press, 1969.

Lempriere, John. *A Classical Dictionary; Containing a copious account of all the proper names mentioned in ancient authors; with the value of coins, weights and measures used among the Greeks and Romans; and a chronological table.* London: Routledge, n.d.

Lettson, William Nanson, trans. *The Fall of the Nibelungers, Otherwise the Book of Kriemhild.* 2nd ed. London: Williams and Norgate, 1873.

Levine, George. "From 'Know-not-Where' to 'Nowhere': The City in Carlyle, Ruskin, and Morris." In *The Victorian City: Images and Realities.* Edited by H. J. Dyos and Michael Wolff. 2 vols. London: Routledge and Kegan Paul, 1973: 2:495–516.

Lewis, C. S. *Rehabilitations and Other Essays.* London: Oxford University Press, 1939.

Lindsay, Jack. *William Morris: His Life and Work.* London: Constable, 1975.

————*William Morris, Writer.* London: William Morris Society, 1961.

Litzenberg, Karl. "The Victorians and the Vikings: A Bibliographical Essay on Anglo-Norse Literary Relations." *University of Michigan Contributions in Modern Philosophy,* no. 3. Ann Arbor: University of Michigan Press, 1947.

London. British Library. British Museum Manuscript 86. William Morris and Jenny Morris. "A List of Books and Manuscripts Bought by William Morris, Compiled about 1876 . . . with Prices Paid."

————British Library. British Museum Additional Manuscript 45,324 613B. William Morris. "The Widow's House by the Great Water."

————British Library. British Museum Additional Manuscript 45,328. William Morris. [Untitled novel; fragments of unfinished romances.]

————Library of J. R. Abbey. William Morris. "A Catalogue of the Library at Kelmscott House."

————Victoria and Albert Museum. R. C. AA. 17. William Morris. *A Book of Verse.*

Lorris, Guillaume de and Jean de Meun. *The Romance of the Rose.* Translated by Harry W. Robbins. Edited by Charles W. Dunn. New York: Dutton, 1962.

MacEachen, Dougald B. "Trial by Water in William Morris' 'The Haystack in the Floods.'" *Victorian Poetry* 6 (1968): 73–75.

Mackail, J[ohn] W. *The Life of William Morris.* 2 vols. London: Longmans, Green, 1899.

Mallet, Paul Henri. *Northern Antiquities; or, An Historical Account of the Manners, Customs, Religion and Laws, Maritime Expeditions and Discoveries, Language and Literature of the Ancient Scandinavians*. Translated by Bishop [Thomas] Percy. London: H. G. Bohn, 1847.

Malory, Sir Thomas. *Le Morte D'Arthur*. Introduction by Sir John Rhys. 2 vols. London: J. M. Dent, 1906.

Mandeville, Sir John. *The voiage and travaile of Sir John Maundeville, kt. which treateth of the way to Hierusalem; and the marvayles of Inde, with other ilands and countryes*. (1725) Introduction by J. O. Halliwell. London: E. Lumley, 1839.

Marx, Karl and Friedrich Engels. *The Communist Manifesto*. Introduction by A. J. P. Taylor. London: Penguin Books, 1967.

Maurer, Oscar, Jr. "William Morris and the Poetry of Escape." In *Nineteenth-Century Studies*. Edited by Herbert Davies et al. Ithaca: Cornell University Press, 1940, pp. 247–76.

Meredith, George. *The Poetical Works of George Meredith*. Edited by G. M. Trevelyan. London: Constable, 1912.

Merrit, James D., ed. *The Pre-Raphaelite Poem*. New York: Dutton, 1966.

Morgan, L[ewis] H[enry]. *Ancient Society; or, Researches in the lines of human progress from savagery through barbarism to civilization*. Edited by Eleanor Burke Leacock. Cleveland: World Press, 1963.

Morris, May, ed. *William Morris: Artist, Writer, Socialist*. 2 vols. 1936. Reprint. New York: Russell and Russell, 1966.

Morris, William. *The Collected Works of William Morris*. Edited by May Morris. 24 vols. London: Longmans, Green, 1910–15. Reprint. New York: Russell and Russell, 1966.

———*The Defence of Guenevere and Other Poems*. Edited by Robert Steele. London: A. Moring, 1904.

———*Early Romances in Prose and Verse*. Edited by Peter Faulkner. London: J. M. Dent, 1973.

———*A Priced Catalogue of a Portion of the Valuable Collection of Manuscripts, Early Printed Books and Etc. of the late William Morris, of Kelmscott House Hammersmith*. London: Sotheby, 1898.

———and E[rnest] Belfort Bax. *Socialism: Its Growth & Outcome*. London: Swan Sonnenschein, 1893.

———and Eiríkr Magnússon, eds. *The Saga Library*. 6 vols. London: Bernard Quaritch, 1891–1905.

———and Eiríkr Magnússon, trans. *The Story of Kormak the Son of Ogmund*. [Kormáks saga] Edited by Grace J. Calder. London: William Morris Society, 1970.

———[and Eiríkr Magnússon], trans. *Volsunga Saga: The Story of the Volsungs and Niblungs*. Introduction by Robert W. Gutman. New York: Collier Books, 1962.

Müller, Max. *Chips from a German Workshop*. (1871–72) 5 vols. New York: Scribner, 1890–93.

Nordby, Conrad H. *The Influence of Old Norse Literature upon English Literature*. New York: Columbia University Press, 1901.

Noyes, Alfred. *William Morris*. London: Macmillan, 1908.

Oberg, Charlotte. "Motif and Theme in the Late Prose Romances of William Morris." In *Studies in the Late Romances of William Morris*. Introduction by Frederick Kirchhoff. Edited by Carole Silver and Joseph Dunlap. New York: William Morris Society, 1976, pp. 33–52.

———*A Pagan Prophet: William Morris*. Charlottesville: University Press of Virginia, 1978.

O'Curry, Eugene. *On the Manners and Customs of the Ancient Irish: A Series of Lectures*. Edited by W. K. Sullivan. 3 vols. Williams and Norgate, 1873.

O'Grady, Standish. *A History of Ireland: Critical and Philosophical*. London: Sampson, Low, 1881.

The Oxford and Cambridge Magazine for 1856: Conducted by Members of the Two Universities. Nos. 1–12, Jan.–Dec. 1856.

Pater, Walter. "Aesthetic Poetry." In *Appreciations: With an essay on Style*. London: Macmillan, 1889.

———*Greek Studies*. (1875–89) Vol. 7 of the *Collected Works of Walter Pater*. London: Macmillan, 1900–1901.

Percy, [Bishop] Thomas. *Folio Manuscript*. (facsimile) Edited by J. W. Hales and F. J. Furnivall. 4 vols. n.p., 1867–68.

———*Reliques of ancient English poetry, consisting of old heroic ballads, songs, and other pieces of our earlier poets, together with some few of later date*. Edited by Henry B. Wheatly, 1886. Reprint. New York: Dover, 1966.

Perrine, Laurence. "Morris's Guenevere: An Interpretation." *Philological Quarterly* 39 (1960): 234–41.

Poe, Edgar Allan. *The Complete Poems and Tales of Edgar Allan Poe*. New York: Modern Library, Random House, 1938.

Praz, Mario. *The Romantic Agony*. Translated by Angus Davidson. 2nd ed. New York: Oxford University Press, 1951.

Prescott, William H. *History of the Conquest of Peru*. 2 vols. New York: Harper, 1847–48.

Press, Muriel, trans. *The Laxdale Saga*. [Laxdoela saga] Edited by Peter Foote. London: J. M. Dent, 1964.

Pugin, Augustus Welby Northmore. *Contrasts*. 2nd ed. Introduction by H. R. Hitchcock. Leicester: Leicester University Press, 1969.

Raymond, Meredith. "The Arthurian Group in *The Defence of Guenevere and Other Poems*." *Victorian Poetry* 4 (1966): 213–18.

Reade, Charles. *The Cloister and the Hearth*. New York: Washington Square Press, 1960.

Reeve, Clara. *The Old English Baron: A Gothic Story*. Edited by James Trainer. London: Oxford University Press, 1967.

Rhys, John. *Lectures on the Origin and Growth of Religion as Illustrated by Celtic Heathendom*. London: Williams and Norgate, 1888.

Ritson, Joseph. *Ancient Engleish Metrical Romanceës*. London: G. and W. Nicol, 1802.

Rossetti, Dante Gabriel. *The Poetical Works of Dante Gabriel Rossetti in Two Volumes*. Boston: Little, Brown, 1913.

Ruskin, John. *The Queen of the Air*. (1869) In *The Works of John Ruskin*. Edited by E. T. Cook and Alexander Wedderburn. Vol. 19. London: G. Allen, 1905.

————*The Stones of Venice*. In *The Works of John Ruskin*. Edited by E. T. Cook and Alexander Wedderburn. Vols. 9–11. London: G. Allen, 1903.

Sadoff, Dianne F. "Erotic Murders: Structural and Rhetorical Irony in William Morris' Froissart Poems." *Victorian Poetry: An Issue Dedicated to the Work of William Morris* 13, nos. 3–4 (Fall-Winter 1975): 11–26.

————"Imaginative Transformation in William Morris' 'Rapunzel.'" *Victorian Poetry* 12 (1974): 153–64.

Scott, Dixon. *Men of Letters*. London: Hodder and Stoughton, 1923.

Scott, Sir Walter. *The Poems and Plays of Sir Walter Scott*. 2 vols. London: J. M. Dent, 1911.

Silver, Carole. "Eden and Apocalypse: William Morris' Marxist Vision in the 1880s." *University of Hartford Studies in Literature* 13 (1981): 62–77.

————"No Idle Singer: A Study of the Poems and Romances of William Morris." Ph.D. dissertation, Columbia University, 1967.

Spatt, Hartley S. "Morrissaga: *Sigurd the Volsung*." In *The After-Summer Seed: Reconsiderations of William Morris's "The Story of Sigurd the Volsung."* Edited by John Hollow. New York: William Morris Society, 1978, pp. 37–67.

Spenser, Edmund. *The Faerie Queene*. 2 vols. London: J. M. Dent, 1910.

Staines, David. "Morris' Treatment of His Medieval Sources in *The Defence of Guenevere and Other Poems*." *Studies in Philology* 70 (1973): 439–64.

Stallman, Robert L. "The Lovers' Progress: An Investigation of William Morris' 'The Defence of Guenevere' and 'King Arthur's Tomb.'" *Studies in English Literature: 1500-1900* 15 (1975): 657–70.

————"'Rapunzel' Unravelled." *Victorian Poetry* 7 (1969): 221–32.

Stevenson, Lionel. *The Pre-Raphaelite Poets*. Chapel Hill: University of North Carolina Press, 1972.

Surtees, Robert. *Handley Cross; or, Mr. Jorrock's Hunt*. London: Bradbury, Agnew, 1854.

Surtees, Virginia. *The Paintings and Drawings of Dante Gabriel Rossetti (1828-1882): A Catalogue Raisonné*. Oxford: Clarendon Press, 1971.

Swinburne, Algernon Charles. *Essays and Studies*. 4th ed. London: Chatto and Windus, 1897.

Talbot, Norman. "Women and Goddesses in the Romances of William Morris." *Southern Review* (Australia) 3 (1969): 342–55.

Tennyson, Alfred. *Poetical Works Including the Plays*. London: Oxford University Press, 1953.

Thompson, E. P. *William Morris: Romantic to Revolutionary*. London: Lawrence and Wishart, 1955. Revised ed. with "Postscript: 1976." London: Merlin Press, 1977.

Thompson, Paul. *The Work of William Morris*. New York: Viking Press, 1967.

Thorpe, Benjamin. *Northern Mythology: Comprising the Principal Popular Traditions and Superstitions of Scandinavia, North Germany, and the Netherlands*. 3 vols. London: E. Lumley, 1851–52.

———, ed. *Yule-Tide Stories: A Collection of Scandinavian and North German Popular Tales and Traditions from the Swedish, Danish, and German*. London: H. G. Bohn, 1853.

Tylor, E[dward] B[urnett]. *Primitive Culture*. (1871) 2 vols. New York: Harper, 1958.

Ugolnik, Anthony. "The Victorian Skald: Old Icelandic and the Evolution of William Morris' *Sigurd the Volsung*." In *The After-Summer Seed: Reconsiderations of William Morris's "The Story of Sigurd the Volsung."* Edited by John Hollow. New York: William Morris Society, 1978, pp. 37–67.

Von Humboldt, Alexander. *Personal Narrative of Travels to the Equinoctial Regions of America*. Edited and translated by Thomasina Ross. 3 vols. London: H. G. Bohn, 1852–53.

Weber, Henry William. *Metrical Romances of the Thirteenth, Fourteenth, and Fifteenth Centuries: Published from Ancient Manuscripts*. Edinburgh: A. Constable, 1810.

Wilde, Lady Jane. *Ancient Legends, Mystic Charms, and Superstitions of Ireland*. Boston: Ticknor, 1888.

Wilson, F. A. C. *Yeats's Iconography*. New York: Macmillan, 1960.

Yeats, W[illiam] B[utler]. "The Happiest of the Poets." In *Ideas of Good and Evil*. London: A. H. Bullen, 1903.

INDEX